W9-CFQ-411

TIME
GOES TO WAR

From World War II to the War on Terror:
Stories of Americans in Battle and on the Home Front

Editor	Kelly Knauer
Art Director	Ellen Fanning
Picture Editor	Patricia Cadley
Writer/Researcher	Matthew Fenton
Maps	Lon Tweeten
Copy Editor	Bruce Christopher Carr
Research Assistant	Rudi Papiri

TIME INC. HOME ENTERTAINMENT

President
Rob Gursha

Vice President, Branded Businesses
David Arfine

Executive Director, Marketing Services
Carol Pittard

Director, Retail & Special Sales
Tom Mifsud

Director of Finance
Tricia Griffin

Marketing Director
Kenneth Maehlum

Assistant Director
Ann Marie Ross

Prepress Manager
Emily Rabin

Associate Product Manager
Jennifer Dowell

Assistant Product Manager
Michelle Kuhr

Special thanks to:
Suzanne DeBenedetto,
Robert Dente, Gina Di Meglio, Kathi Doak,
Dan Donnelly, Anne-Michelle Gallero,
Peter Harper, Raquel Irizarry, Natalie McCrea,
Jessica McGrath, Jonathan Polsky,
Mary Jane Rigoroso, Steven Sandonato,
Bozena Szwagulinski, Cornelis Verwaal,
Niki Whelan.

Copyright 2002
Time Inc. Home Entertainment

Published by TIME Books

Time Inc.
1271 Avenue of the Americas
New York, NY 10020

First Edition

ISBN: 1-931933-22-7
Library of Congress Number: 2002106442

TIME Books is a trademark of Time Inc.

We welcome your comments and suggestions about TIME Books. Please write to us at:
TIME Books
Attention: Book Editors
PO Box 11016
Des Moines, IA
50336-1016

If you would like to order any of our hard-cover Collector's Edition books, please call us at 1-800-327-6388 (Monday through Friday 7 a.m.–8 p.m. or Saturday 7 a.m.–6 p.m. central time).

TIME did not assign writer's bylines to articles in its first decades of publication. However, the magazine did identify the writers of some of its eyewitness accounts during World War II and the Korean conflict, and we have included those bylines in this volume. The work of the following TIME writers is featured in the final two chapters of the book:
Gulf War—Lisa Beyer, Jesse Birnbaum, George J. Church, Hugh Sidey, William E. Smith.
On Patrol—George J. Church, Michael Elliott, Charlotte Faltermayer, Nancy Gibbs, Richard Lacayo, Jodie Morse, Eric Pooley, Romesh Ratnesar, Josh Tyrangiel.
Foreword—Kelly Knauer. Chapter introductory essays—Matthew Fenton.

Hard cover photo credits:
Main image: Aladin Abdel Naby—Reuters—Landov
Back cover (clockwise from top left): Bruno Barbey—Magnum Photos; David Douglas Duncan; Paul Queenan—US Coast Guard—National Archives; Adam Butler—AP/Wide World; Larry Burrows

Soft cover photo credits:
Front cover main image: Aladin Abdel Naby—Reuters—Landov
Inset images (left to right): Paul Queenan—US Coast Guard—National Archives; David Douglas Duncan; Larry Burrows; Barry Iverson—Timepix; David Marck Jr.—US Army—Getty Images
Back cover: David Douglas Duncan

TIME
GOES TO WAR

From World War II to the War on Terror:
Stories of Americans in Battle and on the Home Front

CONTENTS

2

38

72

110

134

Gallery

When Hollywood goes to war, the results are heartwarming
and unexpected, both for the stars and the folks in stripes

The Gulf War

In trouncing Saddam Hussein's Iraq, the U.S. returned
Kuwait to freedom, and the U.S. military regained its pride

Gallery

From victory gardens to yellow ribbons to "United We
Stand," how war leaves its stamp on life in America

On Patrol

All wars aren't major conflicts, all battlefields aren't in lands
across an ocean, and all war heroes aren't soldiers

Tidings of War

Americans see war as a job to be done rather than a calling to be embraced. But as we find ourselves in a new kind of conflict—a war against terror—we listen to stories of old battles with new respect

WAR STORIES. AMERICANS USE THE TERM SAR-castically, as shorthand for boring hours spent with boring elders. Perhaps that's not surprising: war stories speak of the past, and America is famously in love with the future. "History is bunk," said Henry Ford, who taught Americans to love the promise of the highway, not the scene in the rear-view mirror.

War stories? The military ethos has never occupied a central place in American culture. Cossacks, Prussians and Afghans may celebrate the arts of war; Americans cherish religion, family, sports and the almighty dollar far more than epaulets and battle ribbons. The French have their Arc de Triomphe, and the British revere the statue of Admiral Nelson. America's most beloved national monument is a female embodi-ment of the spirit of Liberty, a statue that evokes not war but human rights, immigration and diversity. And that brings to mind another reason Americans don't embrace military life: its authoritarian system of rank runs counter to a society dedicated to the proposition that all men are created equal.

"The American people do not, as a general rule, like or trust the military," said TIME in a 1944 cover story naming General George C. Marshall Man of the Year 1943. Yet if Americans aren't natural soldiers, we respect, admire and cherish the sacrifice of those who serve to preserve our freedom, and we take pride in our distinguished service academies. In this deeply peace-loving nation, it's no accident that we often speak of the "business" of war, and that soldiers down the decades have told TIME, "We're here because we have a job

THE FACE OF WAR: Former Marine David Douglas Duncan took memorable pictures of battle in Korea, then went on to chronicle the war in Vietnam. This picture was taken in Con Thien in 1967.

braced themselves for this new kind of war, it seemed an appropriate time to view our new battle against terrorism within the larger context of America's previous wars. That sent us into the vast archives of TIME's weekly issues, where we discovered a wealth of distinguished reporting—war stories that are as fresh and riveting as the day they were written.

This book celebrates heroes of two kinds: the courageous Americans who have served with valor in wartime and the brave writers and photographers who risked their lives to tell their stories. In these pages you will read the words of TIME correspondent Frank Gibney, wounded while crossing a bridge that was blown up in Korea during the first days of the war. You will see pictures taken by Robert Capa and Larry Burrows, legendary photojournalists who met their death on the battlefield. And you will encounter two current photographers, James Nachtwey and Christopher Morris, who continue to cheat death as they travel to the front lines of the world's battle zones to chronicle war's fury.

The book has a bias: it features stories of common soldiers rather than their leaders. Politicians, diplomats and others who might be classified by our friends in uniform as "rear-echelon personnel" are given short shrift. But in order to present a broad picture of life during wartime, we do offer several portraits of great commanders. And we profile some of our more gifted adversaries, for you can't understand a war without understanding the enemy. We've also featured the contributions of our Allies in the section on World War II, with battle dispatches reporting the British-led effort against the Axis armies in North Africa and the savage fighting in which the Russian army held off, then captured, the Germans in Stalingrad on the Eastern Front.

Some readers may be confused by the datelines of the Dispatches; they are generally dated a week or more after the events they record. Reason: TIME's weekly issues are dated a week ahead of the day on which they appear, for newsstand distribution purposes. The U.S. bombing of Iraq in the Gulf War, for instance, began on the night of Jan. 16, 1991. It was reported in the TIME issue on newsstands the following Monday, Jan. 21, which was dated ahead to Jan. 28, 1991.

Sharp-eyed readers who are intrigued by the correlation of text style to world politics (a small number, we suspect) may note a few style discrepancies in the following pages. We have maintained TIME's original spellings and stylings in the archival Dispatches sections, but not in the new material created for this volume. As a result, you will find Americans fighting Communism in Korea, but you will also find us speaking of "containing communism" in the essays that introduce our chapters. In the decades since 1951, TIME has decided that communism is a political philosophy with many branches, not a monolithic force directed by the Kremlin.

Likewise, the editors have not softened or turned away from language in TIME's original stories that is unacceptable today. Yes, TIME consistently referred to our Pacific enemies in World War II as "Japs." To pretend otherwise or to substitute a less harsh term in accounts that are presented as originals would amount to bowdlerizing history in the service of modern sympathies, and that is both bad journalism and bad history. However, many of our Dispatches have been trimmed from their original length for an obvious reason: so that we could present as many as possible of these gripping, enlightening and deeply moving ... war stories. ∎

to do." As a close friend of General Marshall's told TIME, "He [Marshall] has only one interest: to win this damned war as quick as he can, with the fewest lives lost and money expended, and get the hell down to Leesburg, Va., and enjoy life."

War stories? We'll take our chances: this book is filled with them, and we think readers will find them well worth revisiting. The book had its genesis in the shocking terrorist attacks on America of Sept. 11, 2001. Suddenly Americans found themselves plunged into a new and frightening kind of conflict, in which the battlefield was a city street, the casualties were everyday office workers, and the heroes were fire fighters, police and medics. In the wake of the atrocities, America was swept by a unity of spirit that crossed all our divides: age, class, religion, race and gender. As Americans

TIME GOES TO WAR 1

RUIN WITH A VIEW: As G.I.s chow down in Italy in 1943, a statue of Winged Victory recalls past glories amid present rubble

The Necessary War

It was the largest, most complex war our world has ever seen—but in the most important sense, it was also the simplest

THE TERM WORLD WAR II WAS COINED BY *TIME*. IN the years after what was universally called "the Great War," no one seemed to imagine that there would be a sequel. When it finally came, TIME began referring to the new conflict as "the Second World War" and began referring to the previous conflict as "the First World War." But titles can be deceiving. Although the years 1914-18 had seen a previously unimaginable zenith in mechanized killing, the warfare was confined largely to Europe. The six-year conflagration that was sparked in 1939, when German troops crossed the Polish border, was the first to engulf the entire world.

World War II is remembered as "The Good War"—and if such an oddity is possible, this was probably it. It was a war in which the heroes fought for humane values, and the villains turned out to be far worse than even the fevered imagining of our wartime propaganda. (Indeed, as fragmentary reports of the full depth of our enemies' depravity began to emerge during the war, very few people believed them.) If in later years, and later wars, such stark, simple distinctions, such moral absolutes, would be harder to come by and thus more difficult to believe in, in this conflict they seemed to fit perfectly.

Consider the combatants: in our corner were Franklin Roosevelt and Winston Churchill, who easily rank among the greatest statesmen in their nations' history. Arrayed against us were Nazi Germany and imperial Japan—racist, totalitarian states using evil means to pursue repugnant ends. The contest was nothing less than a titanic struggle for the future of mankind, waged in the skies, the deserts, the mountains, the islands and on the surface of the oceans as well as in their depths. At stake was whether the second half of the 20th century (and beyond) would be an age of slavery, hatred and death or … the world we live in today. And even if it is sometimes possible to imagine a future better than the one our fathers and grandfathers won for us, it is emphatically not possible to imagine a future worse than the one they averted. In victory, they saved the world from a new dark age.

Volumes that would fill several libraries have been written about World War II, and each year more books crowd more shelves on the subject. This book, a survey of several wars, hasn't room to offer a complete report on this immense war. So the pages that follow report on three theaters of the war that are often neglected: the deserts of North Africa, where German forces first met defeat; the islands of the Pacific, where Japan was transformed from conqueror to besieged defender in the 12 months after Pearl Harbor; and the steppes of Russia, where Nazi Germany's fate was sealed. In addition, a portfolio of pictures by legendary photographer Robert Capa offers in-

THEY WENT THATAWAY: An Italian peasant tips off a U.S. soldier in Palermo, Sicily, 1943

delible images from the Allied march through Europe that began in Italy and ended in Berlin with Germany's surrender.

In every passage, in every picture that evokes a specific time and place, we're reminded of a larger truth—that sometimes human beings really are as distinct as heroes and villains, that occasionally we face a clear choice between good and evil, and that once in a great while, life's path is clearly marked in black and white. World War II was just such a moment—and even better, the good guys rose to the challenge—and won. For that, we can never cease to be grateful. ■

Portfolio

Robert Capa

It was Robert Capa who first uttered the words by which all combat photographers live (and sometimes die): "If your pictures aren't good enough, you're not close enough." And Capa meant what he said: he was aboard one of the very first landing craft to hit Omaha Beach on D-day. Within minutes of reaching shore, most of the soldiers from Capa's troop carrier had been killed. Capa himself went missing for two days, which prompted his press

colleagues to assume that he was dead too. Days later, as a group of close friends held an impromptu wake in a barn in the French country-side, Capa strolled in and asked for a drink.

Born André Erno Friedmann, the Hungarian Jew invented the persona of "Robert Capa" so that he and his girlfriend, Gerda Taro, could pose as assistants to the supposedly famous (and entirely fictional) American photographer—Capa—thus earning three fees from European publishers, rather than just one. By the time he waded onto the Normandy beaches, Capa was on his third war: he had already covered the Spanish Civil War (where Taro, the love of his life, was crushed by a tank) and the Sino-Japanese War.

Capa was a larger-than-life figure who helped create the archetype of the dashing wartime photojournalist. His poker buddies included Ernest Hemingway, John Huston and Irwin Shaw; his romantic involvements featured the likes of Ingrid Bergman, Hedy Lamarr and Vivien Leigh. But war trumped romance for Capa. He went on to cover the 1948 Arab-Israeli war and then the twilight of the French colonial empire in Vietnam. It was there that Capa met his end in 1954, stepping on a land mine that killed him just after he had taken a picture.

Yet Capa's legacy lives on—both in the uniquely intense images he captured and in the form of Magnum, the photo agency he helped found to protect photographers' rights to their work. Taking its name from the jumbo champagne bottle, it brings to mind another of Capa's phrases that combat photographers have embraced: "This calls for a drink!"

Beachhead
Omaha Beach shortly after D-day. Capa, who was among the first ashore during the Normandy invasion, shot all his rolls of film in a few short hours, then rode an empty landing craft back across the English Channel to make sure his film was sent safely on its way. After stocking up with more film, Capa hitched a ride aboard another troop carrier and once again landed on the beach, where the battle was still raging. Sadly, almost all his photos of the initial landing were partially ruined by an error in the photo lab.

◀ Spot of Tea?

A 1941 evening in a London air raid shelter. Capa was stranded in Britain from the war's start until 1943, because the U.S. Department of Justice incorrectly believed that, as a Hungarian national, he might be sympathetic to the Axis.

▶ Don't Shoot!

An American soldier accepts the surrender of a German fighter during the Battle of the Bulge, 1944.

▼ Conquering Heroes

Newly liberated Sicilians hail victorious American soldiers as they ride through Palermo. Capa's friend, writer Irwin Shaw, once observed, "He always rode towards the sound of the guns." Or the cheers.

▲ Hit the Dirt!

Spectators at the great parade following the 1944 liberation of Paris fall to the ground when a German sniper, who had remained behind, opens fire.

◀ All Fouled Up

In 1945 an American paratrooper carries a wounded comrade to safety near the Rhine, while another jumper's canopy is snagged on a telephone wire. Capa parachuted into combat with U.S. Rangers several times. He claimed he stowed an extra set of underwear in his pack before jumping into a surrounded Allied position in Belgium, in case his shorts suddenly became unusable. The precaution, he later said, proved prescient.

▶ Sniper's Prey

An American soldier lies mortally wounded on a hotel balcony during the 1945 capture of Leipzig. Moments later, Capa said, his comrades raced downstairs and silenced the German sniper.

ALL ASHORE: Marines unload supplies at Iwo Jima. The initial two hours were easy—not so the deadly battle that followed.

War in the Islands

In a war of aircraft carriers, torpedo planes and amphibious landings, the U.S. and Japan battle for the beaches, skies and atolls of the Pacific

Never before was a war fought over such a vast theater—the thousands of square miles of the Pacific Ocean. And never before was warfare at sea waged over such distances that the ships locked in combat never sighted one another. Instead, pilots flew into battle from aircraft carriers hundreds of miles apart. The war in the Pacific became a struggle to secure runways— on carrier decks or strips of cleared ground. In these dispatches, TIME reports on two great naval air battles that gave the U.S. an early lead in the war at sea. America's island-by-island struggle to bring its airplanes within bombing range of Japan is represented by an eyewitness account of the invasion of Iwo Jima late in the war.

May 18, 1942

In the Coral Sea

It was the greatest battle in the history of the U.S. Pacific Fleet. It was fought below the equator, in the Coral Sea off Australia's northeast coast. For five days, smudged with belching smoke screens and roaring with bomb bursts, a U.S. naval force and Army bombers from land bases took turns tearing into a heavy Jap task force, invasion-bound.

For the Jap the going was too tough. His fleet was badly shot up, largely by one of the greatest concentrations of air power ever sent against a naval force. The straw that broke his back was the unhappy accident of piling into the main U.S. naval force no more than 450 miles off the Australian coast.

Punished until he could stand no more, he turned tail, while 500 airplanes, U.S. and Japanese, roared through the bright subtropical sun over his uneasy head. The U.S. aircraft had the edge. They burst through the Jap fighters again & again, rained bombs and aerial torpedoes at the surface craft.

The battled ended in a nightmare of retreat, with U.S. aircraft hacking at the enemy every step of the way back to the questionable shelter of the islands trailing off the east coast of New Guinea. When the Jap finally got there, only he could count his losses accurately. But by conservative U.S. count he had lost 21 ships, sunk or disabled. And he had unquestionably taken a beating—the first serious defeat of his headlong career through the South Pacific.

The Battle of the Coral Sea was not a clash of a whole fleet against another whole fleet. It was a battle of relentless air bombing and the rapid parry-and-thrust of task forces.

The task force, a varied group of vessels strong enough to carry out a specific job, has become the sea weapon of World War II. Modern naval warfare in the Pacific has kept the slow-footed battleship in port, made the carrier the center of task-force operation, the long-range reconnaissance plane the eyes of the striking force. The airplane has so changed sea warfare that its apostles think they will soon see the day when the plane will drive the battleship completely from the seas.

June 22, 1942

"Abandon Ship!"

Distance and censorship combined to delay Time's *reports of the war in the South Pacific. This account of action during the Battle of the Coral Sea ran weeks after the events it records:*

In the harbor of Tulagi, in the Solomon Islands, the Jap ships lay like dozing ducks when Lieut. Commander Joseph Taylor, of Danville, Ill., saw them through the early-morning clouds. Over his interplane radio he called to the leader of a companion squadron: "Bill, you hit 'em high and I'll hit 'em low!

Dive bombers dipped, torpedo-planes flew low and level at the massed Jap cruisers, destroyers, troop transports, auxiliaries. The attacking pilots swore and yelled into their phones in excitement. Some of their targets sank at anchor; others, aflame, died on the harbor beaches. From three attacks that day, every U.S. plane returned to the mother carriers—the *Lexington* and another, unnamed—waiting 100 miles south of Tulagi with a covering force of cruisers and destroyers.

Two mornings later, scout bombers sighted a Japanese carrier-cruiser force, about 180 miles north of the U.S. force. Attacking U.S. pilots soon saw a stan-

dard Japanese naval pattern; a big carrier (the new, 50-plane *Ryukaku*) steaming astern of two cruisers. The U.S. planes were still ten miles away when the cruisers' guns spat red and yellow flame. At four miles, the enemy anti-aircraft fire was thick and fierce. But the planes ignored the cruisers and flew on toward the carrier.

The *Ryukaku* swerved into a frantic, leftward circle to dodge the U.S. bombs. The maneuver failed. So did the efforts of the cruisers, firing shells into the water ahead of low-flying torpedo planes, hoping they would fly into the geysers. Bombs ripped into the *Ryukaku*, mantling her decks in smoke and flame. A gun mount soared lazily upward, curved overside into the sea. Then the

torpedoes struck home, squarely amidships. Later the Navy said that at least 15 bombs and ten torpedoes hit the Jap ship. The *Ryukaku* had completed her third circle when she sank, with most of her planes still aboard. Aboard the *Lexington*, radio receivers and loudspeakers caught the happy voice of Lieut. Commander Robert Dixon, who was leading a bomber squadron: "Scratch one flat-top, scratch one flat-top!"

That night (as they later learned) the Japanese and U.S. forces passed within 30 miles of each other. Next morning U.S. scouts spotted the Japs in real force: three carriers, with cruisers and destroyers in the usual triangular formations. Wisely the U.S. cruisers and destroyers again stayed with their car-

LOOKOUTS: Douglas SBD-3 Dauntless dive bombers patrol the coral reefs off Midway Island, 1942

FRANK SCHERSCHEL—TIMEPIX

MEN OVERBOARD! Look closely, and you will see sailors climbing down ropes as they follow orders to abandon the U.S.S. *Lexington* before it sinks. More than 90% of the crew survived.

riers. Not once during the battle did the U.S. and Japanese warships get a shot at each other. Off went the planes, into history's first carrier-vs.-carrier combat.

The U.S. planes apparently struck first. Their bombs and torpedoes left the 14,000-ton, 45-plane *Syokaku* flaming and listing so badly that the U.S. pilots doubted her survival (the Navy claimed only that she was severely damaged). When she was hit, the *Syokaku's* flight decks were bare; her planes were attacking the *Lexington*.

Against the *Lexington* and her sister carrier (which was probably damaged but survived) came 108 Japanese planes. Forty were shot down. The *Lexington* dodged nine torpedoes, but could not dodge two others. Three bombs also hit her. Nevertheless her crew took aboard most of her planes,

had three fires under control and another nearly out when an internal explosion (apparently of escaping gasoline fumes) rent the *Lexington*.

At 5:07 p.m., the aircraft carrier's commander, Captain Frederick Carl Sherman (since promoted to Rear Admiral), gave the sailor's saddest order: "Abandon ship!" Before they slid overboard into the sea, to be picked up by destroyers and cruisers, all the men lined their shoes in orderly rows on the flight deck. As Captain Sherman followed the last of his crew overboard, another explosion shook the ship. A little later, lest she fall into Jap hands or endanger other ships, a U.S. destroyer torpedoed the *Lexington's* flaming hulk. "That," said Admiral Sherman, "was the end of the *Lexington*." [The sister carrier, the U.S.S. *Yorktown*, sank at Midway.—ED.] ∎

HIT: A Japanese bomb strikes the U.S.S. *Yorktown* in the Battle of Midway, June 4, 1942. The aircraft carrier sank three days later.

June 22, 1942

Victory at Midway

The U.S. had not merely won a great battle in the Pacific and averted a great disaster: the U.S. had proved its skill and might in a new form of warfare at sea. In the Battle of Midway, U.S. forces met and drove back the first full battle fleet, organized on the grand scale for modern war, which any nation has yet put to sea.

The Japanese Fleet, built around seaborne air power, had to retreat before U.S. air power in a still mightier form: the land-based airplane, now come into its own as a dominant weapon of naval warfare.

Now that the returns from the Coral Sea and Midway are in, these facts seem clear: Japan has lost much of her navy's striking power at sea. Without that power, Japan cannot bring the war to the U.S., or even to the remaining U.S. strongholds in the Pacific. The naval war in the Pacific is now a race to replace striking power. In that race the U.S. has the edge.

On the afternoon of June 3, Navy patrol planes sighted a Japanese fleet, in two forces, some 500 miles west of Midway; a striking force of four carriers, three battleships, many cruisers and destroyers; a supporting force of one carrier, several cruisers and destroyers, troop transports—in all, about 30 Jap ships.

Lieut. Colonel Walter C. Sweeney Jr. led three Flying Fortresses from Mid-

SACRIFICE: A Navy bomber squadron poses before flying into combat at Midway. Only one airman survived.

way to the attack. Clouds compelled his crews to fly fairly low (at about 7,000 feet). The accuracy of the Japs' antiaircraft fire surprised the U.S. pilots and bounced their planes around, but none was brought down. In this first attack, they reported hits on one cruiser, a transport, possibly a second cruiser and a battleship.

In the night, the Japanese maneuvered into assault formations. Cruisers and destroyers led the fleet. Then came three of the carriers, with escorting vessels. About 150 miles behind trailed three battleships, ready to finish off Midway after the carrier planes had attacked. Well behind the battleships were the transports, with their protecting coveys. One of the carriers, also escorted, had sneaked off on its own.

Next morning, Colonel Sweeney's bombers were in the air, headed for what they thought was the main Japanese fleet, when Navy patrols spotted the advance Japanese forces only 125 miles west of Midway. The Japs were then hit with everything Midway could throw at them. Marine Corps dive-bombers struck the leading cruisers and destroyers. Colonel Sweeney's heavy bombers went for the carriers, left one blazing. Four converted bombers, the first Army torpedo planes ever recorded in action, hit the other carriers. Two of the four went down after they had fired their torpedoes; the others limped home to Midway. The Navy had some land-based bombers and torpedo planes on Midway, and these also joined the battle.

This concentration of Midway's air strength was decisive. It dazed the Japs before they were well started. It compelled them to concentrate their planes for their fleet's own defense, after a

single, unsuccessful attack on Midway.

At noon, bombers and torpedo planes from U.S. carriers went into battle. Said a naval flyer: "Ten minutes later the three carriers were blazing from stem to stern." At about the same time, the Army bombers resumed the attack, after refueling on Midway's damaged airfield.

At 1:30 p.m., planes from the fourth, so far unsighted, Japanese carrier attacked a U.S. carrier. Said a torpedo plane pilot who saw U.S. fighters intercept the Japs: "It looked like the sky over there was covered by a curtain of smoke streamers—a curtain of Japanese going down in flames." Only six or

seven Jap bombers got close enough to aim their missiles at the carrier; all were shot down by antiaircraft fire. Two hours later, Japanese torpedo planes attacked the same carrier. Fighters on the flight deck, just in to re-fuel, took off with nearly empty tanks, flew through their own fire, beat off the attackers.

How badly the U.S. carrier was hit, the Navy did not say. But its planes found and attacked the fourth Japanese carrier that evening and again the next morning. The U.S. pilots were sure that this Jap carrier, like the three others, never reached port. [The U.S. carrier was the *Yorktown*.—ED.]

Battered back on the defensive the Jap fleet scurried homeward. As in the Coral Sea, no Jap surface ship had come within sight or range of a U.S. surface ship. Long-range Army bombers continued the hammering pursuit for three days. ∎

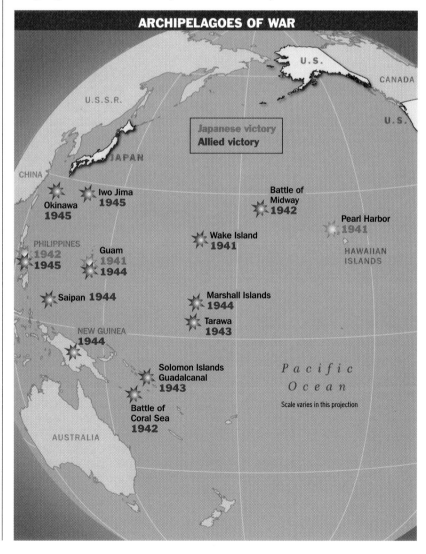

ARCHIPELAGOES OF WAR

U.S.

CANADA

U.S.

U.S.S.R.

Japanese victory
Allied victory

JAPAN

CHINA

Iwo Jima
1945

Okinawa
1945

Battle of
Midway
1942

Pearl Harbor
1941

Wake Island
1941

HAWAIIAN
ISLANDS

PHILIPPINES
1942
1945

Guam
1941
1944

Saipan 1944

Marshall Islands
1944

Tarawa
1943

NEW GUINEA
1944

Solomon Islands
Guadalcanal
1943

Pacific
Ocean

Scale varies in this projection

Battle of
Coral Sea
1942

AUSTRALIA

March 5, 1945

Lives for Yards

• •

On 8-sq.-mi. Iwo Jima last week at least 40,000 Marines fought to the death with 20,000 entrenched Japanese in an area so constricted that the troops engaged averaged twelve men to an acre. Ashore with the Marines, TIME *correspondent Robert Sherrod radioed his account of the battle:*

• •

The Japs will lose Iwo Jima to the men of Major General Harry Schmidt's V Amphibious Corps, and we will have airfields within 750 miles of Tokyo. One reason for this is sheer power, including naval and air supremacy. But the ultimate factor in the fall of Iwo Jima will be the character and courage of the United States Marine Corps. There comes a time when enemy defenses will no longer yield before fire power, however heavy. That is the time when men on foot must pay for yardage with their lives. That is when the Marines are at their greatest. This, said General Holland ("Howlin' Mad") Smith, is their toughest fight in 168 years.

Two hours after the original landings on D-day, we had a toe hold and it looked like a good one. But all hell broke loose before noon. From the north and from the south the hidden Japs poured artillery and 6-in. mortars into the Marines on the beachhead. Nearly all our tanks were clustered near the black-ash beaches like so many black beetles struggling to move on tar paper. A few other chuffing monsters waddled up the steep incline toward the airfield, spouting flames now and then into the pillboxes which were blended into the sandy approaches.

Viewing the scene later, I could only marvel that any men got past those pillboxes. Their openings were mostly to the north and south—naval gunfire might have destroyed them had their vents been exposed to the sea. But somehow these incredible Marines had swept past the pillboxes, tossing grenades into them or shooting flame into them as they inched uphill toward the airfield.

It was sickening to watch the Jap mortar shells crash into the men as they climbed. These huge explosive charges—"floating ash cans," we called them—would crash among the thin lines of Marines, or among the boats bringing reinforcements to the beach, throwing sand, water and even pieces of human flesh 100 feet into the air. Supporting naval gunfire and planes with bombs managed to knock out some of the mortars, but the Japs continued throwing their deadly missiles all afternoon. By noon the assault battalions reported 20% to 25% fatalities.

Some units crossed the island in mid-afternoon and overran the southern extremity of the No. 1 Airfield (the bomber base), but others were thrown back. Five tanks actually got on the airfield; three of them were quickly knocked out and the other two had to return. Our trouble was that the Japs

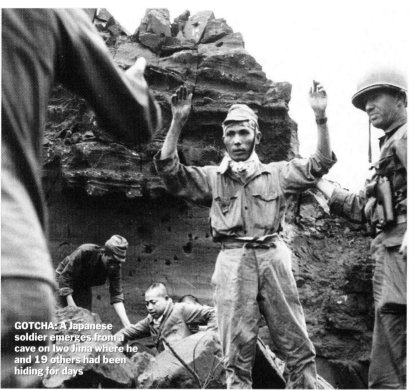

GOTCHA: A Japanese soldier emerges from a cave on Iwo Jima where he and 19 others had been hiding for days

had us covered from both ends of the island. Our men could only advance and die, paving with their bodies a way for the others.

One wonderful factor was in our favor that first day: the weather was fine. A smooth sea enabled us to get more troops ashore and to emplace some artillery. With the rough seas of the second and third days, we might never have accomplished our initial landing. Not all the small boats made the beach that first afternoon, but enough made it to enable us to keep our foothold. By late afternoon we held perhaps 10% of the island—the most dangerous 10%.

The first night on Iwo Jima can only be described as a nightmare in hell. It was partly the weather—Iwo is as cold as Ohio at this season. The front line now has moved out of the tropics into a region of high winds and long periods without sunshine. Soon, U.S. fighting men will long for the dear old steaming jungles and sun-baked atolls. All through this bitter night the Japs rained heavy mortars and rockets and artillery on the entire area between the beach and the airfield. Twice they hit casualty stations on the beach. Many men who had been only wounded were killed. The command post of one of the assault battalions got a direct hit which killed several officers. An artillery battalion based near the beach had twelve men killed. One group of medical corpsmen was reduced from 28 to 11; the corpsmen were taking it, as usual.

Along the beach in the morning lay many dead. About them, whether American or Jap, there was one thing in common. They died with the greatest possible violence. Nowhere in the Pacific war have I seen such badly mangled bodies. Many of them were cut squarely in half. Legs and arms lay 50 ft. away from any body. Only the legs were easy to identify—Japanese if wrapped in khaki puttees, American if covered by canvas leggings. In one spot on the sand, far from the nearest clusters of dead men, I saw a string of guts 15 ft. long.

At the end of six days of bitter fighting, the men of the 3rd, 4th and 5th Marine Divisions hold approximately 40% of Iwo Jima, including half of Airfield No. 2, the fighter field. This is almost in the geographical center of the island and is perhaps the key to the entire defense. Built on a high plateau, it is defended by hundreds of interlaced pillboxes

and concrete casemated caves, apparently connected by labyrinthine tunnels which wind in & out of the cliffsides.

A typical Jap blockhouse below Suribachi was more cunningly contrived than anything on Tarawa. Its outer walls were of reinforced concrete, 40 inches thick. The vent did not open toward the sea, but slantwise toward the upper beaches: the 120-mm gun inside could fire on the beaches and some of our ships, but could not be hit except from a particular angle. There was no sign that it had been touched by anything but a flamethrower. Beside it lay the bodies of eight Marines—the apparent cost of taking what was only one of several hundreds of similar positions, nearly all of which have to be knocked out by men on foot with explosive charges or flame-throwers.

Jap mortars and rockets still fire heavily from the recesses of the northern plateau. Even on the night of D-plus-four we caught hundreds of rounds. There is still no point on the island which the Japs cannot easily bring under fire, though their chances of accuracy diminish as we slowly edge forward up the high ground. Soon they will no longer be looking down our throats.

The 28th Regiment of tall, gaunt Colonel Harry ("The Horse") Liversedge took Suribachi Volcano on D-plus-four. When the U.S. flag was raised over this highest point on the island, some Marines wept openly. ∎

TAKE ONE: Marines raise the flag over Iwo Jima for the first time. The picture of the second hoisting, with a larger flag, is more often seen.

December 22, 1941

Isoroku Yamamoto

The architect of the attack on Pearl Harbor is a proud, driven adversary

A HUMBLE WIRELESS SET TREMBLED LAST WEEK WITH quasi-divine vibrations as the Son of Heaven himself sent Admiral Isoroku Yamamoto, Commander in Chief of the Combined Imperial Fleets, congratulations for the daring execution of a brilliant treachery. Congratulations from Emperor Hirohito fix upon their recipient an incredible joy, but also a certain uneasiness. For they not only bestow praise; they also adjure the congratulatee to continue the good work—or else.

In order to drive the white man from Greater East Asia, Admiral Yamamoto must drive away, or preferably destroy, the white man's bridge to Asia: his fleets. Surveying his assignment, Yamamoto saw that his greatest permanent necessity would be to keep British power and U.S. power from effecting a junction. If, with the help of the Army, he could break off the rungs by which the U.S. Navy has to climb over the shoulder of the Pacific to Singapore, his job would be much easier. Therefore, the attacks of Dec. 7 on Pearl Harbor, Wake, Midway and Guam were important; but the penultimate rung, the Philippine Islands, was most vital to his nation's cause.

In these great projects, air power was the key. By this week Yamamoto's air power had either done or helped to do the following things: sunk one U.S. battleship, capsized another, sunk three destroyers, perhaps one submarine; sunk two British battleships; partly knocked out U.S. and British air power in Hawaii, the Philippines and Malaya by surprise bombardments; established landings in northern Malaya and northern Luzon which promised to provide air bases; captured Guam. He had paid a not-too-exorbitant price: one battleship, one cruiser, one destroyer, perhaps 75 planes.

In every way, by feeling, by training, by detailed experience, Isoroku Yamamoto has all his life been bent to one task: defeat the U.S. and Britain in the Pacific. He is not the grinning, bowing little man with horn-rimmed glasses, eager mustache and super-buck teeth which U.S. cartoonists have selected as Mr. Japan. He is, instead, a hard-bitten professional man. He hates, and all his colleagues hate, the U.S. and British attitude toward Japan, and especially toward Japan's Navy. He has heard for years the U.S. Navy's boast that the Japs would be a pushover. He knows how the cruiser *Mogami*, some of whose welded seams parted when she fired a full salvo on her trials, was exaggerated into a kind of saltwater One Hoss Shay.

He has long hated, and did much to fight, the imputation of inferiority which Britain and the U.S. made in insisting on maintaining the 5-5-3 ratio of naval tonnage in 1934. Referring to a dinner in London, he says: "I was never told there that being much shorter than the others I ought to eat only three-fifths of the food on my plate. I ate as much as I needed."

HUNTED: Yamamoto died in 1943 when his plane was shot down in the Solomon Islands

Unlike the Japanese Army, which has built itself a pretty sordid record in China, Yamamoto's Navy displaces better than its own weight in pride. He graduated from the Japanese Naval Academy in time to lose the first and second fingers of his left hand aboard Admiral Togo's flagship *Mikasa* in the great battle off Tsushima in 1904.

Down the years he has absorbed and fostered the morale of Japan's Navy. Admiral Yamamoto's men, used to negotiating the rip channel tides and foul weathers of their islands, are fine navigators. They work round the clock. They service their ships smartly. They submit to living conditions at which U.S. sailors would mutiny: Japanese ships have superstructures which look like pagodas piled on Shinto shrines astraddle Buddhist temples, and in these great upper horrors the crew lives, to save space, in quarters so crowded that most officers enjoy less room than U.S. enlisted men.

Yamamoto means Base of a Mountain, and the Admiral is solid. He is deliberate, positive, aggressive. His passion for winning has made him the bridge, poker, chess and *go* champion of the Japanese Navy. He is wily as only the Japanese can be. When he crossed the U.S. in 1934, reporters noted that he was short on English, that he answered them through an interpreter. Actually he spoke excellent English then; he used the interpreter to brush off embarrassing questions.

At 57, he is at the top of his powers. He smokes, drinks with gusto, works like a dog, ashore lives a Spartan life in a modest house in Tokyo's suburbs. He has firm control of his heavy-lipped, firm-jawed face, and crops his hairs to look more like the man of action that he is. The Admiral is an adversary who does not want underrating. ∎

November 30, 1942

William Halsey

Steering his battleships to victory, he saves the U.S. troops in Guadalcanal

ADMIRAL CHESTER WILLIAM NIMITZ MEASURED HIS words. With his own hand the Commander in Chief of the Pacific Fleet wrote last week: *"Halsey's conduct of his present command leaves nothing to be desired ... He has that rare combination of intellectual capacity and military audacity ... For his successful turning back of the Jap attempt to take Guadalcanal in Mid-November he has been nominated by the President for the rank of Admiral, which he richly deserves."*

At the moment when these words of praise were being weighed in a map-plastered office in Pearl Harbor, other words were being weighed even more carefully in an office 2,000 miles to the southwest. They were reports on the battle which provoked the tributes. The face which looked down on those reports was itself like a battlefield. Everything about it was big, broad, strong. The weather had been on it, and personal suffering behind it. The huge mouth looked like command, and above it, the nose was pugnacious. The eyes were aggressive. They and their screen of brow above the weariness below were as impressive and busy-looking as a couple of task forces. The face, as it read, was thoughtful.

Time after time Admiral William Frederick ("Bull") Halsey had said: *"Now if these were Japs, this is how I would strike ..."* The reports showed that the stubborn Japs had organized everything which they thought necessary to retake Guadalcanal once & for all. They formed a powerful bombardment task force, including battleships, which was to come in with the most terrifying kind of attack, night shelling, and pound the will to resist out of the U.S. beachhead. Then convoys of transports with over 20,000 troops and with all essential weapons, such as tanks and heavy artillery, were to effect landings. Then, perhaps with the help of carrier-based air attacks, the entire force was to do its final job. That was what the Japs thought. They came piecemeal, in several task forces; but most

BULLDOG: Admiral Halsey aboard the U.S.S. *New Jersey*, en route to the Philippines

CORBIS

of their strength poured down "the slot"—the channel down the middle of the Solomons. They were confident. The U.S. Navy had not, in over three months of fighting, done much fighting with surface units. They had a surprise in store.

Friday the 13th was not lucky for the Japs. At 2 a.m. a U.S. task force of cruisers and destroyers under Rear Admiral Daniel J. Callaghan drove in on the Jap bombardment group. The U.S. flagship was the heavy cruiser *San Francisco.* Behind her steamed a column of heavy and light cruisers. Destroyers flanked the line of battle.

Admiral Callaghan swung his task force right into the main Jap forces. Without hesitation, he drove his ship, whose biggest guns were 8-in., to within 20,000 yards of a Jap battleship, which carried 14-in. guns. He led his force right between two Japanese groups, so that when he pulled out the Japs fired on each other. The *San Francisco*, in running the gantlet, had crippled the Jap battleship, but a 14-in. salvo found the cruiser's bridge and killed Admiral Callaghan and Captain Casin Young (who when blown into the water off the *Arizona* at Pearl Harbor swam back to his ship and resumed the fight). It knocked out Lieut. Commander Bruce McCandless, 31, third in command on the bridge at the time. When McCandless came to, he saw that he was "sopus"— Navy for senior officer present. It was up to him to get the ship out. He got to his feet, took command of the ship, kept her proudly at the head of her column until the battle was over.

The few times the Japs had been hit, while reinforcing the Solomons, they had been hit and run from. But this time there was a new spirit in the U.S. task forces. The Americans came in slugging again and yet again. Another U.S. unit under Admiral Norman Scott took part. He, too, was killed. The next night the Americans attacked once more.

Halsey's victory is no guarantee that the Japs will not try again, powerfully and perhaps dangerously. In the battle of Guadalcanal, he had: 1) repulsed the strongest Japanese attempt to take Guadalcanal; 2) bitten heavily into Japanese strength; 3) restored the Navy's confidence in itself and public confidence in the Navy; 4) given the Marines and Army on Guadalcanal a chance to clean out Japanese observation posts and main forces, possibly win absolute superiority on the island. Halsey's battle saved Guadalcanal. But in the mind of Bill Halsey there is only one ultimate aim: the still distant assault on Japan itself. Just before he saved Guadalcanal, he talked of that assault and said: *I hope I'll be there.* ∎

War in the Desert

Erwin Rommel's Afrika Korps rolls in triumph across North Africa, but his tanks retreat when the Allies, under Bernard Montgomery, strike back

World War II brought war to a host of fronts, and each of them bred weapons and tactics uniquely adapted to the local geography. Desert warfare began when Adolf Hitler sent General Erwin Rommel to shore up the North African colonies of France's Vichy government and Italy's Benito Mussolini, a critical gateway to Europe. Rommel pioneered mechanized desert warfare, thrusting his panzer divisions against the British, sending them in retreat near Alexandria. But the Allies regrouped, named British General Bernard Montgomery to command their forces and pumped arms and men into the region. The Allies attacked Rommel in October, 1942, even as U.S. troops landed in the capitals of the Vichy colonies. Rommel was sent on a long retreat that finally ended German control of North Africa.

July 13, 1942

Into the Funnel

After so many evil tidings, the news looked a little better. Germany's General Erwin Rommel had chased the broken, retreating British 325 miles in eleven days, had rammed his armored spearheads down the coastal desert from Matrûh, taking the flyspeck towns on the railroad to Alexandria like peas ripped from a pod. Now for four days he had not advanced.

The mercurial people of Alexandria, who had shivered and shaken while Rommel rolled, smiled again and went back to their nightclubs. Those who had fled Alexandria talked of coming back "within a few days." Once more Cairo diffused through its screen of censorship a rosy mist of optimism—the same color as that which had preceded the mist-shattering fall of Tobruk.

Lieut. General Neil Ritchie, who lost the first round of the battle, was out, and command of the battered Eighth Army had been taken over by no less a person than the British Commander in Chief of the Middle East, General Sir Claude John Eyre ("The Auk") Auchinleck. The Auk decided to plug Rommel at the neck of a funnel—the 35-mile gap between El Alamein on the coast and the northern tongue of the steep-sided, marsh-bedded Qattara Depression. El Alamein is 70 miles from Alexandria.

Full-steaming into the funnel's neck, Rommel hesitated, then massed his forces and launched them at El Alamein. Thirteen of his Stukas, dive-

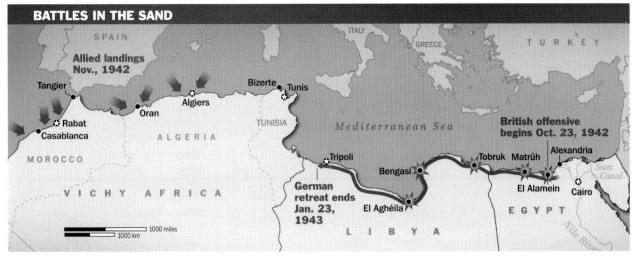

Allied landings Nov., 1942

SPAIN

ITALY

GREECE

TURKEY

Tangier

Bizerte • Tunis

Rabat

Oran

Algiers

Casablanca

MOROCCO

ALGERIA

TUNISIA

Mediterranean Sea

British offensive begins Oct. 23, 1942

Alexandria

VICHY AFRICA

Tripoli

Bengasi

Tobruk Matrûh

El Alamein

Suez Canal

Cairo

EGYPT

German retreat ends Jan. 23, 1943

El Aghéila

LIBYA

Nile River

1000 miles

1000 km

bombing the British guns, were crumpled by fighters from South Africa, and the guns kept firing. Meanwhile, from the south a British light force sped around to harry Rommel's flank. After eleven successive days of relentless attack, Rommel's weary battalions had to withdraw to re-form and prepare for a new attack.

After launching more counterattacks, the British announced the capture of 600 Germans and 40 cannon— some of the guns 25-pounders which the Germans had captured from them. Between the lines of counterattack, Rommel's five divisions of armor and infantry contracted into a solid, sinister oval, pointed at the British center. If that oval should crunch through, the El Alamein defense line that Auchinleck hoped to organize would be lost.

Egypt smiled because Rommel stopped, but the truth was that Egypt's

plight was almost as desperate as when the German charged into the funnel. He was still there, he was always dangerous, he was nearly intact. ∎

November 9, 1942

Wings over the Desert

An empty Chianti bottle lay in the desert where an Italian had dropped it in his retreat. Near by, the moonlight made a complicated and shadowy apparition out of a wrecked Mark III tank, glinted on a German chocolate tin and a bloodied German helmet.

East of this no man's land, headed in the general direction of the Chianti bottle, a squad of British sappers dragged themselves across the sand, pulling the strings of German land mines. Behind them the 51st Highlanders squat-

ted in slit trenches, awaiting the signal to advance another 50 yards. To the rear, British 25-pounders roared, spewing their shells across the line into the darker, hostile horizon.

In the moonlit, light-lanced sky, Allied planes ranged back and forth, their routes marked by bursting bombs behind the Axis front line. West of the Chianti bottle the Axis armies ponderously gave ground.

Somewhere behind the German lines, Erwin Rommel listened with grim interest to the uproar of British guns, and high-domed Albert Kesselring, who designed the bombing of Coventry, brooded over his less than adequate African Luftwaffe. Somewhere behind the Allied lines, tall, affable "Mars" Coningham, R.A.F. chief in the field, guided the performance of his planes. Near by, in a desert caravan, the tough, ubiquitous Bernard Montgomery

AIRLIFT: A U.S. Army supply plane flies over the Pyramids. Superior Allied air power helped defeat Rommel in Africa.

GAMBLERS: U.S. officers and airmen plan a bombing run on Tunisia from a post in the Sahara desert

MARGARET BOURKE-WHITE—TIMEPIX

Promissory Front

This week the Allies offered Hitler a second front. Just when General Rommel's remnants were fleeing before the British in Egypt, U.S. troops landed along the whole coastline of Vichy Morocco and Algeria. Instantly Hitler's already serious problem of trying to keep an Axis foothold in Africa became just twice as serious.

Algiers in the dawn of Nov. 8 was a white, triangular wound against the dun hills behind the harbor. Beyond its jetties, well out in the Mediterranean, a great naval concentration stood in from Gibraltar. A British destroyer nosed past the barges across the entrance to the harbor, darted up to one of the docks, disgorged a small force of U.S. Rangers, who scurried toward the big, white French Admiralty Building on the waterfront. When the docks were clear the destroyer threw a few shells, starting great fires, and dashed out of the harbor.

Unfolding at Algiers that morning was a plan for the conquest of French North Africa. It was thorough and simple. Its initial objective was the seizure of the principal ports of French North Africa: Algiers and Oran on the Mediterranean, Casablanca on the Atlantic and Rabat, the capital of Morocco. With them in hand or enveloped, the larger objectives of the U.S. entry into North Africa could unfold: first the joining of the U.S. forces in the northwest with the British in Libya, then the destruction of the Afrika Korps, the reestablishment of Allied mastery over the southern Mediterranean and finally assault on southern Europe. ∎

kept his finger on every unit of the strongest Eighth Army any British general has yet commanded in the long desert campaign.

Along the 40-mile front there had been no spectacular advance. Unlike previous desert campaigns when wide pendulum swings were measured in hundreds of miles, last week's gains were measured in yards. This was a different kind of desert warfare.

This time minefields, artillery and geography hemmed in the space-devouring tanks. Until infantry clawed a path through the deep and complicated defenses of Rommel's line, there would be no sweeping around flanks. The fighting resembled the trench warfare of World War I. Under a thunderous barrage of cannon fire British troops went forward in short, heavy waves. British ordnance was the week's surprise. Buildings in Alexandria's suburbs, 700 miles behind the line, shook with the reverberations. Axis artillery was only a faint obbligato to the symphony of British guns, which never before in the desert had been able to match the power of Rommel's superb artillery. As the battle wore on, the volume and tempo increased. Germans and Italians left alive were too dazed to fight.

But the most noteworthy Allied performance of the week was in the air. The score, after six days of fighting, was 101 Axis planes downed to 48 Allied. So complete was Allied superiority that aircraft observers were able to hover undisturbed over Rommel's gun positions, directing British fire. ∎

ELIOT ELISOFON—TIMEPIX

TESTING: Indian sappers of Britain's Eighth Army work to clear mines left by the Germans

LOOT: British troops find a souvenir in a destroyed German vehicle

November 30, 1942

The Bells of Tobruk

TIME *correspondent Walter Graebner, en route to the U.S. from Moscow, last week cabled from Cairo:*

I have witnessed one of the war's greatest spectacles—the dash of the victorious Eighth Army and R.A.F. over the Western Desert.

At sundown (5 p.m.) on the first day out we reached the former no man's land at El Alamein. The entire western half of the area was littered with German and Italian guns and shells, helmets, clothing, food, maps and other things, smashed and torn by the Aussies as they crashed through. All about were black, well-made "Jerry cans" (for fuel), a dozen of which we collected and filled with water when we learned that the Nazis had oiled many of the wells farther west. Old tins of British-made "Kiwi" shoe polish lay side by side with empty bottles of Chianti. Pressed into the sand was a letter to a German soldier from his father in Düsseldorf.

Though the Nazi losses in the Alamein battle were colossal, the British also paid heavily. Batteries of German 88-mm guns mowed hundreds of Aussies down before the Germans were driven back for good. But the Aussies proved themselves superior. We viewed freshly made graves of two Aussies and dozens of Germans across the road from where we slept. The bodies were simply laid out and covered with sand. To an Aussie we met up the road I said: "I suppose many of your pals were lost." He just looked at me sadly and then smiled and said: "Yes, of course, but we've got to beat the Hun and the Jap."

Strewn around one Italian tank were papers belonging to Captain Aldo Corbelli. One was a month's pay slip for 3,630 lire. A handbill advertised the Italian edition of Dale Carnegie's *How to Win Friends and Influence People.* A letter from the captain's girl, Mardella, ended "I never stop longing for you." Aldo Corbelli's body lay in the tank.

The second night we spent in the garden of a ruined dressing station along the shore in Matrûh. The Italians had left jars of salve, sulfanilamide, antiseptics, bandages and a big supply of drugs for treating gonorrhea. Though special toilets were built in the garden the Italians found the rooms of the villa more convenient.

West of Matrûh we passed through the greatest dump of motorized equipment in the world, with the possible exception of Stalingrad. The edges of the road and the desert as far as we could see were strewn with wrecked German and Italian tanks, armored cars, motorcycles, lorries and staff cars. In between were tires of Jerry cars and munitions of all kinds from bullets to bombs, tools and helmets, and carcasses of beef.

Wherever there isn't German wreckage in the Western Desert there are British camps. From an airplane the whole of the desert looks like one great tourist camp amid thousands of square miles of wreckage. Cutting through it all is a single band of macadam, alive with vehicles moving westward. We were staggered by the Eighth Army's size, power, organization and mobility. Roaring and rumbling bumper-to-bumper for miles on end were convoy after convoy of tanks, armored cars, Bren-gun carriers, lorries full of troops, petrol, food and ammunition; motorcycles, staff cars and ambulances, red-faced tank men in black berets, Indians, Scots, Tommies, New Zealanders, Australians and Americans, all directed with incredible precision.

Thousands of gallons of fuel, tons of goods and ammunition, and hundreds of men are going west by air. Sometimes the sky above and beyond the supply line is black with craft roaring in both directions. At the R.A.F. advance headquarters, U.S. Army Air Forces General "Lighter-than-Air" Strickland took us over to the tiny blue-doored trailer in which Air Vice Marshal Coningham was directing all R.A.F. operations in the Western Desert. General Strickland says of Coningham: "There's a man for you."

Although Rommel's retreat was orderly, the Allied commanders had not anticipated such a quick Axis collapse in Egypt. On our last day we saw the ruins of Tobruk. The main church is badly damaged but three bells in the tower still ring. Every Tommy who enters yanks the ropes. ■

CAPTURED: A German panzer crewman surrenders to British troops at the battle of El Alamein

July 13, 1942

Erwin Rommel

Hitler's longtime colleague builds a German empire in North Africa

THE ONLY MAN ON EARTH WHOM GENERAL ERWIN Rommel looks up to is Adolf Hitler. And he looks down contemptuously on all other men in the entire continent of Africa. Among military men Rommel is variously appraised as: 1) a bold and brilliant desert commander who makes mistakes like any other man; 2) the best armored-force general of World War II; 3) one of the great military commanders of modern times.

Rommel is such a man as the commanders Napoleon assembled in his youth: tough, untutored, plebeian, successful. In common with Hitler, Rommel is no Prussian aristocrat. His father was a schoolteacher in south Germany. World War I found him serving in the German Army. He started the war as a humble lieutenant, but his war record was remarkable. Commanding a detachment of mountain troops in the first battle of Champagne (1915), he captured an important French position. In 1917 he distinguished himself against the Italians at the Isonzo.

Yet plebeian Rommel had no place in the skeleton post-war *Reichswehr*, and his longing for war turned him very early to the Nazis. He met Hitler in Württemberg, became a Storm Troop leader, joined a murderous raid against the Socialists and communists of Coburg, a raid which Hitler singled out as the turning point in his career. Thereafter Rommel headed Hitler's personal police, the *SS*, and traveled with the leader, sharing with other familiars the honor of sleeping in front of Hitler's bedroom door. When Hitler shook off the shackles of Versailles, Rommel went back to the army, wrote a manual, *Infantry Attacks*. He also studied the techniques of armored forces.

The invasion of Poland found Rommel a colonel. The invasion of France found him a general, commanding the 7th Armored Division, which broke through at Maubeuge and was of great help in the German race to the Channel. The invasion of Egypt finds him a field marshal.

When Hitler in 1940 put Rommel in charge of the Afrika Korps and sent him to strengthen the stumbling Italians in Libya, Rommel began to train the kind of army that could fight a desert war. He established a training ground on a sandy Baltic peninsula. His carefully picked soldiers lived in overheated barracks, learned to get along on dried food and vitamins, little water. Wind machines blew up artificial sandstorms. Rommel acclimated himself in a private hothouse.

Once his men were in Africa, Rommel made them as comfortable as possible. Each man got his own green bivouac tent, with a floor, and a pack containing a camp stove, solid fuel, eye lotion, mouthwash, body powder, washing sets, flashlights. At the rest camps in the rear there were beer gardens, brass bands, playing grounds, movies.

Rommel is vain, arrogant, and autocratic, for when he makes war he takes all the responsibility, all the blame, all the glory. When things go awry in battle, he flies into volcanic rages, showering everyone around him with a stream of vituperation. Dashing about by car and motorcycle in the forward zones of action, he sees his men and they see him. At night Rommel often turns teacher, assembles a quorum of tank officers, lectures them on the beauties of Naziism. He likes to lecture captured British officers on the fallacies of their tactics.

One lesson that many British generals (who have not profited by lectures in captivity) have yet to learn from him is adequate reconnaissance. Rommel, like all good generals, leaves nothing so important as reconnaissance to others. At the risk of his life and of capture, he haunts the front lines at night. When he makes decisions they are based on facts. Rommel's repair cars now come right up to battle zones, often work on disabled tanks during battle. His huge salvage wagons, with their cranes, lumber up as soon as night falls, pick up wrecks—British as well as German—and carry them back to workshops housed in blacked-out tents. Everything captured from the British is promptly put to Rommel's use. Even British tanks, captured one day, go back into action the next, with fresh swastikas printed on their turrets.

Like most production men, Rommel demands results from those who work for him and he lets them understand that he doesn't care what the results cost them. A new aide-de-camp (fifth in a few months) recently arrived to report to him. "Let me wish you luck," the Marshal snapped. "Your four predecessors were killed." ■

CONNECTED: Rommel, one of Hitler's earliest converts and the former leader of the SS, with troops in Africa

HEINRICH HOFFMAN—TIMEPIX

February 1, 1943

Bernard Montgomery

A little-known general takes charge in Egypt and sends Rommel packing

THE ROAD IS A RIBBON ALONG THE FAIR, AZURE SEA. IT twists up arid escarpments. It streaks, hot and straight, for miles across the desert sands. Along its length it is littered with the broken matériel of war and the stiff, broken bodies of German and Italian dead. At the road's end last week stood a wiry man with pale, piercing eyes, hawk's nose and cadaverous cheeks. General Sir Bernard Law Montgomery had traversed half the continent of Africa, leading a victorious army on the heels of a beaten one. This week he was in Tripoli and driving on.

Montgomery had shattered the last vestige of Italy's African Empire. He had opened up a new base for British naval operations and a southern base for Allied ground and air forces from which the Axis' slipping grip on North Africa could be pounded and attacked. He had chased the Germans 1,300 miles in 13 weeks.

Some five months ago Bernard Law Montgomery walked into Cairo's Shepheard's Hotel. Few people noticed the man who had come from England to boss the demoralized Eighth Army. He had been second choice for the job. Outside military circles, the scrawny, gimlet-eyed little man was unknown. The Eighth was holding a thin, 40-mile front between the Qattara Depression and the sea. For two years they had waged a seesaw desert campaign. Sometimes they had been badly led, never had they had adequate equipment. They had driven Graziani westward to El Agheila. General Erwin Rommel had punched them back. Under Auchinleck's command they had regained that ground. Again Rommel had punched them back, this time destroying most of their armored force and driving them eastward to within 70 miles of Alexandria. They were whipped, weary, maligned, discouraged.

Montgomery did not stay long at Shepheard's. At 5 o'clock in the morning the day after his arrival, he rode into the desert with a young cavalry aide. Weeks went by while he mercilessly pounded his army into shape. Supplies poured in to the Eighth. On Oct. 23 Montgomery attacked. Across the sands of Egypt the bagpipes of the 51st Highlanders skirled. Military policemen in white gloves waved yellow lanterns to guide the tanks along the paths which sappers, many of whom gave their lives, had cleared through German minefields. British armor and infantry poured through.

Twelve days later his Eighth Army, after some of the bitterest fighting that Egypt had seen, had cracked the Afrika Korps. Montgomery rode across the bloody sands of Egypt. He rolled through Matrûh, where Rommel's overturned guns and tanks lay like beetles on their backs in the African sun. Rommel with the fleeing fraction of his army escaped through Hellfire Pass, where a few New Zealanders routed his rear guard. Montgomery swept past the white, empty shells of Tobruk's ruined houses. Ahead of him, behind him, was his army. They were Englishmen, Irishmen and Scots; it was a purposeful army behind an impassioned man who was avenging Dunkirk (where he had led the 3rd Division).

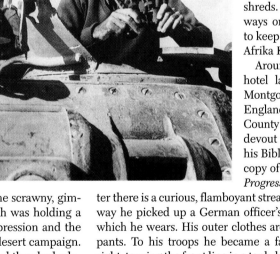

ON THE TRAIL: Buoyed by fresh supplies and troops, Montgomery beat the Afrika Korps

BRITISH WAR DEPARTMENT—NATIONAL ARCHIVES

Rommel abandoned hundreds of tons of new and tip-top matériel. He lost thousands of not so tip-top Italians. Parts of his rear guard vanished in shreds. But his retreat was always orderly and he managed to keep intact a great part of his Afrika Korps.

Around Shepheard's rococo hotel last week the name of Montgomery was better known. England's hero is Irish, born in County Donegal, 55 years ago. A devout man, nightly he reads his Bible. He carries with him a copy of John Bunyan's *Pilgrim's Progress*. In his austere character there is a curious, flamboyant streak. Somewhere along the way he picked up a German officer's suit of silk underwear, which he wears. His outer clothes are informal: sweater and pants. To his troops he became a familiar and spectacular sight, touring the front line in a tank, his hawk's head in a beret protruding from the turret. Sometimes he wore an Anzac's broad-brimmed field hat, on which he pinned the insignia of all the units fighting under him, including the Greeks. His headquarters was an elaborate caravan of trucks captured in 1941 from Italian General "Electric Whiskers" Bergonzoli. His sleeping quarters were the rear end of one of the trucks fitted out with a desk, two chairs, couch, wash basin, toilet and shower. Along the route he added a porcelain bathtub. Over his bed he pinned a picture of his enemy, Rommel. ∎

CHARGE! Evoking the days of Napoleon, Russian cavalry attack the German lines, trying to break the siege of Stalingrad

War in the Steppes

Desperate Russians stop Hitler's armies cold, fighting across the plains and into the streets to capture an encircled German force in Stalingrad

With Western Europe conquered— aside from embattled Britain—Adolf Hitler unleashed an assault on his supposed ally, Joseph Stalin's U.S.S.R., on June 22, 1941. As German armies advanced on a wide front, the Russians gave ground, holding a line in the winter of 1941-42 from Leningrad (St. Petersburg) in the north to Stalingrad in the south. In the summer of 1942, Hitler hurled his armies against Stalingrad, but the gritty Russians held the city in bitter street-by-street fighting. A Russian counteroffensive in the fall trapped a huge German force inside the city. Hitler ordered his generals to fight to the death, but they surrendered—a critical turning point that halted Germany's conquests.

September 21, 1942

For Stalin's City

Over the bodies of Russians who died fighting, the Germans advanced. With every mile lost and every day gone, Russia seemed to have fewer guns, tanks and planes for her sons. Defeat at Stalingrad would mean victory for the Germans in their summer campaign; a Russia dismembered, isolated, weakened; German hordes and German planes free for battle in Western Europe or in the Middle East; a disaster possibly worse than all the other disasters of World War II.

Winston Churchill had said: "It is the eighth of September," inviting the Russians and their allies to believe that winter, if not the Second Front, was coming soon enough to founder the German armies. But if winter is all that Russia's allies can promise, and Russia cannot save herself, then the war in Russia is lost.

The Germans inched on into the environs of Stalingrad. Day by day, for four weeks, they had sent mountains of men and machines to batter the Red Army back across dusty steppes toward the Volga. Colossal expenditures bought each hillock, each ravine, each village, exacting of the Russians losses at least as heavy.

Fresh Russian plane, tank and artillery forces were moved up to the front in an attempt to offset the weight of German numbers. Rested flyers, gunners and tank crews brought with them hope to the stubbornly retreating Red Army.

Sprawling along the Volga for 25 miles, Stalingrad's shoestring outline provides not even a compact area to defend. Stalingrad's precious factories by last week had been stripped of some of their machinery, which was shipped with skilled workers to safety beyond the Urals. River boats and barges, operated entirely by women, had ferried part of the famed Dzerzhinsky tractor plant (now converted to tank manufacturing) up the Volga to Kazan, where it was transshipped on flat cars by the Trans-Siberian railway. ∎

October 19, 1942

Battle of Russia

In September 1942 Adolf Hitler promised his people that Stalingrad "will be taken." Last week the German High Command abandoned the frontal assault on Stalingrad.

The city found salvation in its ruins. Shell-shattered apartment buildings, crumbled houses and bombed factories were converted into makeshift fortresses to help the Red Army defend the city street by street, house by house, man by man. Machine-gun nests, outposts for tommy gunners and small artillery emplacements mushroomed in the smoking debris where even a fragment of wall stood starkly. Each time German detachments crept down a street, crossed an intersection or slipped into an alley, they met a withering crossfire: the Red Army was still in Stalingrad. ∎

November 2, 1942

Apartment 21-A

In Stalingrad Red troops fought not only street by street but room by room. On one of the city's best streets stood Apartment 21-A. It had had a corner sheered off by a German bomb, but Sub-Lieutenant Svetkov and a handful of grenadiers held the building for nine days. Barricades, trenches and machine guns were prepared to control the street intersection. At dawn twelve heavy German tanks, loaded with shock troops, at-

TRAPPED IN STALINGRAD

Rzhev
⊛ Moscow

U . S . S . R .

Don River

Kursk

Volga River

RUSSIA

Serafimovich

KAZAKHSTAN

UKRAINE
Russian pincer movements

Stalingrad

Kotelnikov

Rostov

200 miles
200 km

Caspian Sea

Black Sea

tacked. Hits from anti-tank guns set five afire. Seven rumbled on. Svetkov and his men had no more anti-tank ammo, so they hurled grenades from the windows. Three more tanks were disabled. Four came on.

Suddenly one lanky Russian seized a tank-mine, hugged it to his chest and threw himself in front of an advancing tank. Three came on. At the apartment-house door the tanks let out their shock troops, who fought their way to the staircase.

From a second-floor barricade five Russians with rifles faced 15 Germans. They held off the Germans until another band, clambering up a fire escape, attacked them from the rear. Then they retreated to the third floor, where they fought on. An excited, roaring Russian caught a German grenade before it exploded, tossed it back at the Nazis. Next morning, just as the Russians' ammunition was giving out, a clamor of shouting came from the roof. Red comrades had crossed adjoining rooftops to the rescue. Charging down the stairs, they drove out the Germans, who left 52 dead officers and men. ∎

December 7, 1942

Hitler's Last Gamble

Hitler had lost the gamble. Instead of consolidating his eastern front he had gambled on the capture of Stalingrad. But Stalingrad had held out and now was striking back at his advanced columns. In the midst of Herr Hitler's frantic preoccupation with Africa the Russian winter offensive had exploded. In the central sector around Rzhev the Russians launched another attack. In both sectors Hitler's troops stumbled backward over the frozen graves of Axis soldiers who had already died in the attempt to conquer Russia.

One night a fortnight ago the worn men of Russia's Major General Alex-

SOVFOTO

SNIPERS: Russian soldiers hole up in a bombed-out home in Stalingrad, 1942

SHOT! A Russian soldier is
hit during the 1942 summer
campaign on the steppes
outside Stalingrad

ander Rodintsev's 13th Guards Division crouched in their holes in Stalingrad and listened to sudden thunderous cannonading. The din was the sound of their own artillery.

It was the hour for which the 13th had waited. They were tough, soft-spoken men from Omsk and Barnaul in faraway Siberia. They had arrived in Stalingrad by forced marches—125 miles in one two-day trek—and there in the battered factories had taken up their positions. For six weary weeks, under almost ceaseless shelling and air assaults, hacked at by infantry and tanks, the gaunt 13th had held the ditches, the doorways, the alleys and the gutted buildings.

Southeast of Stalingrad, Russia's forces were moving up. Under cover of subfreezing nights thousands of Russian soldiers were crossing the icy Volga on ferry boats, fishing boats and rafts, carrying with them the artillery, tanks and weapons they would need for a massive counterattack. Behind the bald, rolling Ergeni Hills south of Stal-

ingrad, hidden by mists, they gathered and waited. In the cold dawn of Nov. 20 they attacked.

"The hour of stern, righteous reckoning with the foul enemy, the German Fascist occupants, has struck," said the Order of the Day. "Make the enemy's black blood flow in a river. Comrades, into the attack!"

In the Ergeni Hills the artillery awakened. That was the long-awaited thunder heard by the silent men of the 13th. The cannonading kept up without break for two and a half hours, pouring destruction into the German lines, disrupting communications, softening resistance. Under its cover Russian sappers swept forward to "delouse" German minefields. Over the frozen earth rolled Russian tanks, some of them dragging artillery. Mobile cannon followed, operating in massed groups, blasting holes in German positions that had already been spotted by Russian guerrilla intelligence. Night came and there was no letup.

As the attack started from the south,

Soviet troops north of Stalingrad also launched an assault, moving in a great arc toward Serafimovich. Their purpose was to swing west and south, meet the southern columns and close a ring around the Germans. From Serafimovich prongs spread out like the curving tines of a peasant's pitchfork. From the southern force, prongs also curved off. One jabbed across the Don, severed the Stalingrad-Rostov railway, cut back east to squeeze Axis troops against Stalingrad, where the 13th Division began to bend the stubborn German head backward.

Inside the contracting area the battle became a melee. Distracted Axis troops faced in all directions at once. *Panzer* divisions dug in, using their tanks as pillboxes. Across the steppes galloped Cossacks in their black capes. Around gutted villages roared Russian tanks, swift motor-borne infantry.

Axis troops in suddenly hopeless positions gave up. Across the steppes plodded long lines of Axis prisoners hobbling to Russian bases, some to have frozen limbs amputated, stumbling toward the Volga. According to Moscow communiqués, 66,000 men were seized in ten days of fighting. Into Russian hands fell quantities of booty: food, clothing, more than 50,000 rifles, 3,935 machine guns, 1,380 tanks.

It was possible that many an Italian and Rumanian and even German soldier had lost his appetite for winter combat. Though Hitler had promised his armies that they would be properly clothed, the bitter northeast winds that drove snow and sand across the endless steppes last week blinded eyes, lashed flesh, cut through coats that were lined with mole and rat skins.

But a more likely explanation for the toll of prisoners was the swiftness of the Russian attack. Hitherto Russian assaults have been battering operations carried out largely by pedestrian troops. For the first time in the war Marshal Timoshenko had mounted an agile, Panzer-type, fast-moving attack that encircled and overwhelmed. The Germans were apparently surprised as much by this as by the suddenness of the onslaught.

The Germans suffered also from lack of air support. Hitler had weakened the Luftwaffe, which once ruled Russian skies, to bolster the Axis forces in Tunisia. German air bases had been captured and many German planes had been destroyed on the ground.

Hitler's force of 300,000 troops around Stalingrad were in danger of entrapment and annihilation. In the last ten days some 100,000 of his soldiers had been slain ∎

February 8, 1943

They Won Together

This week the battle of Stalingrad —perhaps the most decisive in the Russo-German war, if not in all of World War II—approached its end. The Red Army had killed or captured most of the German and Rumanian troops that had been hammering the city since last August. In the final stages even the Nazi Commander, Field Marshal Friedrich von Paulus, surrendered along with 16 other generals.

The victory meant much more than the destruction of a great army. It meant the complete failure of Hitler's 1942 strategy in Russia. Last week the Russians revealed how nearly the German Sixth Army had come to capturing Stalingrad. In September the Germans actually occupied the central part of the city. Concentrating their power in the industrial districts, they then stormed into the Stalingrad tank factory, but failed to drive on to the Volga. Often the opposing lines were only 15 yards apart. Most of the fighting was done with hand grenades; one Russian division used more than 100,000 in a single month.

Red Army headquarters was moved five times. At one stage the Russian strategic position seemed so hopeless that Lieut. General Vassili Chiukov, who commanded the Sixty-Second Army, ordered his chief of staff to cross to the east bank of the Volga. His chief refused and told his superior: "We will win or die together." ∎

VICTORY'S PRICE: Russian reserves move into Stalingrad— or what's left of it—during the climax of the battle for the city

RUSSIAN NEWSREEL

December 14, 1942

Georgy K. Zhukov

A rugged, loyal Bolshevik staves off the *Wehrmacht's* drive into Russia

THE GERMANS ARE LOSING THE WAR IN RUSSIA, WHICH means they are losing World War II. On the frozen plains of Rzhev before Moscow, on the Don and in the Volga corridor at Stalingrad, in the snows and floods of the Caucasus, the Russians are on the offensive. But as of this week, the Russian offensives alone are not defeating the Germans. Time is defeating the Germans. Old victories and old defeats are defeating the Germans: the Red Army's stands, retreats and counterattacks; the *Wehrmacht's* losses at Smolensk, Rzhev and Moscow; the men and weapons spent, the weeks forever lost at Sevastopol; the spaces of the Ukraine, the Kuban plains and the upper Caucasus, conquered but nonetheless expensive to their conquerors; and, finally, the pit of Stalingrad. No one of these great battles, sieges or marches in the greatest campaign of history exhausted or defeated the German army. But in the aggregate they saved Russia and they saved the Red Army.

Without this perspective, dispatches and headlines inevitably give the impression that the Russians stand to win all or lose all in their first winter offensives of 1942. The impression is not shared by the hard-eyed, hard-mouthed peasant, Communist and soldier, Army General Georgy Konstantinovich Zhukov, who commands the drive on the Rzhev front and had much to do with planning the others. Army General Zhukov, at 45, officially a Hero of the Soviet Union, wearer of the Order of Lenin and victor over the Japanese in Mongolia, is First Vice Commissar for Defense and second only to Commissar Joseph Stalin in U.S.S.R. military councils.

Georgy Zhukov fought in the Red Revolution, served and studied under the Red Army's famed mentor, Mikhail Frunze. He is a horseman and hunter, was successively a teacher at military schools, a staff officer and a field commander in the pre-1941 Red Army. Even Russians know little else about him, for he has made it his business to stay out of the public eye.

The few foreigners who have seen him remember him best for his "lion's face," his broad and rocky mouth. Like all successful Red Army commanders, he is a professing Communist and (unlike some) he is also a devout one. Said he after the Finnish War: "We would not be Bolsheviks if we allowed the glamour of victory to blind us to the shortcomings that have been revealed in the training of our men. These shortcomings were the result of conventionalism and routine."

Well before the U.S. Army learned the same lesson, General Zhukov began to apply it to the Red Army. Along with Marshals Timoshenko and Shaposhnikov, he braced up Red Army training, brought it as closely as possible to actual conditions of modern warfare. After the Germans suddenly brought war in earnest to the Russians, Stalin entrusted Zhukov with the outer defense of Moscow, and with the winter offensive which pushed the Germans back to their present line at Rzhev. Last summer, when the Germans launched their 1942 campaign, Zhukov still had the central front, and he was responsible for holding the Russians' all-important pivot at Voronezh.

Last August Stalin designated Zhukov First Vice Commissar for Defense but left him in command of the central front. In the months when Stalin was planning his winter offensives he turned more & more to his *Liubimets* (the pet, the favorite, the darling, the beloved), Georgy Zhukov.

General Zhukov shares with most Russians the conviction that the German armies are not yet beaten, that they can be defeated only by a prodigious effort. He also knows that the Red Army, to win this winter, must show more offensive capacity than it has ever

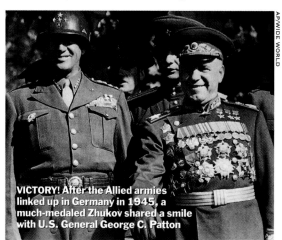

VICTORY! After the Allied armies linked up in Germany in 1945, a much-medaled Zhukov shared a smile with U.S. General George C. Patton

AP/WIDE WORLD

shown before. The offensive on the central front holds the possibilities of a great victory, and the Red Army's position at Stalingrad had the appearance of one in the making. An Axis army of some 300,000 Germans and Rumanians was all but bottled up in Stalingrad and on the Stalingrad steppes. The encirclement, capture or destruction of this army would be for Hitler a catastrophe greater than Rommel's defeat in Libya.

The Red Army is well equipped—superbly equipped considering Russia's wartime poverty—chiefly because its leaders, General Zhukov included, had the wit and courage to retain and build up great reserves of munitions when the richest lands and cities of Russia were falling to the Germans. The true extent of those reserves, known only to the Red Army commands, is one of the factors which will determine the course and outcome of the winter's battles. And if worse comes to worst and the winter offensives fail, Joseph Stalin, Georgy Zhukov and the rest of the Red Army command will save enough of their reserves to try again. ∎

Notebook

Casualties

The identity of World War II's first U.S. fatality is a matter of some dispute. If Pearl Harbor is viewed as the first day in which Americans in uniform can be said to have laid down their lives during World War II, then the distinction belongs to Seaman 2nd Class Warren McCutcheon. The 17-year-old sailor responded to a General Quarters alarm at 7:52 a.m. on the morning of Dec. 7 and took up his post as forward machine gunner on the U.S.S. *Maryland.* McCutcheon began firing to help protect the nearby U.S.S. *Oklahoma.* As Japanese planes turned to make their second pass at the *Oklahoma* (less than a minute after the first shot had been fired), they strafed the deck of the *Maryland,* killing McCutcheon instantly.

The official American death toll for World War II is 405,399.

Heroes

The title for most decorated soldier of World War II is held by two men: the celebrated Audie Murphy—who later became a movie star—and the almost unknown Matt Urban. Murphy was awarded 29 decorations for bravery during the war. Urban was awarded 28, but in 1980 the Defense Department discovered a long-lost recommendation that Urban be awarded the Congressional Medal of Honor. This recent citation brought Urban's total decorations in line with Murphy's.

> ## "[The Jeep] does everything ... It is faithful as a dog, strong as a mule, agile as a goat."
> ## —Ernie Pyle

Hardware

MARGARET BOURKE-WHITE—TIMEPIX

DAVID E. SCHERMAN—TIMEPIX

W. EUGENE SMITH—TIMEPIX

Treads, Wings, Wheels and Decks

Of the 84,160 U.S. tanks built in World War II, more than 60,000 were Shermans. Though faster and nimbler than their German and Japanese counterparts, the Sherman (or M-4) was lightly armored and its gun had a shorter range than those of many enemy tanks.

As war approached, the Army Air Force asked for the impossible: a new bomber that would cruise at 400 m.p.h., with a range of more than 5,000 miles and a bomb payload of more than 2,000 lbs. Result: the B-29, the mightiest bomber of World War II. It entered service in late 1943—in time to soften up Nazi-occupied Europe prior to D-day and to reach across the Pacific to the home islands of Japan.

The Army needed a catch-all vehicle to replace its aging fleet of Model T Fords, motorcycle sidecars and supply horses and mules. Thus was born, in July 1941, the General Purpose (or "Jeep") vehicle. Cost: $738.74. Close to half a million of them were built for World War II.

The U.S.S. *Langley,* a converted cruiser launched in 1922, was the first U.S. aircraft carrier. A stroke of luck found all three of America's Pacific Fleet carriers out to sea from Pearl Harbor on the morning of Dec. 7, 1941. Since the *Langley,* the Navy has built a total of 75 ever larger and more powerful carriers, 12 of which are on active duty today.

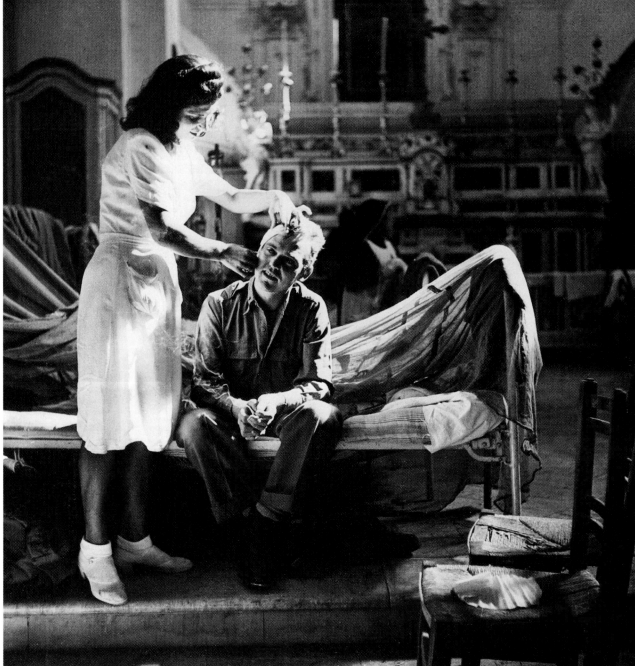

ROBERT CAPA—MAGNUM PHOTOS

They Also Serve

The soldier at the front is only the spearhead of the armed forces' complex fighting machine. No picture of military life would be complete without a salute to this vital supporting cast of medics and chaplains, MPs and nurses, kitchen hands—and four-legged friends

▲ **The English Patient**
An Italian nurse treats a British soldier in a church sacristy converted into a hospital in World War II.

◄ Mule Overboard

Mules land in Sicily in 1943; they will help carry supplies through Italy's mountainous terrain. The last Army mules—loved and hated by their fellow soldiers—were mustered out of service in 1956. Soldiers in Italy staged the "Anzio Derby," racing U.S. Army mules against liberated Italian mules.

▲ Ciphers

A codebreaker uses alphabet strips arranged on a sliding scale to decipher an encoded message in December 1942. Allied knowledge of Axis codes helped win battles—and the war.

► Cranky?

It's the most dreaded job in the military: KP (kitchen patrol) duty. These sailors on a Navy cruiser in 1942 are taking it easy: one of them is operating a hand-cranked spud-peeling machine.

◄ No Time for Scenery

Focusing on the minute against a backdrop of the majestic—the mountains of the Hindu Kush—U.S. Army helicopter mechanics work on a CH-47 Chinook chopper at Bagram Airfield in Afghanistan in 2002.

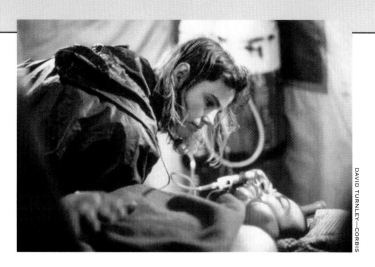

▶ Expert Care

Lieut. Linda McClory, a medic serving with the Army's 5th MASH (Mobile Army Surgical Hospital) Fast Surgical Team, tends to a U.S. soldier wounded by shrapnel while fighting in the Gulf War, 1991.

▲ Digital Technology

As a teletype operator sends messages from a signal corps office in Britain, a poster reminds him: "You are in a position of trust."

▲ Oasis

Sergeant Derek Fuller worships in a mosque at a U.S. military air base in Afghanistan, 2002.

▶ Last Gasp

An Allied soldier is backed up by two members of the French Resistance as they scout for German snipers after the liberation of Paris in 1945.

▲ Surprise Attack!

These women fire fighters are battling the flames at Pearl Harbor on Dec. 7, 1941.

▶ Ground Zero

New York City fire fighters assemble hoses in the first hours after two airliners were crashed into the World Trade Center. The New York Fire Department lost 343 people at the site.

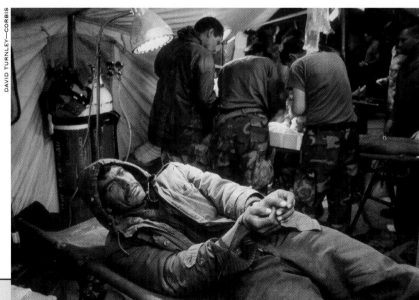

▲ Help on the Way

A wounded, bandaged medic crawls to assist other casualties in heavy 1966 fighting at Bong Son, South Vietnam, as a medical evacuation helicopter flies in.

◄ Ministering to the Enemy

A wounded Iraqi soldier waits his turn for treatment at a MASH unit on the Saudi Arabian front during the Gulf War, 1991.

▲ Mom's Home!

Joy Johnson, a pilot with the Air Force Reserve, gives her daughter Jessica a twirl after returning from a mission to the gulf in August 1990.

▲ Music's Charms

A chaplain plays violin during a service for the leaders of Britain's Eighth Army on the night before an attack in the Africa campaign in 1942.

▲ Making Waves

Trainees for the U.S. Army Signal Corps develop their skills on radio apparatus in 1941 at Fort Devon, Massachusetts.

▲ Liturgy al Fresco

American troops take part in a Mass celebrated by a Filipino priest in front of a devastated church after the liberation of Manila, 1945.

◀ Give Blood

As three generations of concerned locals look on, medic Harvey White gives blood plasma to Roy Humphrey on a street in Sicily in 1943.

▲Why We Fight
A chaplain in Afghanistan leads a memorial service three months after the 9/11/01 strike at America.

▲Attention!
Women's Army Corps recruits brace up in 1942. More than 150,000 WACs served in World War II.

▲Dog Tired
On Sept. 18, 2001, two weary members of the New York City police department rest up while searching for bodies at ground zero.

▶The Heat of Battle
No thermometers are required as Allied surgeons strip down to operate in the summer heat at a hospital in Salerno, Italy, in 1943.

◀ **Skywatch**
With the dome of St. Paul's Cathedral looming in the background, a British aircraft spotter surveys the skies in 1940. The historic church and its dome survived heavy bombing by the Germans during the Battle of Britain.

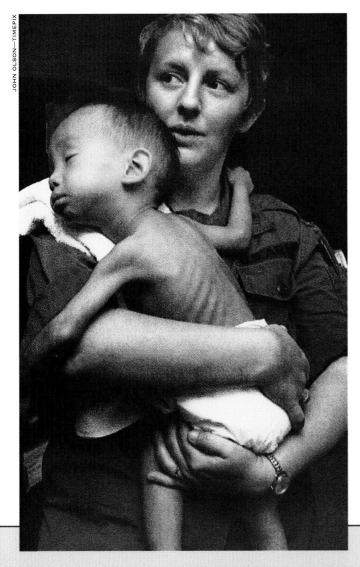

▲ **Lonely Vigil**
A military policeman stands guard at Newport Harbor in Vietnam, 1969. Seldom loved by their fellow soldiers, MPs fill a tough, essential role in the service.

◀ **Someone to Watch Over Me**
Army nurse Donna Hamilton holds a Vietnamese baby at a camp in Long Binh in 1968. It was her second tour of duty in Vietnam.

MOVE UP! On the run, U.S. soldiers race past a dead body

The Unexpected War

Lurching wildly from triumphant victory to humiliating defeat, the Korean War tested U.S. resolve

AMERICA'S CAMPAIGN IN KOREA IS SOMETIMES CALLED "the forgotten war," but the tag doesn't quite ring true. It's closer to the mark to call Korea the war that no one expected. In the spring of 1950, before hostilities erupted there, it is probably fair to say that most Americans would not have been able to locate either North or South Korea on a map. Only months before the war began, U.S. Secretary of State Dean Acheson pointedly omitted South Korea from a list of nations that formed America's "defensive perimeter" in the Pacific.

Our adversary, North Korea, was a country about which we knew almost nothing. Our ally, South Korea, was a client state that Washington ignored. Even the demarcation between the two, the 38th parallel, had been hastily—almost randomly—selected by two young U.S. officers working with a student atlas late at night in the closing days of World War II.

In the five years since, the Truman Administration had pushed the policy of containment, committing the U.S. to stopping the expansion of communism, hopefully through peaceful shows of strength, but with U.S. troops if necessary. Yet when North Korea's army, the Im Min Gun, crossed the 38th parallel and invaded South Korea in the early-morning hours of June 25, 1950, there was probably not a place in the world where the United States was less prepared to make a stand against communist aggression. But we did.

In the first few months of action in Korea, American troops reeled backward in a humiliating, chaotic rout. But on Sept. 15, General Douglas MacArthur led one of the most spectacular military victories in American history—the invasion of Inchon. Within days of this daring amphibious landing, MacArthur retook the South Korean capital of Seoul, cut the peninsula in half and captured or killed tens of thousands of retreating North Koreans. Within weeks, he crossed the 38th parallel, took Pyongyang, North Korea's capital, and pursued the defeated North Koreans right up to the Chinese border.

Then came a defeat every bit as ignominious and staggering as Inchon had been brilliant. Hundreds of thousands of communist Chinese troops crossed into North Korea and counter-

attacked. In bitter winter fighting, they once again drove U.S. and U.N. troops deep into South Korea.

Within months, Harry Truman fired MacArthur. General Matthew Ridgway took his place, rallied the U.S. troops and stabilized the front line near the 38th parallel. The war ground on in a bloody stalemate for another two years, until cease-fire talks formalized the border between two countries that, if not quite at peace, were no longer fully at war either. That situation persists to this day, where troops on either side of the world's most heavily fortified border stand on perpetual alert.

DIVIDING LINE: Control of the border between the two nations seesawed back and forth

YOU ARE NOW CROSS[ING]
38TH PARALL[EL]
US CO.B 728MP

"There is no substitute for victory," MacArthur once said, but he may have been wrong. What America won in Korea was not a victory in the traditional sense. But the U.S. forces—at a cost of 33,629 lives—held the line on communist expansion while avoiding a cataclysmic war with China and the Soviet Union. The final victory came decades later, when the U.S.S.R. collapsed and China remained communist in little more than name. Time, it turned out, was on the side of freedom, democracy and capitalism. Containment bought time. And that is why Korea, the unexpected war, should never be forgotten. ∎

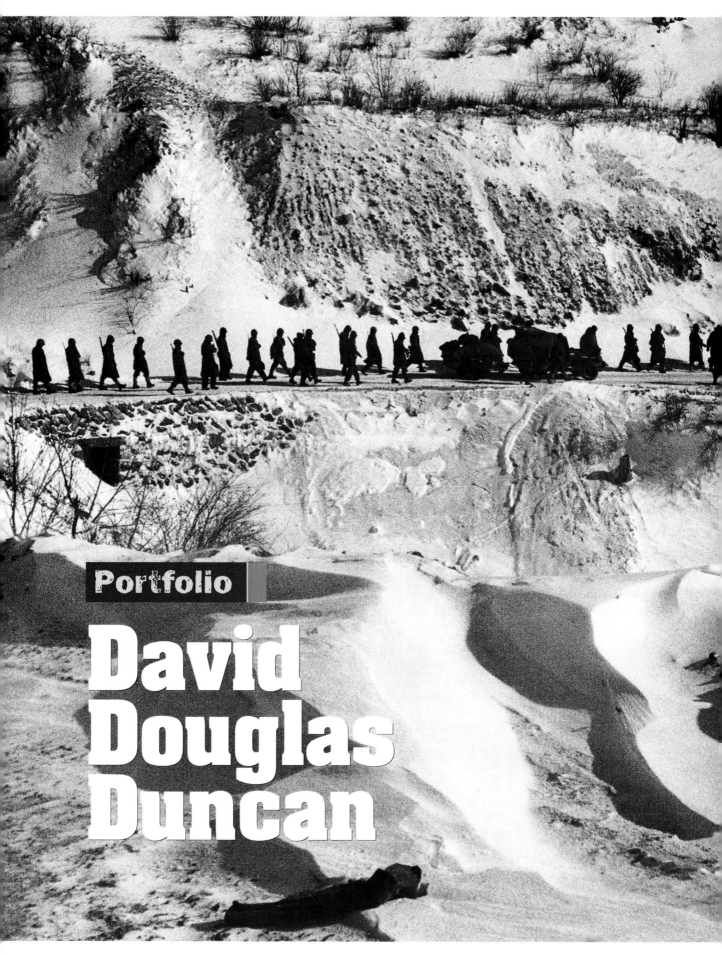

David
Douglas
Duncan

The career of one of America's finest photojournalists was launched in a hasty moment of high drama and unexpected revelation. In 1934, when he was an undergraduate at the University of Arizona, David Douglas Duncan heard that Tucson's largest hotel was on fire. He grabbed a 39¢ camera and ran to the scene, where he shot a picture of a man fleeing the flaming building, clutching his suitcase. Duncan found out the next day that the man he had snapped was the most wanted fugitive in America, John Dillinger, and that the suitcase had been packed full of guns and stolen cash.

Inspired, Duncan embarked on a career in photography that took him to the front lines of every kind of action—military, political and cultural. Describing a lifetime of combat photography that spanned World War II to Vietnam, he said, "I wanted to show the way men live and die when they know death is among them."

Duncan succeeded. Fearless and tough, he shared the risks and hardships of his subjects, making him (and by extension his audience) less an observer to the war's carnage and chaos and more a participant.

He understood soldiers because he had been one. A Marine in World War II, Duncan earned a lieutenant colonel's commission, a Purple Heart, a Legion of Merit, two Distinguished Flying Crosses, six Battle Stars and three Air Medals. When war broke out on the Korean peninsula, Duncan once again hiked into combat with the Marines, this time as a civilian. His classic images of the hardships endured by courageous U.S. soldiers captured the reality of a distant war that the public seemed all too ready to ignore.

Duncan's work outside of battle, from the first-ever photos of the Kremlin's art treasures to intimate shots of his friend, Pablo Picasso, are equally distinguished. But he is still best known for his images of life and death on the battlefield. Duncan once described himself as not a "hawk or dove. I am just a veteran combat photographer and foreign correspondent who cares intensely about my country." Taken in the haste of battle, his pictures still begin in drama and end in revelation.

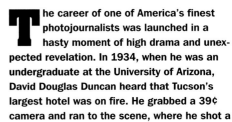

Bitter Retreat

In the depths of Korea's unforgiving winter, a column of Marines marches down "Nightmare Alley." Duncan, a decorated Marine in World War II, said of his decision to cover the Korean conflict with his former comrades, "I knew in the Marines if I got hit, they'd drag me out, they'd patch me up—whatever, I'd get out of there. I knew the code of combat in the Marine Corps. So I joined the Marines in Korea and stayed with them."

◀ Even Marines Cry
With all his ammunition gone and all but two
of his men missing in action, a corporal of the 5th
Regiment sheds a single tear.

▲ Clinging to a Can
An exhausted Marine wrapped in a sleeping bag
holds on to his ration can during the December retreat
from the Chosin Reservoir.

▲ No Exit
Another portrait from the December retreat. Duncan
said that he covered the Korea war "from the point of
view of the dog-tired, shot-up Marine."

▶ Look Away
A recurring theme in Duncan's work is the "thousand-
yard stare"—the blank yet knowing gaze in the eyes
of combat veterans who have looked death in the eye
and are trying to find the strength to go on.

▲ Downhill March

Trudging down "Nightmare Alley" in retreat from the Chosin
Reservoir, a company of Marines passes the dead bodies of
fellow U.S. soldiers at the side of the road. While taking pictures in
Korea, Duncan himself was once hit in the chest by a machine gun
bullet that had reached the limit of its range. It bounced off the
photographer and fell harmlessly to the ground.

▶ Keeping the Trail Open

Clearing a logjam during the December retreat, Marines strip
wrecked trucks of supplies after pushing them off the road
into a ditch to make way for other retreating units.

GOING IN: Black U.S. soldiers from the 24th Infantry Regiment head for the front lines

Reveille

North Korea launches a surprise attack, hurling South Korean troops— along with a rapidly assembled U.S. force—reeling south in disarray

Attacking in a well-coordinated blitz on six fronts in late June, North Korea drove the South Koreans out of their capital city of Seoul. Within days, the evacuation became a panic-stricken flight, joined by several thousand hastily deployed U.S. troops. By Aug. 14, 60,000 U.S. soldiers and 50,000 South Korean troops had retreated to a shrinking perimeter around the port city of Pusan, surrounded by some 100,000 North Koreans.

As the perimeter grew smaller, it seemed that a Dunkirk-style evacuation from Pusan might be necessary. But the allies' surprise Sept. 15 landing at the port of Inchon, ten miles west of Seoul, cut off the Northern troops and handed the advantage to the allies.

July 3, 1950

Challenge Accepted

It was 4 a.m. Sunday in Korea; it was still only 3 p.m. Saturday in Washington. Just before a gray dawn came up over the peninsula, North Korea's Communist army started to roll south. Past terraced hills, green with newly transplanted rice, rumbled tanks. In the rain-heavy sky roared an occasional fighter plane. Then the heavy artillery started to boom.

All along the 38th parallel—the boundary between North and South Korea—the invaders met little resistance. In a six-pronged drive the Communist troops swept south. The North

Korean radio broadcast war whoops. According to the Communist versions of events, the Southerners had invaded the North and were being "repulsed." In South Korea's bustling capital of Seoul, army jeeps carrying loudspeakers roared through the streets, urging soldiers: "Go and join your units immediately."

The South Korean army made a valiant effort to overcome its initial confusion. The Korean navy (consisting of small patrol craft) announced that it had sunk a Russian gunboat in Korean territorial waters. All night long, Seoul was kept awake by convoys rumbling through the streets. Next morning Northern planes machine-gunned the city streets. At the U.S. Embassy, clerks burned secret papers. President Singman Rhee and his cabinet moved to Taejon, 90 miles to the south. Communist tanks were reported entering Seoul. The Northern radio broadcast a triumphant appeal to the South to surrender.

But the Communist mood of triumph was premature. General Douglas MacArthur's headquarters in Tokyo called reports that Seoul had fallen a result of "war hysteria." For hours, hope teetered in precarious balance with despair. Then came the electrifying news from Washington: the Yanks were coming. President Harry Truman had forcefully committed U.S. air and sea forces to give the Korean government "cover and support." ∎

July 10, 1950
A Bridge Is Blown

• •

TIME *correspondent Frank Gibney cabled an eyewitness account of the first days of the war in Seoul. This selection begins in the early-morning hours of Wednesday, June 28.*

• •

A t 2:15 a.m. the telephone rang. We got a warning: "It looks bad. I think they've broken through. You'd better get out of here as fast as you can. Head south for Suwon."

We decided to check in at KMAG headquarters [the U.S. military command in South Korea—ED.] for directions. There we found a major giving quiet instructions to a Korean staff officer. "It's bad," he said. "Tanks have broken into the city and we don't know how much longer the lines will hold. The enemy will be here any minute."

We ran down the stairs. As we reached a landing my eyes fell on a bright new poster on the KMAG bulletin board. It read: "Don't forget—Tuesday, June 27—bingo."

Traffic was heavy on the road running south to the big steel Han River bridge. There were no signs of a military rout. Most soldiers, even those in retreat, were singing. Guided by MPs, automobiles kept strictly in line.

The only disorder was outside the military line of march, among the thousands of poor South Korean refugees, women toting bundles on their heads and men carrying household goods in

KOREAN PENINSULA, 1950

CHINA

NORTH KOREA

Pyongyang

Sea of Japan

38th Parallel

Inchon • ✪ Seoul

SOUTH KOREA

Yellow Sea

Pusan Perimeter

• Pusan

JAPAN

100 miles
100 km

wooden frames fastened to their backs.

Traffic moved quickly until we reached the bridge. There the pace slowed, then stopped. We found ourselves almost halfway over the bridge, our jeep wedged tightly between a huge six-by-six truck full of soldiers in front and other jeeps behind. The roar of guns from the north grew louder and we wondered how long the lines around Seoul would hold. We got out of the jeep and walked forward to find

out what was delaying traffic. The milling crowds of civilians pouring over the bridge made that impossible. We returned to the jeep and sat waiting. Without warning the sky was lighted by a huge sheet of sickly orange flame. There was a tremendous explosion immediately in front of us. Our jeep was picked up and hurled 15 feet by the blast.

My glasses were smashed. Blood began pouring down from my head over my hands and clothing. New York *Times* correspondent Burton Crane's face was covered with blood. I heard him say: "I can't see."

Thinking at first the explosion was some kind of air raid, we raced for the gullies leading off from the bridge, Crane's wound looked very bad. He ripped off his undershirt and had me tie a crude bandage around his head. As it turned out, neither of us was seriously hurt.

All the soldiers in the truck ahead of us had been killed. Bodies of the dead and dying were strewn over the bridge. Scores of refugees were running pell mell off the bridge and disappearing into the night beyond.

At the time we thought that the bridge had been mined by saboteurs. We learned later that it had been dynamited by the South Korean army demolition squad on orders of the chief of

CORBIS

MINERS: G.I.s from the 1st Cavalry Division pull a "daisy chain" of mines across a bridge near Yongdong in late July

WE'RE BACK: Marine Luther Leguire raises the U.S. flag atop the U.S. consulate in Seoul after the Inchon invasion in September

ifestation of joy. Above us, flying north-ward in neat formation, were six American B-26s.

Someone dragged me out of the jeep and began patting my back. An old man knelt before me weeping and clasped his hands around my arm. All of us found ourselves swept into a sea of smiling faces. There was more clap-ping, more cheers. The Americans had come at last. We were just as surprised as the Koreans. We had no idea whether the U.S. Government would have the guts to live up to its obligations here. But however mixed our emotions, the joy and relief of the Koreans were over-powering. For the first time in the long trip we felt we could hold up our heads among the Koreans. ∎

July 24, 1950

Battle at a Pusan Pass

Near Pusan, Gibney joined a regiment of the U.S. 4th Infantry Division that had been fighting steadily for 31 days.

James Shelton, a 21-year-old private from Company D, 1st Battalion, 19th Infantry Regiment, was awak-ened from the sleep of the exhausted by the zing of Communist bullets over his foxhole. For an hour before, confident Communist infantrymen, their conical Russian helmets sticking up like mush-rooms through the early-morning mist, had marched along a steep dirt road to a mountain pass commanding the U.S. positions. Wakeful U.S. sentries heard the Reds singing snatches of Commu-nist marching songs as they pulled an aged, creaking Russian heavy machine gun up the steepening slope.

As the lead platoon of Communists approached the pass, some over-eager G.I.s opened fire, instead of waiting to trap the next unit. "I was asleep when they cut loose," Shelton said, "then the next thing I knew, enemy bullets were coming into my hole." But the soldiers discovered that their buddies had the situation under control. Blasts from U.S. BARS and salvo after salvo from 75-mm. recoilless rifles ripped into the advancing Reds, pinning some to the cliff-like wall of the pass, hurling others into the roadside ditches. Within min-utes, the first wave of the Communist attack had been shattered.

---

staff. The Korean army command had panicked and ordered the bridge blown too soon. The demolition squad, instead of roping off the bridge at both ends, had incredibly told only the traffic in the middle what was about to happen.

We headed toward a KMAG housing area on Seoul's outskirts. It was then about 3 a.m. Inside the abandoned U.S. military reservation it was quiet except for the boom of guns in the distance. We found one house with a light still burning inside.

This hastily evacuated house still had the stage props of any typical American home. There were brightly colored children's phonograph records, a woman's lacy hat, copies of *Collier's* and the *Saturday Evening Post,* and bottles of Coca-Cola in the refrigerator. Something inside this comfortable house seemed to say: "It can't happen here." Outside, the field guns rumbled.

Before dawn, we made a run for it.

∙∙

Gibney and his party crossed the Han River a few miles outside of Seoul and joined Korean refugees heading south.

∙∙

Soldiers also joined us, told the story of Seoul's fall. "Their tanks were too many," said one, "and their guns too big." "Where are the American air-planes?" asked an MP sergeant-major bitterly. As we traveled south, with our jeeps slipping and miring down in the narrow muddy roads, lines of refugees paused in flight to cheer the first Amer-icans they had seen that day.

At 10:25, as we entered a town, sud-denly a shout went up from Korean sol-diers on tops of jeeps and from dirty, wearied refugees. Wildly cheering people ran into the dusty roads and pointed at the sky. All traffic stopped. Never had I seen such a heartfelt man-

GRIEF: U.S. soldiers mourn the loss of a friend while a corpsman at rear fills out casualty tags

Almost on the heels of the first wave of Reds came a U.S. counterattack. Spearheaded by five tanks and two M-8 reconnaissance cars, truckloads of G.I.s from the 19th Infantry Regiment roared through the pass and down into the valley below. Heavy Communist fire damaged the two recon cars and three tanks. The G.I.s, supported by covering fire from the pass, spilled out of their trucks, began fighting a day-long melee in the valley and on the crests of the surrounding hills.

Slowly the weight of two full Red regiments pushed the undermanned U.S. units back toward the pass. But, at the pass, the G.I.s stuck. Time and time again, Red charges smashed against the Americans' guns. As the Reds rushed up reserves, frantic G.I. gunners manning 13 guns lobbed a torrent of 155-mm and 105-mm shells into masses of green-clad North Koreans trying to move up along the hillsides. But the Reds kept on coming. Two "Mansei" (the Korean equivalent of the Japanese "Banzai") charges rolled up against the U.S. positions—and broke.

By late afternoon the battle was almost over. The slopes leading down to the valley belonged to the dead. Along the wall of the cliff in the pass lay the hideously twisted bodies of North Korean soldiers. Red machine-gun crews were lashed in death to guns they had never had a chance to serve.

Sitting by the road and munching their cold rations, the G.I.s discussed the battle. Some meager loot—a few Russian Tommy guns and occasional pistols—was the object of interest. But the G.I.s had found, in the pockets of dead Korean Reds, all too many reminders that the Reds, for their part, had looted the American dead. One G.I. said wryly: "Every time I hit one of those lucky bastards, I get a fresh package of Lucky Strikes."

They spoke of the dead with a quiet casualness that seemed callous. "Too bad about the sergeant," two boys said to me as they watched stretcher bearers carry the blanketed form of their platoon sergeant downhill. The sergeant had been killed by a mortar shell. "Hey, Al, your buddy got it," shouted a jeep driver at a G.I. eating by the roadside, "down on the hill this afternoon." The G.I. looked at the driver and nodded; then he went back to eating. Many men had died; it was not an unusual thing.■

September 25, 1950

Invasion at Inchon

The enemy knew that a U.N. landing was hanging over him. But the enemy did not know where the main amphibious blow would fall. The mighty battleship *Missouri* steamed far up Korea's eastern shore, firing salvos. Then South Korean marines struck at Kunsan on the peninsula's west coast. But that too was a feint. The enemy did not suspect that the place would be Inchon, the port of Seoul, 150 miles northwest of Taegu.

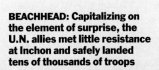

BEACHHEAD: Capitalizing on the element of surprise, the U.N. allies met little resistance at Inchon and safely landed tens of thousands of troops

But Inchon it was, in spite of a formidable high tide and a treacherous, silt-filled channel.

Massive U.N. air strikes softened Inchon's beaches and all land approaches to the port. As Admiral James H. Doyle's task force approached, six destroyers gamely plowed ahead, drew and silenced the fire of hidden enemy batter-

SUPPORT: Inbound troops watch smoke rise from the pre-landing bombardment of the Inchon beach

HANK WALKER—TIMEPIX

ies on Wolmi Island. Several ships were damaged, one severely. Then the U.S. 1st Marine Division hit the beaches. The enemy's beachhead resistance was negligible.

• •

TIME-LIFE photographer Carl Mydans was aboard General MacArthur's command ship. His report:

• •

On landing day last week, in the dawn's early light, MacArthur picked his way through a confusion of men in helmets and life jackets, climbed into the admiral's bridge chair. He wore his old, braided sweat-stained garrison cap. Then the naval bombardment began and he raised his glasses to watch. The planes came. We could see the streaks of their rockets, and minutes later hear the booms.

When the ship's speaker blared: "The first wave of the attack force is ashore," MacArthur nodded to Admiral Doyle. Then the speaker called: "All boats are ashore from the first and second waves. The troops are fanning out rapidly. No casualties so far." MacArthur lowered his head a little, and then a broad grin spread across his face. When the speaker announced: "The American flag is flying on the heights of Wolmi Island," MacArthur stood up, looked around with a smile. Admiral Doyle said: 'Let's go below and get some coffee." The General, who, at 70, had conceived an operation with the daring and imagination of a young officer, walked off the bridge. A bit later the radio sent off an old fighter's message: "The Navy and Marines have never shone more brightly than this morning. MacArthur."

October 9, 1950
Seoul Is Taken

• •

After the landing at Inchon, the North Koreans retreated swiftly. TIME *correspondent Dwight Martin cabled an eye-witness account of the capture of Seoul.*

• •

On Tuesday morning I entered Seoul up Mapo Boulevard. Three months ago, Mapo was a bustling, cheerful, tree-lined thoroughfare with a doubletrack trolley, grocery, wine and tea shops. This morning Mapo wore a different look. The burned and blackened remains of the boulevard's shops and homes sent clouds of acrid smoke billowing over the city. Buildings still ablaze showered sparks and ashes high into the air to cascade down on red-eyed, soot-faced marines.

In the center of the street, six Pershing tanks wheeled into position to advance. Directly in front of the lead tank lay the body of a Red soldier who had been caught in the burst of a white phosphorous shell. The corpse was still burning as the tank's right tread passed over it, extinguishing the flame and grinding the body into a grisly compost of flesh and cinders.

At a burned-out police substation, a group of marines waited behind a wall, tending three of their wounded and a wounded enemy soldier. The corpsmen shouted for an ambulance. A marine from the other side of the street replied, "Bring 'em out on litters. The major says we've lost four ambulances, seven corpsmen and four drivers since last night. We ain't got the ambulances to replace 'em." The medics swore softly, placed the wounded on litters and started back to the C.P.

Farther along, behind a barricade just seized by the marines, we saw another amazing sight. Less than 50 yards away, through dense smoke, came 40 to 50 North Korean soldiers. They dragged a light antitank gun. Apparently they thought the barricade was held by their side. The marines first stared at them in disbelief, then opened fire with every weapon available. The Reds screamed, buckled, pitched and died on Mapo's pavement. ∎

"FROZEN CHOSIN": Two Marines rest during the battle near the Chosin Reservoir in December. Thousands of U.S. troops suffered frostbite when temperatures in the area hit 30 degrees below zero.

Reversal

In a stunning surprise, Chinese army troops attack the allies, hurling the South Koreans and U.N. troops south in a bitter wintertime retreat

The war in Korea rode a seesaw. The U.S. and its U.N. allies (Britain, Australia, New Zealand, Turkey and others) began the conflict in retreat, holding a perimeter that allowed hundreds of thousands of South Koreans to retreat safely from Seoul to Pusan. The allies swung the balance of power their way with the Inchon landing, quickly retaking Seoul and all the rest of South Korea, then driving into North Korea and occupying Pyongyang ("the first Communist capital to be liberated by the forces of the free world," TIME crowed).

But when Douglas MacArthur sent his forces close to China's border, Mao Zedong unleashed his enormous army against the stunned allies. Once again, U.N. and South Korean forces retreated, this time in the depths of a bitter winter. Waging a heroic rear-guard action, most of the allied soldiers survived, but only ten weeks after China's army attacked, North Korea's flag again flew over Seoul.

October 30, 1950

"Damn Good Job"

At 6:30 one morning last week, two U.N. columns jumped off for the final assault on the North Korean capital, Pyongyang. The 5th Regiment of the U.S. 1st Cavalry Division drove out of the mountains 16 miles south of Pyongyang. The R.O.K. 1st Division punched in from a point eight miles southeast of the city. The R.O.K. troops were commanded by Brigadier General Paik Sun Yup, a man with a grim ambition to be the first into Pyongyang. Five years ago the city's Communist rulers had sawed off the head of General Paik's baby.

The cavalrymen, firing from their vehicles, drove swiftly through Pyongyang's outer defenses, left the enemy on their flanks to be mopped up by the men who followed them. At 11 a.m. the 5th's 2nd Battalion blasted its way into the southern edge of Pyongyang.

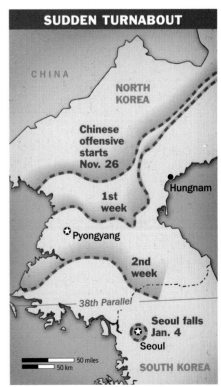

SUDDEN TURNABOUT

CHINA

NORTH KOREA

Chinese offensive starts Nov. 26

Hungnam

1st week

Pyongyang

2nd week

38th Parallel

Seoul falls Jan. 4

Seoul

50 miles
50 km

SOUTH KOREA

FLIGHT: With Chinese troops close behind, Koreans flee Pyongyang across a shattered bridge over the Taedong River, Dec. 4, 1950. This picture won the Pulitzer Prize for Max Desfor.

About the same time, soldiers of the R.O.K. 1st Division entered Pyongyang's tree-lined streets from the east. While diehard North Korean snipers blazed away, U.S. and R.O.K. troops met on an avenue flanked with burning buildings. Paik, a veteran of the Japanese army, slapped the back of every American in sight, repeated exultantly: "Damn good job. Damn good job."

U.N. commanders, who had expected to pay heavily for Pyongyang, found the city dotted with carefully prepared 76-mm. gun positions and innumerable sandbag barricades. But many of the positions had been left unmanned, and most of the Red soldiers who had been assigned to defend Pyongyang quickly threw up their hands.

••••••••••••••••••••••••••••••••••••

With the U.S. troops was TIME *correspondent Dwight Martin. His report:*

••••••••••••••••••••••••••••••••••••

The people of Pyongyang cheered, waving South Korean flags, British flags, Chinese Nationalist flags and improvised U.N. flags which had been designed from hearsay. At Seoul, which had been devastated by both the retreating Communists and the U.N. assault, the people had shown a restrained enthusiasm for their liberators. Here, they were staging the most spontaneous demonstration seen in any Asiatic city since the World War II liberation of Shanghai from the Japanese.

At one intersection we slowed down to pass a sandbag barricade. The crowds lining the street surged out around us, offered us sesame cookies and handshakes. Farther down the street a South Korean cavalryman put his horse through a victory prance while waving his rifle aloft, a Communist battle flag impaled on his bayonet. ∎

November 6, 1950

Slight Delay?

Early last week nothing but bad roads and poor maps slowed the U.N. advance toward the border dividing Korea and Manchuria. R.O.K. officers whose divisions were racing through northwest Korea jubilantly reported to Eight Army headquarters: "We will not stop until we bathe our sabers in the Yalu River."

Before the Koreans had a chance to wet a saber, the roof fell in. Throughout northwest Korea the Communists started unexpectedly strong counterattacks, supported by tanks, artillery and mortars. One North Korean force cut the main supply road to Chosan, isolated the R.O.K. 7th Regiment on the Yalu. Three more Red battalions surrounded part of the 6th Division near Onjong, 50 miles south of Chosan. Thirty miles west of Unsan, U.N. air strikes failed to break stubborn North Korean resistance which stalled the drive of the British Commonwealth 27th Brigade toward Sinuiju on the Manchurian border.

R.O.K. commanders in the northwest claimed that the enemy punch had been delivered by Chinese Communist troops brought down from Manchuria. But with or without Chinese aid, the North Koreans were still capable of making trouble. ∎

November 13, 1950

Winter War

With shocking suddenness the U.N. victory march in Korea was stopped and hurled back. Driven from advanced positions near the Manchurian border, U.N. troops settled grimly to holding a defense line which in some places was only 45 miles north of Pyongyang. Generals who two weeks before had promised to have their forces on the Yalu River in a matter of days now discussed a "winter war." Said one U.S. officer grimly: "I think we can hold them." A seemingly sure victory had been snatched from the U.N.'s grasp. What happened next depended chiefly on the Chinese Communist government.

Throughout Korea U.N. troops had abandoned the easy optimism of previous weeks. U.N. pilots who had long had the air almost to themselves were meeting increasing numbers of Yak fighters. Last week they had their first brushes with enemy jets coming from north of the Yalu—Soviet MIG-15s with swept-back wings and a speed of 600 miles an hour. Ground troops faced enemy units heavily equipped with tanks, automatic weapons, 76-mm. howitzers and multiple rocket launchers. The men who handled the weapons displayed skill and high morale. Said one G.I. last week: "Those guys who hit us last night are the best we've run up against in Korea." ∎

November 13, 1950

Crazyhorse Rides Again

Few soldiers now with the U.S. 1st Cavalry Division were in the outfit when it sadly traded its horses for trucks and tanks eight years ago. But today's troopers still cherish traditions of the days of boots and saddles and of dashing General George Custer, who once commanded the division's famed 7th Cavalry Regiment.

Last week the past seemed to rise up and haunt the cavalrymen. On its way to bolster up crumbling R.O.K. forces in northwest Korea, the division's 8th Regiment dug in for the night near Unsan, 70 miles north of Pyongyang. When morning came, the few troopers who were awake could not believe their ears. Said Pfc. Henry Tapper: "Someone woke me up and asked me if I could hear horses on the gallop. I couldn't hear anything, but then bugles started playing, far away." Pfc. William O'Rama, who was sitting in a machine-gun emplacement, heard the bugles too— "very faint-like."

Lieut. W.C. Hill thought he was dreaming. "I heard a bugler ... and the beat of horses' hooves in the distance. Then, as though they came out of a burst of smoke, shadowy figures started shooting and bayoneting everybody they could find."

The infiltrating Red force, probably Chinese, achieved complete surprise. O'Rama and his buddies were still talking about the bugles "when a hand grenade was thrown into our hole." Some cavalrymen thought their attackers were insane. Said a U.S. sergeant: "They would stand right up in front of you laughing to beat hell."

At first the cavalrymen offered no organized resistance. Said one trooper: "I couldn't see anything until a tank came along. I climbed on and fell off three times or was pulled off by others trying to get on. Then the tank burst into flames and we all started running." Most of the men who escaped the confused, swirling battle swam the icy Kuryong River to safety.

Eight hundred troopers were still holding out, trapped on a ridge. Helicopters flew in to them, brought out 20 of the most seriously wounded. Twice 1st Cavalry Division reinforcements tried to break through to the trapped remnants, but each time the relief columns ran into "stone-wall" resistance.

More than twelve hours after the attack, the relief columns gave up. By that time more than 500 cavalrymen had filtered through the Red lines to safety. To the men still on the ridge went orders to get out as best they could. Next day a bitter cavalry officer said: "It was a massacre like the one which hit Custer." ∎

December 11, 1950

Defeat

The U.S. and its allies stood at the abyss of disaster. The Chinese Communists, pouring across the Manchurian border in vast formations, had smashed the U.N. army, this week were clawing forward to pursue and destroy its still-organized fragments. Caught in the desperate retreat were 140,000 American troops, the flower of the United States Army—almost the whole effective Army the U.S. had. With them, fighting to establish a defensive position, were 20,000 British, Turkish and other allies, some 100,000 South Korean soldiers. It was defeat—the worst defeat the U.S. had ever suffered.

Last week the conservative military textbooks, the old ways of war, caught up with the U.S. and with a daring champion of new ways of war, Douglas MacArthur. In North Korea, he tried what he called a "massive compression envelopment" against greatly superior forces. He undoubtedly underestimated the size and the quality of the Chinese troops. The enveloped Chinese broke through the envelopment. Their thrust was so wide, deep and strong that his inadequate reserves could not check it. MacArthur's center was gone and the Reds lapped around the two

SPENT: Exhausted Marines of the 5th and 7th Regiments rest after a battle in which they held off three Chinese divisions

FRANK C. KERR—NATIONAL ARCHIVES

inside flanks of his divided army, pushing both wings back toward the sea.

His forces on the west began pulling back early, but in the east, four days seem to have elapsed between the Red breakthrough and the order to the X Corps to try to fight their way to the coast. At week's end, it seemed doubtful that the U.N. forces could get out of Korea without a very severe mauling. ∎

December 18, 1950

Retreat of the 20,000

The best to be said of Korea was that the worst had not happened. The U.S. forces threatened with annihilation a fortnight ago had not been destroyed, and were not likely to be destroyed. Lieut. General Walton H. Walker's rapid withdrawal of the Eighth Army saved most of it; the fighting retreat of the X Corps in the northeast saved most of that command too.

The battered but not broken Eighth Army rolled south, with vehicle col-

ON THE SPOT: During a North Korean attack, Marine Captain Francis "Ike" Fenton learns that his first sergeant has been killed and that his unit has run out of ammo

DAVID DOUGLAS DUNCAN

umns bumper-to-bumper on the roads and a million refugees alongside. Jeeps and trucks that broke down were not repaired—they were shoved off the road and burned. Said a reconnaissance pilot, looking down on the dreary spectacle of U.S. defeat and retreat: "This hurts. It hurts where I can't scratch."

The Chinese Communists surged into burning Pyongyang and its port, Chinampo. At the port some 7,000 allied wounded and civilians were evacuated by sea. Chinese troops crossed the Taedong estuary in a vast fleet of power junks and small craft; farther back they waded the Congchon and tinged the icy river with blood when allied airplanes strafed them. But the locustlike swarm of the enemy never stopped.

Retreat is contagious. Already some Korean civilians were leaving Seoul for the south, and the price of a truck ride to Pusan hovered around three million won ($700).

"Retreat, hell!" snapped Major General Oliver Prince Smith, commander of the 1st Marine Division, with which he had fought on Guadalcanal, New Britain, Peleiliu, Okinawa. "We're not retreating, we're just advancing in a different direction."

Said Colonel Lewis ("Chesty") Puller, famed battle-scarred commander of the 1st Marine Regiment: "We'll suffer heavy losses. The enemy greatly outnumbers us. They've blown the bridges and blocked the roads ... but we'll make it somehow."

The running fight of the Marines and two battalions of the Army's 7th Infantry Division from Hagaru to Hamhung—40 miles by air but 60 miles over the icy, twisting, mountainous road—was a battle unparalleled in U.S. history. It had some aspects of Bataan, some of Anzio, some of Dunkirk, some of Valley Forge, some of the "Retreat of the 10,000" (401-400 B.C.), as described in Xenophon's *Anabasis.*

Assembled in Hagaru, south of the frozen, blood-stained beaches of the Chosin Reservoir, the 1st Marine Division and the 7th had already suffered heavy casualties in battles with the encircling Communists. They had heard the screams of their comrades when the Reds lobbed phosphorous grenades into truckloads of U.S. wounded. When the order came to start south, the enemy was already closing in on Hagaru's makeshift airstrip, whence thousands of wounded and frostbite victims had been flown out. The last plane waited an extra hour for one desperately wounded man.

The Marines abandoned one of their disabled men, but bulldozers pushed the dead into mass graves by hundreds. The flight to Koto, six miles down he road, was the worst. The crawling vehicles ran into murderous mortar, machine-gun and small-arms fire from Communists in log and sandbag bunkers. The U.S. answering fire and air attacks killed thousands of the enemy and held the road open. When the lead vehicles reached Koto, the rearguard was still fighting near Hagaru to keep the enemy from chewing up the column from behind.

Three miles from the city of Koto on the narrow mountain road which led to safety, encircling Communist troops had blown the only bridge across a reservoir. With the bridge gone, the 20,000 men had no choice but to abandon their vehicles, take out on foot and make a 20-mile detour through enemy-infested hills. The commanders were informed that 80,000 to 120,000 Chinese were in the country around them.

Had they been members of any other army the Marines and soldiers would have made the detour and perhaps been annihilated in the process. As it was, even before the crucial crossing was reached, eight spans of a 16-ton bridge had been parachuted down out of the sky to the U.S. troops seemingly isolated in the midst of the enemy. Eight C-119s, each hauling a single span, had carried out the world's first airdrop of a bridge. The retreating col-

TAKE FIVE: Marines of the 1st Division share a smoke after their passage through "Nightmare Alley." A relief column arrives at the rear.

umn was free to move ahead, vehicles and all. ∎

January 15, 1951
Scorched-Earth Retreat

Said a U.S. officer, who had hoped that Douglas MacArthur's coast-to-coast line below the 38th parallel could be held: "What are you going to do when the enemy doesn't care how many men he loses?" The suicidal fury of the Reds' first attack north of Seoul was astounding. The vast mass of the enemy pressed on by day as well as by night, ignoring U.S. artillery zeroed in on their lines of advance, ignoring the swarm of planes that hammered them from the air.

Having forced their way across the frozen Imjin River, the Chinese ran into minefields and barbed wire. The leading elements marched right through the minefields, most of them blowing themselves up, and those who followed advanced over their own dead. When they reached the barbed wire, hundreds of Chinese flung straw mats down on the wire, then threw themselves down on the mats, and the others trod the living bridge over the wire.

Then the planned allied retreat began. Once more, the bumper-to-bumper vehicle columns rolled south. It was a scorched-earth retreat: the troops and the aircraft burned every building in which the pursuing foe could take shelter. An icy north wind followed the retreating G.I.s and seared the faces of rearguards firing from the back slopes of paddy-field dikes.

From the north, northwest and northeast, the Chinese converged on Seoul. Allied evacuation of the capital was carried out efficiently and without undue haste. "After all," said a U.S. officer bitterly, "we've had a lot of practice."

••••••••••••••••••••••••••••••••

TIME *correspondent Dwight Martin, in Seoul again before it fell to the Communists, cabled:*

••••••••••••••••••••••••••••••••

Seoul was all but dead. During the day, occasional bands of laborers trudged off to the north to work on the city's last-ditch defenses. The rest of the remaining population seemed to be mostly kids, some hawking U.N. and South Korean flags from sidewalk stands. At night, the city lay black, empty and desolate in the moonlight. The crack of small-arms fire rang incessantly through the streets, much of it directed at jeep thieves who worked steadily every night. Seoul's Capitol Club, where two weeks ago a plate of potato chips had sold for $2.50, was dark and deserted. In its stead, a few blocks away, stood Seoul's last-ditch nightspot, the Consolation Club, which advertised "Fifty Beautiful Women Fifty." Inside, a dozen-odd bedraggled beauties gyrated round a scarred dance floor, their swirling Korean skirts revealing singularly unattractive expanses of olive-drab G.I. long johns.

Two days later, from morning till night, the retreating U.N. forces rolled back down the two main roads through Seoul—down the same roads on which outnumbered South Korean troops and a handful of U.S. advisers had fled six months before. ∎

January 1, 1951

The U.S. Fighting Man

Destiny's draftees, the G.I.s in Korea are TIME's Men of the Year 1950

THE U.S. FIGHTING MAN HAS BEEN CALLED SOFT AND tough, resourceful and unskilled, unbelievably brave and unbelievably timid, thoroughly disciplined and scornful of discipline. One way or another, all of these generalizations are valid. He is a peculiar soldier, product of a peculiar country. His two outstanding characteristics seem to be contradictory. He is more of an individualist than soldiers of other nations, and at the same time he is far more conscious of, and dependent on, teamwork. He fights as he lives, a part of a vast, complicated machine—but a thinking, deciding part, not an inert cog.

RETREAT: Marines pull back before the Chinese onslaught in December

Better trained, more experienced and older than the G.I.s of World War II, the U.S. Army in battle in Korea was the nearest approach to a professional army that the U.S. had ever sent into war. The men in it did not lend themselves to easy characterization. Nobody could find a typical U.S. soldier of 1950. There was no one type; there were as many types as there were men. Here are some of the men:

CPL. HIDEO HASHIMOTO, a Japanese-American who had been interned in the U.S. during World War II, kept hurling hand grenades at the storming Reds; after he ran out of grenades, he threw rocks.

2ND LIEUT. JOHN CHARLES TRENT, of Memphis, captain of West Point's 1949 football team, was killed by a rifle bullet while he was walking from foxhole to foxhole to see that his men—fighting for three days and nights—had not fallen asleep.

PFC. DONALD PATTON, who in his frontline foxhole slept through the bloodiest night attack which the Reds hurled against the U.S.'s position on the famed "Bowling Alley" near Taegu, woke up the next morning, looked at the smoking, knocked-out Red tanks and cried in a frightened voice: "Holy cow! What happened?"

T/SGT. WAYNE H. KERR, of Cleveland, was on safe desk duty but got into an L-5 at night when other pilots had refused the mission; holding a flashlight in one hand to light up the instrument panel, he landed on a tiny, badly lighted mountain strip and flew out a wounded Marine.

CAPT. "WHISTLIN' JOE" ROGERS, 26, of the 36th Squadron, Eighth Fighter-Bomber Group, had probably killed more North Koreans and Chinese than any other flyer. During World War II, to his disgust, he had been an instructor, saw no combat. He had made up for it in Korea. Air Force men liked to talk about Joe's exploits—his trick of barrel-rolling when he came in for a strafing run, the time he attached a whistle to one of his wings to scare the enemy, thus earned his nickname.

The story they like best was the one about Joe chatting at the bar with a B-26 pilot who, not knowing Joe's record, was beefing because he had to fly combat two days in a row. "How many missions you got?" asked Joe. "Eight," said the other flyer. Joe didn't say anything. At that point a third man joined them and asked Joe how many missions he had. "Hundert an' fifty-three," said Joe. The B-26 man quietly set down his glass and faded away.

MARINE SGT. ROBERT WARD is a full-blooded Cherokee Indian who grew up in Los Angeles. If there is one story of a U.S. fighting man that can sum up the best in all the stories, it is his. He got to be a wonderful marksman with a bow and arrow. Ward's two older brothers were killed in action in World War II. Robert served in the Navy, then joined the Marines. After he went into action in Korea last summer, his mother wrote to President Truman and to the Marine Corps, begging that Sgt. Ward, her only surviving son, be transferred from the combat zone. The Marines' General Clifton Gates agreed to apply the "only surviving son" rule. Leather-faced Sgt. Ward intercepted the transfer orders, went on fighting. Eventually, despite his protests, Ward was transferred to a desk job in Japan.

Last week his mother received a letter from Sgt. Ward. He wrote:

"I'm no hero, but … if these people aren't stopped here on their own ground, we will have to share the thing which so many have died to prevent their loved ones from sharing—the sight of death in their own backyards; of women and children being victims of these people. I went on the warpath for the right to do my bit to keep our people free and proud and now I'm shackled to a useless job. I ask you, my mother, to free me … I need them—my dirty, stinking and loyal platoon."

Sergeant Ward was sent back to Korea and his dirty, stinking and loyal platoon. His mother said: "When men in our tribe say something, they mean it." ■

April 23, 1951

Douglas MacArthur

He preferred to run his own show—but so did President Harry Truman

A WHITE HOUSE AIDE, LEAFING THROUGH A ROUTINE sheaf of wire copy from the news ticker, started with surprise. He had come across the report of Republican leader Joe Martin's speech, made that afternoon in the House, containing General Douglas MacArthur's letter endorsing the employment of Chiang Kai-shek's troops to open a second front in China. The aide rushed into the President's office. As he read, Harry Truman flushed with anger. He made his decision then and there—Thursday, April 5—that Douglas MacArthur must go.

After the Cabinet meeting next day, Truman asked Chairman of the Joint Chiefs of Staff Omar Bradley and Defense Secretary George Marshall to stay behind. Truman told them his decision and his reasons. Marshall agreed that MacArthur must go, and Bradley added that the Joint Chiefs emphatically felt the same way.

For five days, Truman hugged his secret. The Joint Chiefs held emergency meetings to discuss MacArthur's successor. They decided on Lieut. General Matthew Ridgway. Just before lunch Tuesday, Harry Truman told his staff to draw up MacArthur's firing orders— just as the afternoon papers bloomed with headlines: MACARTHUR DEMANDS FREER HAND IN WAR. By 9:30 the documents and statements were ready and taken over to Blair House. Harry Truman looked them over and signed. By midnight, stencils had been cut, and Press Secretary Joe Short gave the switchboard orders to summon the regular White House reporters at 1 a.m. The press got mimeographed sheets: "It is fundamental … that military commanders be governed by the policies and directives issued to them in the manner provided by our laws and the Constitution."

In Tokyo, just a little after 3 o'clock in the afternoon, General Douglas MacArthur was eating a chicken leg at a late lunch when an aide handed him a note. It was a radio news flash. Holding the drumstick in one hand and the note in the other, MacArthur read the news. His mouth opened in astonishment.

CARL MYDANS—TIMEPIX

AP/WIDE WORLD

TOP DOG? MacArthur at Inchon, above, and meeting President Truman at Wake Island in 1950, right

Abruptly, the luncheon ended. It was 20 minutes later that he got the official dispatch informing him of Truman's decision.

Seldom had a more unpopular man fired a more popular one. Harry Truman, completing his sixth year as President, had written a record of courage in crises—in enumerating the Truman Doctrine against the Communist threat in Greece, in his firmness over the Berlin blockade, in the way he rallied his party and won the 1948 election, in his quick decision to counter the Korean aggression. But the six years had provided increasing evidence of shabby politicking and corruption in his administration, of doubts about his State Department, and distaste for his careless government-by-crony.

The man he fired was a military hero, idolized by many. MacArthur had done a superb job as Supreme Commander for the Allied Powers in the occupation and reconstruction of Japan. But strong-minded General Douglas MacArthur had set himself firmly against the policy of Truman, of his Secretary of State Dean Acheson and of the U.S. itself. Despite repeated efforts to silence him, he had spoken up defiantly and deliberately. On the record, there was little doubt that Douglas MacArthur had ignored the wishes, intent and specific orders of his Commander in Chief.

Unable to silence MacArthur by teletype, Harry Truman staged the dramatic Wake Island meeting in 1950, from which emerged public statements of agreement (and MacArthur's private assurance to Truman that the Chinese would not come into Korea).

Then, late in December of 1950, the Chinese surged across the Yalu. They forced a bruising defeat on MacArthur's ill-deployed forces, shaking the J.C.S.'s confidence in his military judgment. MacArthur was for forceful retaliation. But the State Department laid down the line: U.S. policy would be to fight China only in Korea. MacArthur launched a fresh barrage of dissent, complaining of the enemy's "privileged sanctuary."

A few weeks later, over the morning coffee, the nation read of Harry Truman's action and fumed. That night, Truman took to the air with an explanation. "I believe that we must try to limit the war to Korea … Events have made it evident that General MacArthur did not agree … We are trying to prevent a world war—not to start one." As the first of 18,000 telegrams and 50,000 letters poured in, Truman knew that he faced that biggest political storm of his stormy political career. ∎

SHELL: Having changed hands for the fourth time, Seoul lies in ruins in June 1951

Stalemate

Buoyed by a new commander, the U.S. and allied troops regain their morale, stand their ground, win back Seoul—and end the war in a draw

After the unexpected Chinese assault, U.S. forces fought their way to safety; some 60,000 men were evacuated from the port city of Hungnam. When Eighth Army commander Lieut. General Walton Walker was killed in a jeep crash in December, dynamic leader General Matthew Ridgway took over and restored morale; allied troops began to regain ground in the spring. In April President Harry Truman shocked America by relieving General Douglas MacArthur from the top command for insubordination; Ridgway replaced him. By June allied troops again took Seoul. With both sides exhausted—and holding roughly the same territory as at the war's start—peace talks began in July.

February 5, 1951
Brawl in the Alley

Lieut. Colonel William E. Bertram of Chicago was heating water on a gasoline burner—for a bath in the half-shell of a discarded belly tank. Bertram gave his story of last week's first big battle between the enemy's Russian-made MIG-15s and U.S. F-84 Thunderjets: "We were hitting a bridge halfway between Sinuiju and Sinanju. I saw a MIG on the tail of one of our guys and went to help, and then four more MIGS went through me. I went up into the sun and skidded around and caught some more tracers going by.

"Then I saw another 84, called for him to team up and we slid over behind two MIGs and went in wide open. I felt better chasing my MIG with some protection behind me. About 2,500 feet out I gave him a burst, and it seemed to hit him all over. I got in a close burst and he poured big white smoke and fire. He rolled over at 8,000, hit the deck and blew up."

U.S. jet pilots have their own name for the northwestern corner of Korea, where the MIGs have been darting back and forth from their sanctuaries beyond the Yalu. The name: "MIG Alley." Two days after Bertram's victory, speeding up the alley to hit the Communist airfield at Sinuiju, 33 U.S. F-84 Thunderjets fought a screaming series of dogfights with enemy MIGs.

JOSEPH SCHERSCHEL—TIMEPIX

Said Lieut. Jacob Kratt, flying top cover: "I rolled over and came down fast, and got in a good long burst on the No. 2 MIG. Smoke poured out of his tail, and he turned to the Manchurian side, and that apparently disorganized their attack, as two more of our flights made passes at the field, and nobody got bounced on his run. My wingman said that when he passed my MIG it was flaming."

Said Captain Allen McGuire: "We flew east to get out of flak from across the Yalu. Then we turned south and west, and when I looked at the air over the Sinuiju field, it looked like a Mixmaster. We turned north, and I saw a MIG turning in front of us. I don't think he saw us. I gave the MIG a burst from 2,500 feet. My wingman said that he saw MIGs coming in from 6 o'clock and would have to leave me in a minute. Three seconds later he said, 'I am gone.' I followed my MIG from 12,000 down to 4,000, and gave him a burst that knocked pieces off him. Then I turned right. I guess they call it a 'probably.' "

After this battle, the total MIG score for the U.S. was 20 destroyed, ten probably destroyed, 32 damaged. The Air Force announced that five U.S. jets had been lost since Nov. 1. Said Captain William Slaughter: "Let's admit it—the MIG is all right. It's a damned fine airplane. The F-84 is all right too. But if we were flying the MIG and they were flying the 84, I think we would be murdering them." ∎

February 19, 1951

Red Strike

This week the Communists, who had been giving ground before Seoul and shifting strength to the east, launched a vicious 60,000-man assault on a 30-mile front in the central mountains of Korea. Outnumbered South Koreans, who were out in front with a U.S. division backing them up, promptly collapsed. The Communists—Chinese and North Koreans—drove an eight-mile wedge in the allied line.

Some observers had the same shivery feeling that accompanied the Chinese breakthrough of last November and the wholesale U.N. retreat that followed. But the situation this time was quite different. Largely as a result of

THE END OF THE STORY

The U.S. never declared war in Korea; President Truman called the conflict a "police action." He feared that declaring war might compel North Korea's communist allies, China and the U.S.S.R., to attack America, and Truman was determined to avoid a wider war.

After the first truce talks in 1951, the war continued for two years, in a fitful and inconclusive manner. The talks proceeded in much the same way—months of diplomatic stalemate, followed by short bursts of frantic activity. When the fighting ended in July, 1953, the 38th parallel became a border frozen in time. Fifty years later, hostile troops still stand at the ready, poised to resume fighting a war that was never formally declared and that never technically ended.

General Matt Ridgway's morale-boosting, the Eighth Army was no longer suffering from "bug-out fever" (an overquick tendency to retreat in case of trouble).

Instead of being strung out in vulnerable "pursuit formation," Ridgway had been advancing carefully, compactly, on constant guard against surprise attacks and flank threats. Moreover, when they struck in November, the Chinese were fresh, confident, unhurt. Now they had been weakened by allied air attacks and ground action, and by cold, hunger and disease.

Meanwhile, as the U.N. forces below Seoul closed in on the Han River, Communist anti-tank guns firing from a hill briefly stalled the advance. A company of G.I.s, led by Captain Lewis Millett of South Dartmouth, Mass., charged the crest with fixed bayonets, spitted 47 Chinese, shot down 50 more as they ran down the north slope. The advance continued.

Allied fire from tanks and artillery reached such a furious volume that some Chinese who surrendered had blood streaming from nose and ears because of concussion. On Hill 431, which had changed hands five times in battles between Turks and Reds, the Chinese finally put up the white flags of surrender.

Loss of Hill 431 seemed to make the enemy's position south of the river untenable. Into Yongdungpo, Seoul's industrial suburb where U.S. marines had such a rough time last September, the doughfeet now walked without opposition. The town was silent and empty. After a while an old man and some boys appeared, clapped their hands, cried: "O.K.! O.K.!" At a road crossing

HEAT! Former U.S. and Australian POWs warm up after being handed over to the allies

CAUGHT: Three enemy soldiers in a fishing boat surrender to forces from the U.S.S. Manchester, May 1951

where one road branched off toward Seoul, a fur-hatted old man stood alone. The Communists had gone that way the night before, he said, pointing toward Seoul.

General Ridgway quickly brought up four divisions to the Han, while a few North Korean rearguards scrambled across the thawing and treacherous ice. While British tanks dueled across the river with Communist self-propelled guns, two armored U.S. task forces sped northwest and west to take Kimp Airfield, Korea's biggest, and Inchon, Seoul's port, without a fight. Both were almost total ruins. ∎

March 26, 1951

Way Out

The Communists had finally found a way to beat General Matt Ridgway's "killer" offen-

sive: they pulled back out of range, faster than Ridgway dared to follow, and Chinese casualties due to ground action fell off sharply. In his own good time, Ridgway was following, however, and there was some political uproar last week over whether he should or should not cross the 38th parallel.

The Peking radio admitted that Seoul had fallen, but called it a "temporary withdrawal." General Ridgway had been wisely unwilling to accept the casualties of a frontal attack. Instead, he had put a bridgehead across the Han River east of the capital. When the bridgehead outflanked the Red defenders, they pulled out.

The fourth fall of Seoul was a sad business, something like the capture of a tomb. Only 200,000 of Seoul's original 1,500,000 population were still there. The broken city brooded over its own destruction.

None of the utilities were operating.

Streetcar and light wires dangled from poles. A few women dipped water from manholes in gourds fastened to long poles. The capital building, which the Reds had fired last autumn in a senseless act of spiteful arson, had its lobby fouled by manure from horses stabled there by the enemy. ∎

May 7, 1951

The Strange War

Last week the U.S. State Department began to wake up to a question: How do we settle this thing, anyway? The first phase of the great Chinese spring offensive—South Korea's third Red invasion—was over, and it was a failure. The Chinese had failed to inflict serious damage on the U.N. forces, had not come anywhere near their stated objective of driving the allies into the sea.

The Eighth Army moved back fast enough to keep out of serious trouble, slowly enough to inflict vast damage on the Chinese. The Eighth was trading space for enemy blood—all that the U.N. forces could do in Korea. In a valley south of Chorwon, where hundreds of Reds were ambushed, other Reds slipped and staggered in puddles of blood while trying to remove their dead.

Said an officer: "They're spending people the way we spend ammunition." The Americans were spending plenty of ammunition. Some busy gun crews, stripped to the waist in the warm weather, hardly had time for a drink of water. ∎

July 16, 1951

Sunday in Kaesong

At 8:50 a.m. Sunday, Korea time, two big green U.S. helicopters windmilled up from Munsan, the allied "advance outpost" for truce talks, and vanished to the north in the morning haze. They flew slowly. In ten minutes they were across the Imjin River; in a few more minutes their pilots sighted Kaesong, three miles south of the 38th parallel, the war-battered town the Communists had picked as the place to talk peace.

Kaesong (meaning "open castle") was the first major South Korean town

HOMELESS: South Korean women and children take to the road as enemy forces advance again, 1951

to fall to the North Korean invaders, in the war that began on another Sunday, 54 weeks earlier; it fell five hours after the aggressors crossed the frontier. Although the Sunday meeting was only a preliminary to set the stage for cease-fire negotiations to begin this week, the West's hopes, fears and doubts converged, along with the green helicopters, on Kaesong.

The man whose eyes were fixed most intently on Kaesong was General Matthew Bunker Ridgway. Rarely had a military commander found himself in the kind of situation that Ridgway was in this week. It was Matt Ridgway who had rallied the Eighth Army against the overwhelming Chinese onslaught last year, and turned his troops north again. To Ridgway, as to any soldier, the best way to finish the job in Korea could only be to defeat the enemy. Ridgway knew that, with more ground strength in Korea—and perhaps with air blows at

Manchuria—he could drive the Chinese back behind the Yalu. Yet with the Chinese licking the wounds that Ridgway's punches had inflicted on them, he was trying to negotiate a truce. The job was not designed for the liking of a hard-hitting combat leader, but Good Soldier Ridgway did the job as well as he knew how.

In its wary hope for peace, in its tense preoccupation with the great struggle between freedom and Communism, the world is apt to forget one fact: one of the items on the agenda at Kaesong is a country called Korea and some 30 million people who live there.

After a year's fighting, 375,000 South Korean civilians are dead or missing, 125,000 more have been wounded. No one can be sure how many people were killed in North Korea. At least 6,000,000 Koreans North and South, are homeless.

Peace, if it comes, will find Korea's

cities dead. Humbler and more complete than the city ruins is the destruction of the grass-roofed villages. They have vanished—more than 12,000 of them—into heaps of bluish-gray ash. Bleak stone walls still stand in front of them, and mulberry and acacia bushes, covered with heavy dust.

One of the observations heard repeatedly last week was that, no matter how the truce talks turned out, there could be no victory for the Korean people. The Koreans' plight is a great tragedy, but they know that there are differences even in suffering. Amid death, destruction and hopelessness, millions of Koreans held on to a simple fact: they would rather live where the Americans are than where the Communists are.

To the bulk of Koreans, it still makes a great difference whether or not their country—or half their country—is run by Communists. ∎

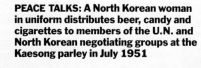

PEACE TALKS: A North Korean woman in uniform distributes beer, candy and cigarettes to members of the U.N. and North Korean negotiating groups at the Kaesong parley in July 1951

March 5, 1951

Matthew Ridgway

A tough, experienced leader starches up America's overwhelmed soldiers

AS USUAL ON A MARINE JUMP-OFF, THE LEATHERNECKS were not losing any time. Corporal Ardrick Hammon of Alton, Ill., radioman for an artillery observer, slogged his way north, so loaded with fighting and communications gear that he could not stoop to tie the flapping lace of one combat boot. He felt a tap on his shoulder, looked into a lean face under a pile cap with three stars and a paratrooper's silver badge on it.

"Don't you want your shoe tied?" asked Lieut. General Matthew Ridgway.

"No, sir," Hammon replied. Ridgway knelt down and tied the shoe. "Is that too tight?" he asked.

"No, sir," said the abashed Hammon.

It was an odd gesture for a lieutenant general. Hammon and his fellow marines would never forget it. But for Matthew Bunker Ridgway, a soldier who possesses a passionate sense of detail, an instinct for the bonds that unite a commander and his troops, and a nice flair for showmanship, it was no effort at all. A few minutes later the general climbed into his helicopter and whirred off to another sector of his front line.

This week, with the precision of a machine, the marines and other divisions of Ridgway's Eighth Army ground their way northward over the mountains of central Korea. In the last two weeks of battle Ridgway's men had inflicted an estimated 30,000 casualties on Chinese and North Korean Communists, at small cost to themselves. The U.N. army had regained its self-confidence and vindicated the contention of U.S. artillerymen that a compact, mobile fighting force, long on organization and heavy in firepower, can stand up against the mass levies of a Communist war machine.

When last week's U.N. attack began, Matt Ridgway, an austerely handsome man of 56, tramped alongside the lead tank of a column, critically watching the two lines of infantrymen shuffle up the road a few hundred yards ahead. Neatly hooked to the web harness he wore over his trench coat were a paratrooper's first-aid kit and the hand grenade that has become as famous a trademark as George Patton's legendary pearl-handled pistols.

Each day Ridgway shuttled across the front in his helicopter, marshaling his troops as carefully as a Roman general. He brought to his G-1 a complaint that the envelopes G.I.s used for letters home were sticking together. (This week the Air Force announced that it had delivered 27 tons of new envelopes and writing paper to U.N. troops in Korea.) He ordered the division G-4 to provide fresh meat for his units seven out of ten days. When the G-4 mentioned the lack of refrigerators, Ridgway snapped, "The winter will give you time to work out the refrigeration problem."

In his hectoring, driving way, Matt Ridgway had changed the Eighth Army out of all resemblance to the command, riddled with defeatism, that he had found two months before, reeling in retreat before the Chinese Communist advance.

Matt Ridgway began his Army career informally some 45 years ago, when he used to shout a sentry's challenge to visitors from the porch of the family quarters at Fort Walla Walla, Wash. He entered West Point in the class of 1917. He managed the football team, played on the hockey squad. Commented the West Point yearbook: "Beyond doubt the busiest man in the place." Like Eisenhower, Ridgway missed the fighting in World War I, but began building a reputation as a staff officer. In 1942 he became commanding general of the 82nd Division, succeeding Omar Bradley. A few weeks after he took over, the Pentagon decided to convert the 82nd into one of the first two U.S. airborne divisions. To show his men what paratrooping might be like, Ridgway, who had no particular airborne qualifications, hied himself to Fort Benning to make a parachute jump. "It was the most glorious feeling in the world," he told the dubious infantrymen. "You feel like the lord of creation."

For the next three years the 82nd's war diary read like a history of the development of airborne operations. Ridgway and his staff, with few precedents to go by, wrote their own field manuals as they went along. Ridgway jumped into battle at Normandy, later led the XVIII Corps at Nijmegen and the Ardennes.

A fellow officer says: "It makes him personally offended to be shot at." In Normandy, Ridgway and an aide were surprised by a German tank which rumbled up from the rear. The aide dived into a hole. Ridgway whipped his rifle to his shoulder and fired. For some inexplicable reason, the tank turned and clanked away. "I got him," bellowed Ridgway.

Ridgway ruthlessly drives his subordinates. Asked what it was like to work for him, one former aide said, "Tense." "Ridgway—tense?" "No," said the officer, "we're tense." ∎

DRIVEN: Ridgway pulls desk duty

JOHN DOMINIS—TIMEPIX

Notebook

The Buildup

The week the Korean War began, there was a total of 485 U.S. military personnel in South Korea. One month later, at the end of July 1950, there were more than 48,000 American soldiers in the country. By year's end, that number had more than tripled, to 163,507 men. A year after the war started, the total had risen to 229,291 troops.

The Longest Siege

Before the Korean War, the Civil War Battle of Vicksburg was the longest siege (42 consecutive days of naval bombardment) ever mounted by any branch of the American military. This record was surpassed in early March 1951, when the U.S. Navy's shelling of the North Korean coastal cities of Wonson, Songjin, and Hungnam reached 43 consecutive days. The Navy shelled all three cities for an astounding 861 days without pause, until the signing of the July 1953 cease-fire.

Heroes

The Battle at the Chosin Reservoir yielded the greatest number of decorations conferred for a single engagement in the history of the America's Armed Forces: 17 Congressional Medals of Honor, 70 Navy Crosses and nine Distinguished Service Crosses were awarded. The fighting in Korea, though concentrated in a single year, earned the Congressional Medal of Honor for 131 Americans in uniform, 93 of which were awarded posthumously.

The official American death toll for the Korean War is 33,686.

Hardware

NATIONAL ARCHIVES

Dawn of the Jet Age

The F-86 Sabre, the Air Force's first swept-wing jet fighter, took to the skies in May 1948 and soon set a new world speed record of more than 670 m.p.h. It faced a tough competitor when North Korean pilots began flying the state-of-the-art Russian-made MiG-15, which could outfly and outfight every U.S. Air Force plane other than the F-86. The U.S. jet soon proved as well suited to duty as an interceptor and a fighter-bomber as it was to high-level dogfights. But the F-86's first and best role was as a hunter and killer of enemy aircraft. By the end of the Korean War, F-86s had shot down 792 MiGs (credit for three of those kills went to fighter pilot and future astronaut John Glenn), at a loss of only 76 Sabres—a kill ratio of more than 10 to 1.

"Red China ... lacks the industrial capacity to provide adequately many critical items necessary to the conduct of modern war."
—General Douglas MacArthur

AP/WIDE WORLD

At Ease

Take five … the smoking lamp is lit. Military life can involve long stretches of downtime as well as fevered moments of combat. Filling those empty hours may call for a drink or a smoke, a game or a movie, a bath or a song—or, perhaps best of all, a good long snooze

▲ **Do Not Disturb**
A rubber container used to haul helicopter fuel makes a fine berth in Vietnam, 1966.

◀ **Cheers!**
Celebrating the liberation of her city, a young Frenchwoman decants the national beverage for Allied soldiers.

▼ **Jump Ball!**
Navy pilots hoop it up in the forward elevator well of the U.S.S. *Monterey* in the Pacific. The jumper on the left is future President Gerald Ford.

▲ **Always Room for One More**
A much-tattooed sailor proffers additional canvas for a shipmate aboard the U.S.S. *New Jersey* in 1944.

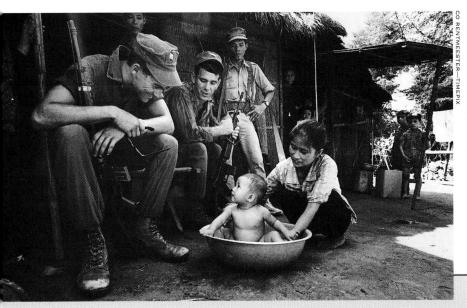

◀ **Friendlies**
Marine Corporals Ronald Schaedel and David Nielson monitor nautical maneuvers as South Vietnamese soldiers look on.
Location: Hoa Hiep, South Vietnam, 1967.

▶ **Significant Other**
November 1990:
On duty in Saudi Arabia for
Operation Desert Shield,
1st Cavalry tank driver
Clinton Raacke snuggles up
with a Christmas present
sent by his girlfriend.

▲ **Dear Mom**
Dwight Exe of the 5th Cavalry
Regiment finds a protective nook in
which to write a letter to his
parents. Korea, 1951.

▲ **Networking**
Members of the
U.S. Navy's 2nd
Medical Battalion
pass the time near
the Kuwaiti border
in 1991.

▶ **Gender Ender**
Male and female
MPs clean up at an
ingenious outdoor
bathroom during
Operation Desert
Storm, 1991.

GUN FIGHT AT COMMANCHE CREEK AUDY MURPHY

▲ Busman's Holiday

Off-duty Marines in Vietnam look forward to the evening's offering at the local theater. Star Audie (not Audy) Murphy was one of the most decorated soldiers of World War II.

▶ Rubba Dubba Bubba

We've heard of motor pools … but inflatable pools? President Bill Clinton chats with U.S. soldiers who are beating the heat in Haiti during the U.S. peace-keeping mission in 1995.

◀ **Fez or Bandage?**
Headgear told tales in 1942 at one the century's most fabled watering holes—the bar at Shepheard's Hotel in Cairo.

▼ **Information Gap**
A soldier struggles to read a censored newspaper during the Marine deployment to Lebanon, 1958.

▲ **For That Country-Fresh Feeling ...**
Marine Capt. Manlee Herrington heats up a second-hand Taliban stove: it's laundry day in Afghanistan.

◀ **Working Both Ends**
One is a cranial-protection device. The other is a hydraulic metatarsal relaxation receptacle. And this soldier in Korea in 1950 could probably identify many more strategic uses for the humble helmet.

▲ Pawns or Kings?
David Severance, left, and Jeff Flaig of the 82nd Airborne Division play chess by a light armored vehicle in the Gulf War, 1991.

▶ What War?
Robert Capa photographed two young ambulance drivers who made time for knitting outside Cassino, Italy, in 1943.

◀ The Pause That Refreshes
An Australian soldier enjoys an al fresco bath in Libya's shattered city of Tobruk during the African campaign, December 1941.

▼ Asia Is Mine!
Everyday soldiering isn't enough for these would-be Napoleons—they're playing Risk during downtime in Afghanistan in 2002.

▲ Oooof!

Nick Downey lifts barbed-wire weights at the airport in Kandahar, Afghanistan, in January 2002.

▲ Good Ball!

A U.S. soldier admires a local lad's footwork after the U.S. invaded and pacified Grenada in 1983.

▲ Pinup Palace

Korea, 1952: Marines of the "Devil-cats" squadron hunt for girlie pictures to brighten their Quonset hut. Tally: 3,000—and counting.

▶ Just Visiting

Late in the Vietnam War, in 1973, U.S. airmen enjoy a chat with the local girls in Saigon. The official term: fraternizing. Headline supplied by Hollywood.

◄ **Pair of Jokers**
A permanent floating card game takes up residence in a town square in Sicily in 1943. These Airborne troops are waiting to board a ship that will take them to fighting on the front in mainland Italy.

▲ **The Sound of Peace**
French and American voices unite in song to celebrate the liberation of Cherbourg by Allied troops in July 1944.

◄ **Battlefield Philosopher**
Khe Sahn, South Vietnam, 1971: A machine gunner strikes a classic pose, one foot atop a guard shield that states his religious beliefs.

NOW WHAT? The expression on this soldier's face, caught by photographer Larry Burrows in 1966, seems to sum up America's indecisive path in Vietnam

War of Futility

Struggling against committed, savvy guerrillas on their home ground, the mighty American war machine bogged down

WE REMEMBER MOST WARS WITH A PHRASE OR A sentence: "We won our independence" or "We freed the slaves." It speaks volumes about America's involvement in Vietnam that the war brings to mind questions rather than slogans. Questions like, "What were we doing there?" Or perhaps, "What went wrong?" Or worse, "Did they die in vain?"

These nagging doubts hang like an epitaph over a war that was both well intended and ill conceived. If Korea, the war that preceded Vietnam (and in some ways inspired it), began with an unmistakable bang—communist forces pouring over the border by the tens of thousands in the dead of night—America staked its honor and fortune in the Land of the Ascending Dragon much more gradually and subtly.

So imperceptible was America's growing commitment to Vietnam that President Dwight Eisenhower could predict before leaving office that the major strategic test of U.S. influence in Asia during the 1960s would take place in Laos. Robert Kennedy would boast dismissively in 1962, in answer to a reporter's query: "We have thirty Vietnams a day."

The tale begins in 1956, when French colonial forces were decisively beaten at Dien Bien Phu. Paris decided to pull out, but after seeing China lost to Mao Zedong and after sending Americans to die for South Korea, Washington couldn't afford to allow a new communist victory in Asia. So we stepped in. The ante was small: a few dozen advisers, then a few hundred, to teach the South Vietnamese how to win a war. But the bidding was steep. By 1960, there were more than 1,000 U.S. military personnel in Vietnam, then more than 3,000 by early 1962. Four years later there were 300,000. By 1968, 600,000 Americans found themselves at war very far from home.

For nearly 20 years, occupants of the Oval Office from both parties—each of whom was determined not to be the first U.S. President to lose a war—stepped a little bit farther into the quicksand. When the essential question was asked—What vital interest is at stake here that justifies the risk of American lives?—the answer was always the same: America's credibility as leader of the free world is at risk. But as time went by, the price of defending this abstraction came to seem too high. America's tattered credibility began to resemble the famous South Vietnamese village cited by a loose-lipped U.S. officer: in seeking to save it, we were destroying it.

A war that had been sold to the American people as a struggle on behalf of freedom and against communism looked from the other side like a war of Vietnamese nationalists and patriots against foreign invaders and colonialists. And as the war dragged on, more Americans saw it from the other side. The war came home, dividing the nation. In the end, more than

IN DEEP: U.S. paratroopers of the 173rd Airborne Brigade seek the enemy in 1965

America's credibility was at stake: the nation's unity, pride and sense of purpose all went missing in action in Vietnam.

Yet America's fighting men there did what they have always done: they answered the call, fought bravely and laid down their lives by the tens of thousands. Perhaps the most tragic element of this war is that its brave veterans returned to a nation too discouraged to honor them. Decades later, the wounds are still healing. And the doubts remain, because of the questions we got wrong from the beginning. Sadly, the one question we should have examined more closely then is the one we are still asking now: "Why?" ∎

HENRI HUET—AP/WIDE WORLD

LARRY BURROWS

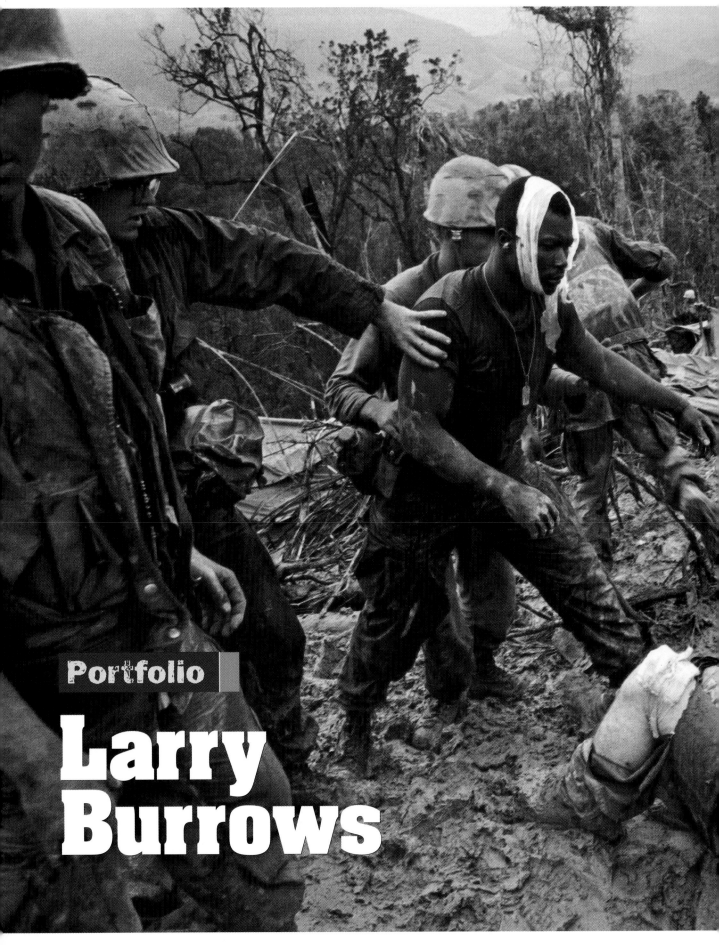

Portfolio

Larry Burrows

Friendly Fire
In one of the most famous images of the Vietnam War, wounded Marine Gunnery Sgt. Jeremiah Purdie is led past other fallen G.I.s after watching his commanding officer and radioman die seconds earlier in an artillery barrage— later found to be misdirected U.S. fire.

L arry Burrows found the inspiration that would make him a great photographer years before he ever touched a camera. As a child in London, he lived through the German bombing. "I didn't have the equipment or the ability to express my feelings about war," he recalled decades later. "That has a great deal to do with my feelings now—to show the interested and shock the disinterested people into realizing and facing the horrors of war."

It was this commitment to brutal honesty that would bring fame to Larry Burrows, who was in some ways an unlikely chronicler of warfare. Terrified of heights, frightened of snakes and spiders, Burrows spent nine years crisscrossing the skies of Vietnam and hiking through its jungles, documenting the human cost of America's effort to stave off Ho Chi Minh's gutsy guerrillas. But as long as he was looking through a camera lens, Burrows was fearless: he once had himself strapped to the wing of an airplane so that he could take pictures from outside the cockpit.

The one thing that could make Burrows stop shooting, even briefly, was a chance to alleviate the agony to which he bore witness. "Do I have the right to carry on working and leave a man suffering?" he once asked. "To my mind, the answer is, 'No, you've got to help him.'" What made this exceedingly gentle man pick the camera up again each time was the "feeling that I can contribute a little to the understanding of what others are going through."

On Feb. 10, 1971, days before he was scheduled to leave Vietnam, Burrows boarded a helicopter to photograph Operation Lam Son 719—an interdiction effort meant to sever the Ho Chi Minh Trail as it wound through Laos. The chopper was shot down; Larry Burrows died in the crash. But years earlier, he had written his own epitaph, when he said, "I concluded that what I was doing would penetrate the hearts of those at home who are simply too indifferent." As indelibly demonstrated on the pages that follow, he succeeded.

TIME GOES TO WAR 75

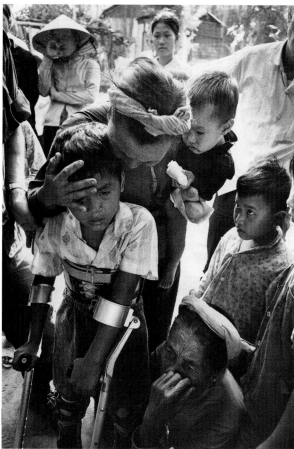

▲In Sorrow Assembled

Mourning monks proceed past Vietnamese Boy Scouts toward the funeral of two young Buddhists killed during religious rioting in 1964. Burrows was among the first to document the Buddhist-Catholic strife in Vietnam and the brutal repression of Buddhists by the South Vietnamese government.

◄ Coming Home

Nguyen Lao is reunited with his family in 1971 after he was treated in the United States for wounds suffered in a mortar explosion.

► Men Down!

In this scene from 1965, helicopter crew chief James Farley struggles with a jammed machine gun and calls for assistance while Lieut. James Magel and Sgt. Billy Owens lay wounded at his feet. Owens lived; Magel died. Burrows wrote in his notebook a few days later, "A glazed look came into the eyes and he was dead. Nobody spoke for a few seconds."

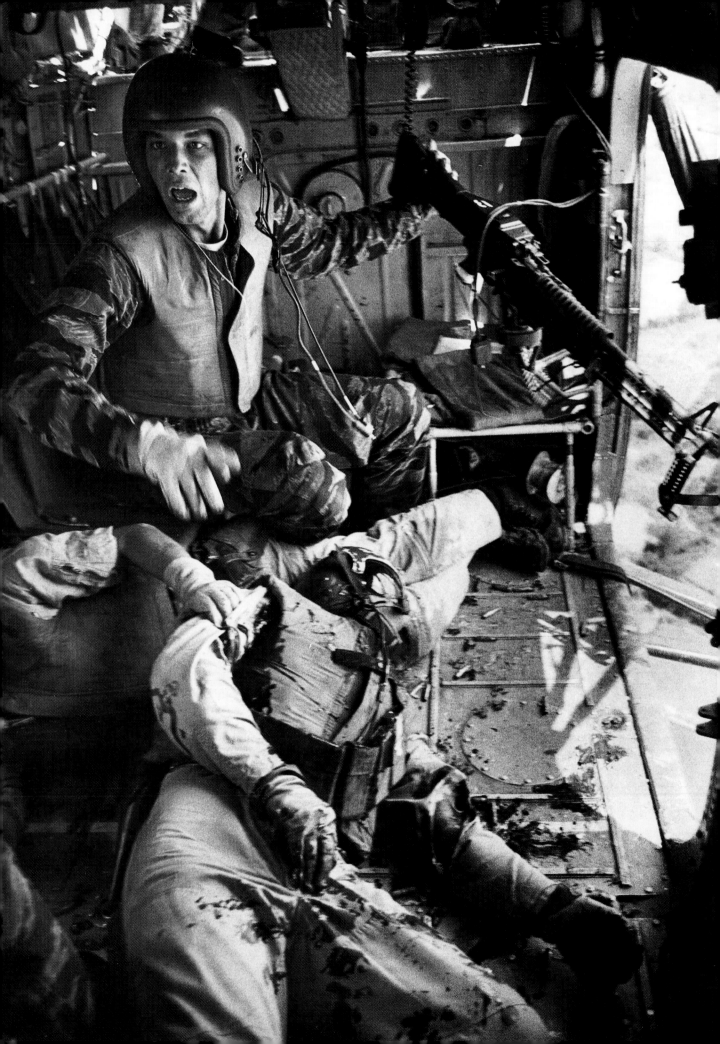

◄ **"Talk!"**
A South Vietnamese paratrooper
brandishes a bayonet while
interrogating a Viet Cong suspect
in 1962. Burrows once said of his
work, "I will do what is required to
show what is happening."

◀ **Cavalry to the Rescue**

The U.S. 1st Air Cavalry airlifts ammunition and supplies into a Marine outpost during the 77-day siege of Khe Sahn in 1968. Burrows often became so intimate with the units he photographed that he was accepted as a comrade in arms. A helicopter squadron's commanding officer once awarded the cameraman a set of air wings.

▲ **Scorched Earth**

Special Forces Capt. Vernon Gillespie contacts his base camp while South Vietnamese soldiers torch a Viet Cong "hootch," or hideout, in 1964, early in the war. Burrows' photographs were among the first images to bring home to the U.S. public the reality of the brutal conflict in a country that few Americans had heard of.

Going In

AIRBORNE: Under
Operation "Eagle's
Claw," U.S. Air Cavalry
helicopters arrive outside
Bong Son in February 1966

STEVE VAN METER—UPI—CORBIS

President Lyndon Johnson commits the U.S. to defend South Vietnam, and 200,000 young Americans find themselves at war in a faraway land

In reading TIME's *coverage of the war in Vietnam, we can trace the unhappy arc of the U.S. intervention: early chest beating, growing dismay and, finally, bitterness and shame. In 1965, as the buildup began,* TIME *echoed the White House line, trumpeting the U.S. arsenal of high-tech weaponry and the enormous deployment of American troops as harbingers of victory. The cover story at right offers more cheer-leading than analysis and guarantees eventual triumph in Southeast Asia. But only two weeks later,* TIME's *fine story of the siege at Plei Me reveals that the situation on the ground was perilous indeed. In retrospect, its headline, "Winning, Not Wishing," would be more accurate if reversed.*

October 22, 1965

A New Kind of War

It was only three months ago that the lethal little men in black paja-mas roamed the length and breadth of South Vietnam marauding, maiming and killing with impunity. No highway was safe by night, and few by day; the trains had long since stopped running. From their tunneled redoubts, the Communist Viet Cong held 65% of South Vietnam's land and 55% of its people in thrall. Saigon's armies were bone weary and bleeding from defec-tions. As the momentum of their mon-soon offensive gathered, the Commu-nists seemed about to cut the nation in

half. The enemy was ready to move in for the kill, and South Vietnam was near collapse.

Today South Vietnam throbs with a pride and power, above all an *esprit*, scarcely credible against the summer's somber vista. Government desertion rates have plummeted and recruitment is up, and it is now the Communists who are troubled with rising defections. Roads are being reopened for the first time in years, and the much-vaunted Viet Cong plan to move into their mass-attack "third phase" is now no more than a bedraggled dream.

The remarkable turnabout in the war is the result of one of the swiftest, biggest military buildups in the history of warfare. Everywhere today South

Vietnam bustles with the U.S. presence. Bulldozers by the hundreds carve sandy shores into vast plateaus for tent cities and airstrips. Howitzers and trucks grind through the once-empty green highlands. Wave upon wave of combat-booted Americans—lean, laconic and looking for a fight—pour ashore from armadas of troopships. Day and night, screaming jets and prowling helicopters seek out the enemy from their swampy strongholds. The Viet Cong's once-cocky hunters have become the cowering hunted as the cutting edge of U.S. fire power slashes into the thickets of Communist strength. If the U.S. has not yet guaranteed certain victory in South Vietnam, it has nonetheless undeniably averted certain defeat. As one top-ranking U.S. officer said: "We've stemmed the tide."

It was late July when the President of the U.S. summoned his aides to a three-day secret session to deliberate Vietnam. When Lyndon Johnson announced his decision, it was the most significant for American foreign policy since the Korean War: "We will stand in Vietnam." To stand meant in fact that the U.S. would go to Vietnam in overwhelming force and stay until the job was done. Why? "If we are driven from the field in Vietnam," the President told the nation and the world, "then no nation can ever again have the same confidence in American promise or in American protection."

By then 75,000 American servicemen already were present in South Vietnam or were pledged to go. The President promised 50,000 more by the end of this year, and the promise was soon outstripped by the deed. Today the total is 145,000, and it will pass 200,000 by New Year's Day. Target by next summer: 280,000.

The U.S. military has been in Vietnam in an advisory role to government forces ever since the French were swept out in 1954—a role that grew with the swelling magnitude of the Viet Cong threat until eventually it required 24,000 men. But it was not until last March, when the 9th Marine Expeditionary Brigade of 3,500 men swarmed ashore at Danang, that the first U.S. combat troops entered the fray. Like the 7,500 men of the 173rd Airborne Brigade, and the 191st Airborne's Danang 1st Brigade that soon followed, the marines' first assignment was de-fensive: creating a protective enclosure around the bustling Danang airbase and harbor. The 173rd was thrown around Bien Hoa airbase, together with the 2nd Brigade of the 1st Infantry Division—the Big Red One—which arrived in July. The Screaming Eagles of the 101st helped reopen Route 19 from the coast to An Khe, deep in the Viet Cong–infested Central Highlands, then stood watch while the 1st Air Cavalry's advance party hacked out a helipad for their covey of "Huey" copters. Predictably, the well-turfed 12,000-sq.-ft. helipad is now widely known as "the golf course."

Standing watch was all that many critics thought U.S. combat troops would—or could—do in Vietnam. Even as the number of G.I.s swelled, the myth remained that Americans were not up to the wiles of the Viet Cong or the woes of the Asian jungle.

U.S. troops were soon besting the Viet Cong in fire fights from Chu Lai to An Khe. Meanwhile, the Marines, day in and day out, in methodical, grinding patrols against the Viet Cong, are killing an average of 40 Viet Cong a week—at roughly the cost of one marine dead and five wounded a day.

Typical was a night's work last week. After dusk a Marine platoon surrounded a hamlet in which V.C. had been re-ported hiding out, split into five squads and sat down to wait. No one spoke, no cigarettes were allowed, nor was mosquito repellent, despite the stinging swarms, for a trained soldier can smell the chemical 50 yards away.

Around 3 a.m. a drenching monsoon rain roared in from the northeast, but still not a Marine moved. It lasted two hours. Finally the wan moon reappeared and picked out four men, its light gleaming from their weapons, heading out of the village. The Marines opened fire, a grenade exploded, and the leathernecks had one more kill and three wounded V.C. prisoners.

"I hate this goddamned place like I never hated any place I've ever been before," growled a leathery Marine sergeant, "but I'll tell you something else: I want to win here more than I ever did in two wars before."

The Communists themselves chose South Vietnam as their test case and springboard to the conquest of all Southeast Asia. There are signs that they are already beginning to regret it. The U.S. has picked up the gauntlet, and it is not only Vietnamese nationhood but all of free Asia that stands to be strengthened by the extraordinary—and still burgeoning—commitment of the lives and talent and treasure of America in Vietnam. ∎

SWAMPED? Special Forces Captain Vernon Gillespie leads a *montagnard* patrol through a jungle stream in 1964

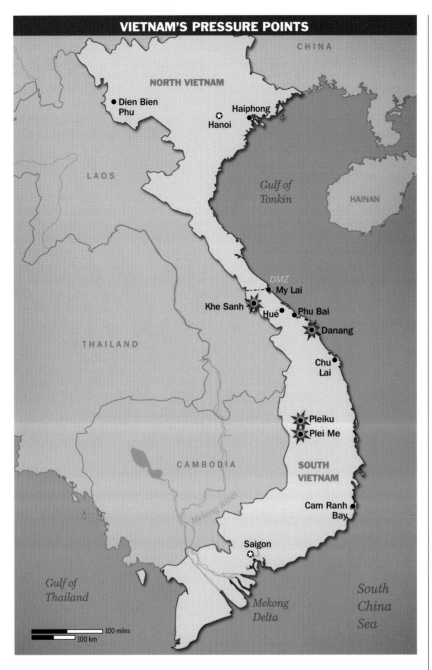

VIETNAM'S PRESSURE POINTS

CHINA

NORTH VIETNAM

Dien Bien Phu

Haiphong

Hanoi

LAOS

Gulf of Tonkin

HAINAN

DMZ

My Lai

Khe Sanh

Hué Phu Bai

Danang

THAILAND

Chu Lai

Pleiku

Plei Me

CAMBODIA

SOUTH VIETNAM

Cam Ranh Bay

Mekong River

Saigon

Gulf of Thailand

South China Sea

Mekong Delta

100 miles
100 km

November 5, 1965

Winning, Not Wishing

Despite all the headlines, all the vignettes of heroism and horror, all the demonstrations in the U.S. itself, the average American, cushioned by prosperity and a span of 8,500 miles, has found it hard to realize that the struggle in Southeast Asia is indeed a war. But it is—and that fact was driven home last week as never before when a fresh, division-strength Communist force laid the bold and bloody siege of Plei Me in the rugged jungle highland

215 miles northeast of Saigon.

Between the flat, metallic blasts of occasional mortar shells, the only sound in the camp was the rustle of rats shuffling over sleeping men. In the rifle pits behind the sandbagged perimeter of Plei Me, weary defenders sniffed the sour stench of cordite and unwashed clothes and grumbled about the duty. "Shut up," said a grizzled major. "This is what we're getting paid for."

The American soldiers weathered 178 hours of constant mortar and recoilless rifle barrage, fanatical assaults by wave on wave of mustard-uniformed North Vietnamese regulars, the end-

less thrum and thunder of close air support ("The Skyraiders looked like they were wired nose to tail," marveled one survivor), night after night in which land flares and blazing napalm turned the landscape into a Bosch-like rendering of the pit. By the end of the siege, only three of Plei Me's dozen Special Forces men were unwounded and on their feet. But the Americans were all ready to fight some more. "Are you a tiger, Swanson?" a doctor asked a gut-shot trooper at the hospital in nearby Danang. The man grinned weakly: "Yes, sir."

The siege of Plei Me began two unsuspected days before the first shot was fired. Up to the triangle-shaped fort 20 miles from the Cambodian border crept sappers from two recently infiltrated North Vietnamese regiments. Working in darkness just 40 yards from the camp's wire-strung perimeter, the cautious *bo doi* (infantrymen) cut trenches and L-shaped firing pits, hauled the dirt away in baskets and camouflaged their labors with brush. Though the camp's 400 *montagnard* defenders were patrolling assiduously up to ten miles away, no one thought to poke around his own front yard.

Into each Communist pit went tidy stacks of ammo, a Chinese automatic rifle at one end, an ugly snub-snouted 12.5-mm antiaircraft machine gun at the other. Every emplacement was manned by a single gunner and designed so that he could scuttle quickly between his submachine-gun, trained on the camp, and the antiaircraft gun whenever fighter-bombers appeared.

With the siegeworks complete, fully 6,000 fresh Communist troops waited silently in the jungles around Plei Me. They had carefully set up another Dong Zai–style battle, hoping to draw relief force after relief force into a merciless meat grinder. At 7:30 p.m. on Tuesday, Oct. 19, the Reds turned the handle.

First hit was a *montagnard* patrol; it was decimated by a scythe of small-arms fire. Then a 20-man outpost in a clearing below the first was overrun—the defenders died in their bunkers. At the main fort, U.S. Special Forces Captain Harold M. Moore radioed for help. Soon flare ships were splashing naked light over enemy positions as the Reds' recoilless rifles slammed round after round through the camp's longhouses.

HURRY! Under sniper fire, medics carry a wounded paratrooper to an evacuation helicopter near Thuong Lang, June 1965

The 2,300-odd *montagnard* women and children also living at Plei Me disappeared underground for a week-long hibernation. All, that is, except the older boys—twelve years and more—who grabbed carbines nearly as tall as themselves, strapped grenades to their frail waists, and ran to the rifle pits.

At II Corps headquarters in Pleiku, a government relief force was quickly assembled but more cautiously dispatched. While its tanks, armored personnel carriers, artillery and a thousand infantrymen crept in by road, a helicopter landing force of 250 Vietnamese Rangers dropped boldly into Plei Me at first light. Commanded by burly, boulder-bellied U.S. Army Major Charles H. Beckwith, 36, of Atlanta, the Rangers quickly filled the vacuum caused by the Reds' initial assault.

Some six miles away on the road to Plei Me, the tank-led relief column was braced for ambush. When it erupted from a thorn thicket, the tanks wheeled into something resembling the old Wild West wagon-train circle—but there the similarity ended. Loaded with heavy canister (finned, inch-long small shot), the tank guns blazed away point-blank at the jungle, mowing the brush to stubble as if a huge rotary mower had cut a 40-yd. swath on each side of the road. Dozens of shredded enemy bodies—arms, legs, heads, viscera—were plastered against the shattered tree trunks beyond. U.S. Air Force

planes then swept in to strafe and bomb. "It was awesome," said a U.S. officer. "Through it all, the Communists never quit firing. Not one pilot got a free run." And it was accurate fire: during 600 sorties, 20 planes were hit, three shot down.

Back at Plei Me, the besieged defenders were also learning to respect the attackers' endurance. "Old Charlie just stands up in his hole and shoots back at the whole Air Force," said one man. An American officer saw a single Red soldier charge a squad of *montagnards* ("yards" in G.I. parlance) brandishing grenades and screaming fiercely. The yards broke and ran, while the U.S. officer dropped to one knee, adjusted his sights, and in six rounds felled the sprinting Viet Minh attacker. "Damn," he said later. "Give me 200 men that well disciplined, and I'll capture this whole country."

As the camp's supplies and ammo dwindled, U.S. C-123s roared in—flaps down—to drop load after load of parachuted packages. Two men were killed by one pallet of supplies; another load crashed through the mess-hall roof; colored parachute silk festooned the camp, giving it an incongruously festive air. The whole place took on the

paramnesiac air of unreality; men sipped soup bowls of steaming coffee or washed their feet in cold coffee as water ran short; lice swarmed through every man's uniform; in the steamy sky over the fort, a tiny, gold-fringed souvenir American flag fluttered bravely. "If we're going to get zapped," cracked Sergeant Joseph Bailey, of Lebanon, Tenn., "let's get zapped under our own flag." An hour later, pushing toward a downed U.S. helicopter, Bailey was zapped—dead.

Not until Wednesday, Oct. 27—after more than seven days—was the siege finally broken. Then, as elements of the U.S. 1st Cavalry (Airmobile) swarmed in by low-flying helicopter, the Viet Minh faded reluctantly away from Plei Me.

At Plei Me, where the stomach-wrenching task of burial was going on, the women and children emerged from their bunkers. A pretty little girl in a blue store-bought dress pranced among the corpses while the defenders counted captured Communist arms. "Man," said one American Special Forces private, "if those were supposed to be the underfed and diseased Communist troops I've been reading about, I'd hate to tangle with them when they're healthy." ∎

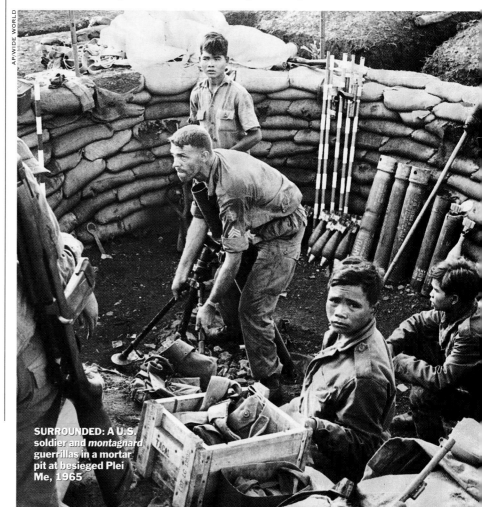

SURROUNDED: A U.S. soldier and *montagnard* guerrillas in a mortar pit at besieged Plei Me, 1965

June 17, 1966

Vo Nguyen Giap

He beat the French at Dienbienphu. Now he battles an even stronger foe

THE MASSIVE INFUSION OF U.S. TROOPS INTO VIETNAM, now some 275,000 strong, has taken the initiative away from the enemy. Not since the bloody battle of Ia Drang last November, when the U.S. 1st Cavalry (Airmobile) destroyed 20,000 North Vietnamese soldiers, have Communist troops ventured out in regimental strength to do battle of their own choosing. What will the Reds do next? The North Vietnamese *éminence grise* with the answer to that question is tiny, plump General Vo Nguyen Giap (pronounced Zhop), 55, Commander in Chief of the North Vietnamese army, Hanoi's Defense Minister and Deputy Premier, who shares with China's Mao Tse-tung a reputation as the world's foremost practitioner of the dark art of insurgency warfare.

Though Vo, his family name, means "force," and Giap, his given name, means "armor," the architect of North Vietnam's army was born near the city of Vinh, the son of a bourgeois landowning family that had fallen into penury. By the time he was 14, he was a member of a clandestine, anti-French sect; four years later the French clapped him in jail for political agitation. It proved a fortuitous incarceration. Behind bars he met Fellow Militant Minh Thai, who became his first wife. And the French police *commissaire* for Vinh took a liking to the brilliant, angry young Giap, got him out of prison, and sent him off to one of the best French schools in Indo-China. He won his baccalaureate, and for four years taught history at a lyceum in Hanoi. An accomplished lecturer, he "could step to a blackboard and draw in the most minute detail every battle plan of Napoleon," one of his former students recalls.

When the Communist Party was banned by the French in 1930, Giap fled to China. His wife stayed behind, was arrested by the French, and died in prison. Under the aegis of the Chinese Communists, the Viet Minh was founded, with Giap a 1941 charter member along with Ho Chi Minh. Ho ordered the little professor to specialize in military affairs, and the career of the Red Napoleon began. His first self-education was in guerrilla operations against the Japanese who then occupied Vietnam. The OSS supplied Giap with American weapons to that end, but Giap was looking to the future; he cached most of them for use in the resumed struggle against the French. On Aug. 15, 1945, as the Japanese surrendered, he led his guerrillas into Hanoi and took over the city for Ho Chi Minh, and the Democratic Republic of Vietnam was born.

When negotiations with the French failed to gain independence for North Vietnam, Giap was delighted, and his eight-year war against Paris got under way. He had already remodeled his guerrillas along Communist people's army lines, with political commissars seeded through the ranks and political indoctrination as much a part of a soldier's training as bayonetry. He had even recruited Japanese jungle-warfare instructors from the retreating enemy he had just fought, and had carefully collected every weapon the Japanese military left behind. It took four years before he launched the first of his major offensives against the French forces.

He scored some successes but suffered more signal defeats, largely because he lacked artillery to compete with the French in set-piece conventional battles. After a stinging series of losses in 1951, Giap retreated into the hills and paddies to reassemble his forces. The chance for annihilation came at Dienbienphu, when the French, thinking Giap still had no heavy artillery, dropped paratroops into a valley, hoping to draw Giap into combat. But Giap had obtained over 100 American 105-mm howitzers from the Red Chinese, carted them through the jungles and over the mountains, and pounded the French forces to pieces in the valley below. In fact, at Dienbienphu he annihilated only 4% of the French force in Vietnam, but it was psychologically the end for the French. They were thoroughly fed up with the eight-year war that had cost them $10 billion and 172,000 dead or missing.

Giap's French adversaries had once dismissed him with St.-Cyr-bred contempt as a sometime schoolmaster who had been awarded his general's stars by Communist bush politicians. But after Giap's native army destroyed the will of the politicians back in France to fight on, he became the first modern commander to drive a white European nation out of Asia. And this victory made Giap nearly as much of a legend throughout Vietnam as Ho Chi Minh. ∎

NIHON DENPA NEWS, LTD

ALL DRESSED UP: Giap at a formal banquet in 1965, with Ho Chi Minh at right

January 7, 1966

William Westmoreland

A battle-tested general in a faraway land is TIME's Man of the Year 1965

AS COMMANDER IN CHIEF OF ALL U.S. FORCES IN SOUTH Vietnam, General William Childs Westmoreland, 51, directed the historic buildup, drew up the battle plans, and infused the 190,000 men under him with his own idealistic view of U.S. aims and responsibilities. He was the sinewy personification of the American fighting man in 1965 who, through the monsoon mud of nameless hamlets, amidst the swirling sand of seagirt enclaves, atop the jungled mountains of the Annamese Cordillera, served as the instrument of U.S. policy, quietly enduring the terror and discomfort of a conflict that was not yet a war, on a battlefield that was all no man's land.

There is an almost machine-like singlemindedness about him. His most vehement cuss words are "darn" and "dadgum." A jut-jawed six-footer, he never smokes, drinks little, swims and plays tennis to remain at a flat-bellied 180 lbs.— only 10 lbs. over his cadet weight. Says Major General Richard Stilwell, commander of the U.S. Military Advisory Group in Thailand: "He has no gimmicks, no hand grenades or pearl-handled pistols. He's just a very straightforward, determined man." Few who know him doubt that he will some day be Army Chief of Staff.

Westmoreland belongs to the age of technology—a product not only of combat but also of sophisticated command and management colleges from Fort Leavenworth to Harvard Business School. The son of a textile-plant manager in rural South Carolina, Westmoreland liked the cut of a uniform from the time he was an Eagle Scout. Though he never made the honor roll at West Point, he was first captain of cadets (class of '35) and won the coveted John J. Pershing sword for leadership and military proficiency.

As a young artillery officer, Westmoreland worked out a new logarithmic fire-direction and control chart that is still in use. During World War II he got a chance to try it out as commander of an artillery battalion in North Africa and Sicily. In the months of front-line combat from Utah Beach to the Elbe, he had two bouts of malaria and a brush with a land mine that blew a truck out from under him but left him almost unscathed.

Volunteering for Korean duty in 1952, Westmoreland went over as commander of the tough 187th Regimental Combat Team, made a couple of paratroop jumps. Fretful that the cease-fire was playing havoc with his men's discipline, Westmoreland set them a spartan regimen: reveille at 5, a two-mile run, digging fortifications all day, baths in an icy creek and, after dinner, 2½ hours of intramural sports, especially boxing. "By 10 o'clock every night," he grins, "they were so exhausted they couldn't make mischief of any kind."

After a round of Pentagon assignments, he became the Army's youngest major general at 42. Named superintendent of West Point in 1960, he expanded its facilities, increased enrollment (from 2,500 to 4,000). In 1964 "Westy" was summoned to Saigon as Paul Harkins' deputy. By midyear he was the natural choice for the top job—and a fourth star—when Harkins returned to the U.S.

Westmoreland has the politically sensitive job of top U.S. adviser to South Vietnam's armed forces and boss of the 6,000-odd U.S. advisers attached to Vietnamese units. As commander of Military Assistance Command, Vietnam, he has under him all U.S. servicemen—115,000 soldiers, 10,000 sailors, 17,500 airmen, 45,000 marines, 250 coast guardsmen; more than 1,000 Army helicopters and light aircraft, as well as some 550 U.S. Air Force planes—soon to be increased to 1,200—and a Navy seadrome at Cam Ranh Bay.

To keep this vast establishment operating, Westmoreland heeds—and invariably exceeds—the advice he gives newcomers to Vietnam: "Work like the very devil. A seven-day 60-hour week is the very minimum for this course." Rising at 6:30 in his two-story French villa, Westmoreland does 25 push-ups, usually breakfasts alone. At his desk by 7:30, he rarely leaves it before nightfall, even then lugs home a fat briefcase. He zips around by Beechcraft U-8F and helicopter, often galloping to and from his craft at a dead run so that he can squeeze in one more visit to one more outpost in the "boonies." Marvels a Vietnam veteran in the Pentagon: "Imagine a really gung-ho West Point officer worrying about growing corn for peasants!" Westmoreland, who is so gung-ho a West Pointer that he looks well-pressed in swimming trunks, does worry. "Today's soldier," he says, "must try to give, not take away." ∎

> **TOUGH JOB: The general would be lampooned as "Waste-more-land" by U.S. protesters**
>
> PIX INC.—TIMEPIX

WESTMORELAND

TRAPPED: Under heavy enemy fire during the Tet Offensive, U.S. marines take cover in Hue. U.S. forces won control of the city only after seven days of fighting.

Quagmire

After years of fighting, America is bogged down in Vietnam—in the *Tet* Offensive, at My Lai and in trouble at home, our sense of purpose is lost

The Tet *Offensive in 1968 proved that the U.S. was losing, not winning, the war.* TIME's *account of* Tet *includes the quote by a U.S. officer that summed up the futility of the cause: "It became necessary to destroy the town to save it." The enemy's success began to turn the American public against the war, and support further deteriorated after U.S. soldiers were discovered to have murdered scores of innocent civilians at My Lai. The war drove President Lyndon Johnson from office, and when Richard Nixon expanded the conflict by sending U.S. troops into Cambodia in May 1970, college campuses exploded in protest. Americans sighed with relief when Nixon began removing troops, and when the war seemed to end with a 1973 peace agreement.*

February 9, 1968

Tet: Giap's Gamble

Though ominous harbingers of trouble had been in the air for days, most of South Vietnam lazed in uneasy truce, savoring the New Year's festival of *Tet*, the happiest and holiest holiday of the Vietnamese year. Vietnamese soldiers made a special effort to rejoin their families. Relative visited relative, threading through thousands of firecrackers popping and fizzing in the moonless night. The Year of the Monkey had begun, and every Vietnamese knew that it was wise to make merry while there was yet time; in the twelve-year Buddhist lunar cycle, 1968 is a grimly inauspicious year.

Through the streets of Saigon, and in the dark approaches to dozens of towns and military installations across South Vietnam, other Vietnamese made their furtive way, intent on celebrating only death. After the last firecrackers had sputtered out on the ground, they struck with a fierceness and bloody destructiveness that Vietnam has not seen even in three decades of nearly continuous warfare. Up and down the narrow length of South Vietnam, more than 36,000 North Vietnamese and Viet Cong soldiers joined in a widespread, general offensive against airfields and military bases, government buildings, population centers and just plain civilians.

The Communists hit in a hundred places, from Quang Tri near the DMZ in the north all the way to Duong Dong on the tiny island of Phu Quock off the Delta coast some 500 miles to the south. No target was too big or too impossible, including Saigon itself and General William Westmoreland's MACV headquarters.

The raiders attacked 28 of South Vietnam's 44 provincial capitals and occupied some. South Vietnam's capital, which even in the worst days of the Indochina war had never been hit so hard, was turned into a city besieged and sundered by house-to-house fighting. In Hué, Vietnam's ancient imperial city and the architectural and spiritual repository of its history, they seized large parts of the city—and only grudgingly yielded them block by block under heavy allied counterattacks.

The Communist attack, admitted Brigadier General John Chaisson, Westmoreland's combat operations coordinator for South Vietnam, was "a very successful offensive. It was surprisingly well coordinated, surprisingly intensive and launched with a surprising amount of audacity." Westmoreland himself called the enemy campaign "a bold one," though marked "by treachery and deceitfulness." The attackers embarrassed the U.S. They succeeded in demonstrating that, despite nearly three years of steady allied progress in the war, Communist commandos can still strike at will virtually anywhere in the country.

It was undoubtedly an extraordinary tour de force, unprecedented in modern military annals: the spectacle of an enemy force dispersed and unseen, everywhere hunted unremittingly, suddenly materializing to strike simultaneously in a hundred places throughout a country. Nowhere was the feat more impressive, or its part more instructively displayed, than in the assault on Saigon.

Into the capital in the days just before *Tet* slipped more than 3,000 Communist soldiers armed with weapons ranging up to machine-gun and bazooka size. Some came openly into the open city, weapons concealed in luggage or under baskets of food. Others came furtively: some of the Viet Cong who attacked the U.S. embassy had ridden into town concealed in a truckload of flowers. Once in town, they hid their weapons. Only after the attack did Vietnamese intelligence realize that the unusual number of funerals the previous week was no accident: the Viet Cong had buried their weapons in the funeral coffins, dug them up on the night of the assault. They even test-fired their guns during the peak of the *Tet* celebrations, the sound of the shots mingling with that of the firecrackers going off.

PEOPLE'S WAR: Civilians patrol the hamlet of Ben Cat, 1968

The most daring attack—and certainly one of the most embarrassing—occurred when 19 Viet Cong commandos of the C-10 Sapper Battalion made the U.S. embassy in Saigon their target. When Ambassador Ellsworth Bunker opened the white reinforced-concrete complex last September, few American missions ever settled into more seemingly impregnable quarters. Looming behind a 10-ft.-high wall, the six-story symbol of U.S. power and prestige is encased in a massive concrete sunscreen that overlaps shatterproof Plexiglas windows. Saigon wags soon dubbed it "Bunker's Bunker." Yet the Viet Cong attackers gained access to the embassy compound and rampaged through it for 6½ hours before all were

FRESH AMMO: While Marines fire a mortar barrage against the enemy in Hué, comrades bring new shells on the run

IN OUR HOUSE: With two soldiers down, MPs of the 101st Airborne Division fight guerrillas inside the American embassy compound during the *Tet* campaign

killed and the embassy was once again secure.

At 3:03 a.m., supporting V.C. troops positioned around the embassy began lobbing mortar fire onto the grounds. Then the 19 commandos appeared, wearing civilian clothes (with identifying red armbands) and carrying automatic weapons, rockets and enough high explosives to demolish the building. Attacking simultaneously, some of the guerrillas blasted a hole into the concrete wall with an antitank gun and swarmed through it; others quickly scaled a rear fence. Though allied intelligence had predicted the attack, the embassy's defense consisted of only five U.S. military guards—just one more than normal. They fought back so fiercely that only their courage denied the enemy complete success. Sergeant Ronald W. Harper, 20, a Marine guard, managed to heave shut the embassy's massive teakwood front doors just seconds before the guerrillas battered at

them with rockets and machine guns, thus denying the V.C. entry to the main building.

Unable to penetrate the main chancery, the V.C. commandos ran aimlessly through the compound, firing on everything they saw. Meanwhile, small groups of Marines and MPs began arriving outside the walls of the embattled embassy. The Viet Cong burst into the embassy's consular building and various other buildings in the compound, but the Americans on the scene threw such heavy fire at them that the guerrillas were kept too busy to set off their explosives.

Finally, just before 8 a.m., Pfc. Paul Healey, 20, led a counterattack through the front gate, personally killing five V.C. with grenades and his M-16 rifle. Minutes later, two paratroop platoons from the 101st Airborne Division at nearby Bien Hoa landed on the embassy's rooftop helipad. Working their way down, they met no resistance. As

the troopers advanced, a wounded guerrilla staggered into Mission Coordinator George Jacobson's white villa behind the embassy. When U.S. troops tried to flush him with tear gas, he started upstairs, spotted the 56-year-old retired Army colonel there, and fired three shots. The guerrilla missed, and Jacobson finished him off with a .45 that had quickly been tossed up to his second-floor window by troops below. That fearsome finale ended the battle. Five Americans lay dead.

On the outskirts of Saigon, an enemy force of at least 700 men tackled the city's most vital military target: Tan Son Nhut airstrip and its adjoining MACV compound housing Westmoreland's headquarters and the 76th Air Force Command Center, the nerve centers of U.S. command in the war. The Communists breached the immediate base perimeter, slipping past some 150 outposts without a shot being fired, and got within 1,000 feet of the runways before they were halted in eight hours of bloody hand-to-hand combat. All told, the Communists attacked from 18 different points around Tan Son Nhut, getting close enough to MACV to put bullets through Westy's windows. Staff officers were issued weapons and sent out to help sandbag the compound, and Westmoreland moved into his windowless command room.

At week's end, Saigon was still a city shuddering with the roar of bombs and the splat of bullets. After five days of fighting, the stubborn attackers of Tan Son Nhut airstrip were still entrenched near the field as F-100 jets, skyraiders and helicopters blasted at their positions. Fighting flared in one part of the city, and when troops moved in with air support to damp it down, broke out in another area.

The violence in Saigon was only a small portion of the fighting that raged through the rest of the country. In its surprise, its boldness, the sweep of its planning and its split-second orchestration, the general offensive bore all the unmistakable marks of General Vo Nguyen Giap's genius. ∎

Picking Up the Pieces

Still stunned by the speed and brutality of the Communists' countrywide onslaught, South Vietnam and its allies last week began the enormous task of recovery. The job was not made easier by the fact that no one knew for sure exactly what had happened, or why; nor was there any certainty that it would not happen again. The roll of cities and towns nearly literally leveled to the ground read like a grim Vietnamese gazetteer.

Pleiku, a highland town of 66,000, was 50% destroyed and 11,000 of its people made homeless. In the Delta, Vinh Long was 25% destroyed and burdened with 14,000 new refugees. Ben Tre (pop. 35,000) was one of the hardest-hit towns in all Vietnam: 45% destroyed, nearly 1,000 dead, 10,000 homeless. Estimates of the damage to Hué ran as high as 80%. One out of five of Dalat's 82,000 people was without a roof over his head.

The problem likely to plague South Vietnam the longest is the widespread destruction of its cities, its towns, its homes. It was the Viet Cong's decision to bring the war into the midst of the cities, and the initial damage was wrought by Communist guns and mortars. But the bulk of the actual destruction occurred during the allied counterattacks to oust the Viet Cong. For allied commanders, these posed a grim dilemma that was summed up bluntly—and injudiciously—by a U.S. major involved in the battle for Ben Tre. "It became necessary to destroy the town to save it," he said.

In his blitzkrieg, General Giap showed that not even American power could protect urban Vietnamese from Viet Cong guns. The demonstration equally undermined the South Vietnamese government's stature in the minds of many South Vietnamese. The attacks enhanced the mystique of the Viet Cong as a stealthy, dedicated foe, unmindful of death. The V.C. took the initiative away from the allies. Most important, Giap managed to create in Washington and across the U.S. a fresh and profound agonizing about the war. ∎

AP WIDE/WORLD

FLIGHT: The *Tet* campaign brought the war into the cities. Here, refugees flee a Saigon neighborhood.

HELP! This medic from the 101st Airborne Division is calling in a helicopter, but his stance seems to sum up the Americans' plight in Vietnam

ART GREENSPAN—AP/WIDE WORLD

December 5, 1969

An American Tragedy

Only a shadow of a doubt now remains that the massacre at My Lai, which took place in March 1968 but did not come to public attention until the weeks past, was an atrocity, barbaric in execution. Yet almost as chilling to the American mind is the character of the alleged perpetrators. The deed was not performed by demented men. Instead, according to the ample testimony of their friends and relatives, the men of C Company who swept through My Lai were for the most part almost depressingly normal. They were Everymen, decent in their daily lives, who at home would regard it as unthinkable to maliciously strike a child, much less kill one. Yet men in American uniforms slaughtered the civilians of My Lai, and in so doing humiliated the U.S. and called in question the U.S. mission in Vietnam in a way

that all the antiwar protesters could never have done.

In March of 1968, most members of C Company of the American Division's 11th Infantry Brigade had never been tested in direct combat with any large numbers of the enemy. Trained together in Hawaii, they had been in Vietnam only one month. Yet as part of Task Force Baker, their assignment in March was a fearsome one: to clear the Viet Cong out of Quang Ngai province, an area long known as "the cradle of revolution" in Vietnam. Despite repeated sweeps, in which more than 3,000 Communist deaths were reported, the province remained a stronghold of the Viet Cong's 48th Local Force Battalion, an outfit with an unnerving ability to disperse, then reappear to strike again.

The inexperienced Charlie Company, commanded by Captain Ernest Medina, 33, thus had ample cause for fear as it prepared to assault My Lai, a village with bricked-up huts and extensive hidden tunnels. The U.S. sol-

diers were angry. Repeatedly lashed by booby traps and sniper fire by unseen Viet Cong, the company's strength had already been cut from 190 to about 105. Of those, about 80 men were helicoptered into a grassy spot on the outskirts of My Lai on the warm, sunny morning of March 16, 1968.

Precisely what happened next will be the subject of multiple investigations. But enough participants have spoken up to make the general outline painfully clear.

The edgy company, expecting a firefight and anxious to at last even the score for their comrades picked off by an invisible enemy, split into three platoons. Two were assigned to take up flank positions and block the escape of anyone from the village. The central platoon (apparently about 30 men), commanded by Lieut. William Calley, 26, headed into the village. It met no resistance on the outskirts. But despite the lack of enemy fire, Calley's men in less than 20 minutes ignited "hootches" and chased all the villagers, whether fleeing, standing or begging for mercy, into groups, and shot everyone. All were either elderly men, women or children. Estimates of the dead ranged from 109 to 567. [The final body count remains unknown in 2002—ED.]

Each man in such an action sees only a fraction of what happens. Yet many such personal recollections were chilling ones. "Everyone was scared going in—we thought there'd be enemy troops there," recalls Charles A. West, 23, a Charlie Company sergeant. "I was frustrated, same as the rest of the guys." On the way in, he said, "some individuals jumped out of a hedge 15 to 20 yards ahead of us. They had what we thought were guns. It was a surprise and we opened fire. When something like this happens, you don't stop to ask questions." West learned that his group had slain four women and two old men. Their "guns" turned out to be the traditional sticks that peasants use to carry belongings.

West, a squad leader in a platoon commanded by Lieut. Jeffrey La Cross, followed Calley's platoon in My Lai. "Everyone was shooting," he says. "Some of the huts were torched. Some of the yanigans [his term for young soldiers] were shooting kids." In the confusion, he claims, it was hard to tell "mama-sans from papa-sans," since both wear black pajamas and conical hats. He and his squad helped round up the women and children. When one of his men protested that "I can't shoot these people," West told him to turn the group over to Captain Medina. On the way out of the village, West recalls seeing a ditch filled with dead and dy-

MURDERED: A child and an adult lie dead in a ditch at My Lai, victims of U.S. troops

RONALD S. HAEBERLE—TIMEPIX

ing civilians. His platoon also passed a crying Vietnamese boy, wounded in both a leg and an arm. West heard a G.I. ask: "What about him?" Then he heard a shot and the boy fell. "The kid didn't do anything," says West. "He didn't have a weapon."

A detailed account came from Paul David Meadlo, 22, a member of Calley's platoon. As they walked toward the village, he told CBS, "there was one gook in a shelter, he was all huddled down in there—an older man. And Sergeant [David] Mitchell hollered 'Shoot him.' And so the man shot him." Meadlo says his group ran through My

Lai, herding men, women children and babies into the center of the village— "like a little island."

"Lieut. Calley came over and said, 'You know what to do with them, don't you?' And I said 'Yes.' And he left and came back about ten minutes later, and said, 'How come you ain't killed them yet? And I told him that I didn't think he wanted us to kill them, that he just wanted us to guard them. He said, 'No, I want them dead.' So he started shooting them. And he told me to start shooting them. I poured about four clips [68 shots] into them. I might have killed 10 or 15 of them.

"So we started to gather more people, and we had about seven or eight and we put them in the hootch and then we dropped a hand grenade in there with them. And then they had about 70-75 people all gathered up by a ravine, so we threw ours in with them and Lieut. Calley told me, 'Meadlo, we got another job to do.' And so he walked over to the people, and he started pushing them off and started shooting. We just pushed them all off and just started using automatics on them."

Sergeant Michael Bernhardt said no one shot at the G.I.s. "We met no resistance, and I only saw three captured weapons. As a matter of fact, I don't remember seeing one military-age male

ON THE SPOT: A chopper lands on the flight deck of an armored troop carrier, described as the Navy's smallest aircraft carrier

U.S. NAVY

ALL WET: Troops of the 1st Air Cavalry Division take a breather. Forecast: monsoon rains will begin next week.

AP/WIDE WORLD

in the entire place, dead or alive."

For shocked Americans, what happened at My Lai seems an awful aberration. For the Communists in Viet Nam, the murder of civilians is routine, purposeful policy. Terror is a part of the guerrillas' arsenal of intimidation, to be used whenever other methods of persuasion have failed to rally a village or province round the Viet Cong flag. During the past eleven years, the Communists are known to have killed more than 26,000 South Vietnamese, injured hundreds of thousands, kidnapped at least 60,000 in their reign of terror ∎

May 11, 1970

Raising the Stakes

Vietnam has been called a war without fronts. Yet for five long years, U.S. combat troops were halted time and again by one seemingly impenetrable enemy line: South Vietnam's twisting 600-mile border with Cambodia. Although the line shielded no fewer than five large North Vietnamese and Viet Cong sanctuaries, the U.S. refused to violate Cambodia's neutrality by crossing the border to destroy them. Frustrated American military men, peering across valleys at one or another of the inviolable areas, often wished aloud: "If only they'd let us lose the map." Last week their Commander in Chief, Richard Nixon, ordered them

to do exactly that. Pointing to the Communist sanctuaries on his own White House map, Nixon announced that he had ordered thousands of U.S. combat troops onto Cambodian soil to knock them out.

Even as he spoke, U.S. air cavalrymen thrust into Cambodia's Kompong Cham province, located inside a Communist-infested zone called "the Fishhook." Their mission: a strike at the Communist high command hidden in groups of heavy concrete bunkers at several points beyond the border. Farther south, troops of the South Vietnamese army (ARVN), aided by U.S. advisers, helicopters and medical teams, swept into another Communist stronghold known as "the Parrot's Beak," located only 35 miles from Saigon. U.S. planes, meanwhile, began bombing the three other enemy sanctuaries on the President's list.

Nixon and his aides carefully argued that this was not an invasion of Cambodia, partly because the areas involved had long been held by the Communists, not the Cambodians. The President insisted that the U.S. move was merely the tactical extension of the Vietnam conflict. He promised to keep U.S. combat forces to a minimum and indicated that the entire operation would be concluded in six to eight weeks. Despite such assurances, he had—temporarily at least—turned the long and tortured conflict in Southeast Asia into a new war. ∎

May 18, 1970

Martyrdom That Shook the Country

It took half a century to transform Kent State from an obscure teachers college into the second largest university in Ohio, with 21,000 students and an impressive array of modern buildings on its main campus. But it took less than ten terrifying seconds to convert the traditionally conformist campus into a bloodstained symbol of the rising student rebellion against the Nixon Administration and the war in Southeast Asia. When National Guardsmen fired indiscriminately into a crowd of unarmed civilians, killing four students, the bullets wounded the nation.

After a Friday-night confrontation between students and local police that seemed bred more by campus spring fever than by protest against the war, Saturday began quietly. But in the evening, protesters at a gathering in the ten-acre Commons approved by the university set fire to the school's ROTC building, then pelted firemen with stones and cut their hoses with machetes until police interceded with tear gas.

Ohio Governor James Rhodes quickly ordered National Guardsmen transferred from points of tension in a Teamster strike elsewhere in Ohio. Within an

ANGELS OF DEATH: Larry Burrows took this picture of a U.S. tank crew in Cambodia

LARRY BURROWS

hour, about 500 Guardsmen, already weary from three nights of duty, arrived with fully loaded M-1 semiautomatic rifles, pistols and tear gas. Order was restored by midnight.

On Sunday, Governor Rhodes arrived in Kent and told newsmen that campus troublemakers were "worse than Brown Shirts and Communists and vigilantes—they're the worst type of people that we harbor in America." He refused to close the campus; instead, he declared a state of emergency and banned all demonstrations on the campus.

On Monday, the campus seemed to calm down. In the bright sunshine, tired young Guardsmen flirted with leggy coeds under the tall oaks and maples. Classes continued throughout the morning. But the ban against mass assemblies was still in effect, and some students decided to test it again. At high noon, youngsters began ringing the school's Victory Bell, normally used to celebrate a football triumph but rarely heard of late. About 1,000 students, some nervous but many joking, gathered on the Commons. Another 2,000 ringed the walks and buildings to watch.

From their staging area near the burned-out ROTC building, officers in two jeeps rolled across the grass to address the students with bullhorns: "Evacuate the Commons area. You

OHIO FRONT: National Guardsmen fire tear gas at demonstrating students at Kent State

have no right to assemble." Back came shouts of "Pigs off campus! We don't want your war." Students raised middle fingers. The jeeps pulled back. Two skirmish lines of Guardsmen, wearing helmets and gas masks, stepped away from the staging area and began firing tear-gas canisters at the crowd. The Guardsmen moved about 100 yards toward the assembly and fired gas again. A few students picked up canisters and threw them back, but they fell short of the troops. The mists of stinging gas split the crowd.

A formation of fewer than 100 Guardsmen—a mixed group including men from the 107th Armored Cavalry Regiment based in neighboring Ravenna, and others from a Wooster company of the 145th Infantry Regiment—pursued fleeing students between the two buildings. The troopers soon found themselves facing a fence and flanked by rock-throwing students, who rarely got close enough to hit anyone. Occasionally one managed to toss one of the gas canisters back near the troops, while delighted spectators, watching from the hilltop, windows of buildings and the roof of another men's dorm, cheered. Many demonstrators were laughing.

Then the outnumbered and partially encircled contingent of Guardsmen ran out of tear gas. Suddenly they seemed frightened. They began retreating up the hill toward Taylor Hall, most of them walking backward to keep their eyes on the threatening students below. The crowd on the hilltop consisted almost entirely of onlookers rather than rock throwers. The tight circle of retreating Guardsmen contained officers and noncoms from both regiments, but no single designated leader. Some of the troops held their rifles pointed skyward. Several times a few of them turned, pointing their M-1s threateningly at the crowd, then

THANKS FOR COMING: The first U.S. troops to be withdrawn from Vietnam receive gifts at Danang in 1969

February 5, 1973

Exhaustion, Relief And a Truce

At last, a truce. At last, after a season of false moves and false dawns, the papers were signed. At last, after years of death and destruction, the war that four U.S. Presidents had considered a necessary act of resistance against international Communism was ending in an ambiguous stalemate. For the U.S., at least, it was over. In Vietnam, fighting may well resume—or never entirely stop. Yet for the moment, those on all sides who had once sought victory now felt an exhausted sense of relief.

The ending of the longest war in U.S. history, with its bitter sacrifice of lives and money, undoubtedly deserved more of a tribute. But the American public was in no mood to celebrate. Peace had been promised so often that even now some people were not sure that it had really come, or would last. Others had been so emotionally numbed by the war that they found it hard to react at all. There would be no heroic memories to cherish—no Valley Forge, no San Juan Hill. And not many heroes either.

Vietnam was not the bloodiest war in U.S. history—despite nearly 50,000 dead by enemy action plus another 300,000 wounded. Americans suffered more casualties in the Civil War and the two World Wars. Physically speaking, most Americans were untouched by the war. Business went on pretty much as usual. Psychologically, however, Americans had never endured such a war.

Increasingly the long struggle in Vietnam seemed to lack meaning and justification. The official arguments for continuing to fight it kept changing—and kept being undermined. How could a war to stop Communist expansion be explained when President Nixon was making friends with the leaders of the two great Communist powers? To a country that prides itself on being practical, the Vietnam dilemma seemed too expensive by any reckoning. Morally expensive as well. Too many memories, from My Lai to the massive bombings of last Christmas, would continue to weigh on the American spirit. ∎

continued to retreat.

When the formation reached the top of the hill, some Guardsmen knelt quickly and aimed at the students who were hurling rocks from below. A handful of demonstrators kept moving toward the troops. Other Guardsmen stood behind the kneeling troops, pointing their rifles down the hill. A few aimed over the students' heads. Several witness later claimed that an officer brought his baton down in a sweeping signal. Within seconds, a sickening staccato of rifle fire signaled the transformation of a once-placid campus into the site of a historic American tragedy.

"They are shooting blanks—they are shooting blanks," thought Journalism Professor Charles Brill, who nevertheless crouched behind a pillar. "Then I heard a chipping sound and a ping, and I thought, 'My God, this is for real.'" An Army veteran who saw action in Korea, Brill was certain that the Guardsmen had not fired randomly out of individual panic. "They were organized," he said. "It was not scattered. They all waited and they all pointed their rifles at the same time. It looked like a firing squad."

The shooting stopped—as if on signal. Minutes later, the Guardsmen assumed parade-rest positions, apparently to signal that the fusillade would not be resumed unless the Guardsmen were threatened again. "I felt like I'd just had an order to clean up a latrine," recalled one Guardsman in the firing unit. "You do what you're told to do."

The campus was suddenly still. Horrified students flung themselves to the ground, ran for cover, or just stood stunned. Then screams broke out. "My God they're killing us!" one girl cried. They were. A river of blood ran from the head of one boy, saturating his school books. One youth held a cloth against the abdomen of another, futilely trying to check the bleeding. Guardsmen made no move to help the victims. Geology Professor Glenn Frank, an ex-Marine, ran up to talk to officers. He came back sobbing. "If we don't get out of here right now," he said, "the Guard is going to clear us out any way they can—they mean *any* way."

In that brief volley, four young people—none of whom was a protest leader or even a radical—were killed. Ten students were wounded, three seriously. Another is paralyzed below his waist by a spinal wound. ∎

May 26, 1967

Clide Brown Jr.

In Vietnam, black American soldiers win a battle for respect and equality

DEEP IN "INDIAN COUNTRY," THE VIET CONG'S JUNGLED heartland, a lone U.S. helicopter flapped furiously down on an abandoned dirt roadway. Even before the Huey hit the ground, its six passengers were out and running. Their faces streaked with camouflage paint, their black and green "tiger suits" blending into the foliage, their black-stocked M-16 automatic rifles at the ready, they faded softly into the perennial twilight of the 80-ft. trees, impenetrable bamboo thickets, and tangles of thorn and "wait a minute" vines. This was "Lurp Team Two," a long-range reconnaissance patrol (LRRP) of the 173rd Airborne Brigade, sent to seek out two Viet Cong regiments that this outfit was itching to locate, engage and destroy. Within moments, Team Two was itself in imminent danger of destruction.

It did not take long for the patrol to discover that it had landed smack in the midst of a Viet Cong concentration. As skilled as Victor Charlie in the deadly blindman's bluff of jungle warfare, Team Two realized that the enemy was following its every move. Each time Staff Sergeant Clide Brown Jr. halted his men, he could hear footfalls close behind—and then a bristling silence. As the jungle dusk deepened into blackness, Brown set up a defense perimeter and listened more closely. Above the keening of insects, geckos and night birds, he heard the snap of two fingers and the snick of a rifle bolt not 30 yards away. "We're getting out of here," he whispered. "They're just behind us."

Linked up head and tail like circus elephants by their "escape ropes," each humping half a hundredweight of gear, the muzzles of their rifles still taped to keep out gunk, the scouts took advantage of distant artillery salvos to mask their footfalls on the way back to a prearranged retrieval zone. Brown, in the lead, groped his way back through the blackness by memorizing the map and counting his own steps; each time his left foot hit the ground 67 times, he calculated the team had covered 100 meters. Back at the landing zone, Brown's whispered message filtered into the radio transceiver: "Four seven, this is Papa Two. I'm in trouble. This is Papa Two ..." No reply. The triple-tiered jungle canopy drowned his call to the pickup helicopter. Brown moved his men soundlessly across the clearing and set up a radial defense—each man flat on his back, head to the center of the circle, his M-16 ready—behind a tangle of fallen trees.

Team Two measured the passage of the night in careful inhalations, silent exhalations, and the clack of bamboo signal sticks used by the Viet Cong patrols that passed within 50 feet of its hideout. Then, at 2 a.m., a single shot blasted the night: Brown's radioman, shifting his M-16, had accidentally triggered a tracer round—almost certainly disclosing the team's position. Brown hung tough, hoping that the cross-weave of jungle echoes would confuse the enemy searchers. It did; at dawn the team moved back in to hunt out the Viet Cong base camp.

Only after Brown had spotted a concentration of black pajamas did Team Two withdraw. As enemy sniper bullets stitched around and between them, the scouts blasted back with fragmentation grenades and bursts of automatic fire that chopped the brush into jungle salad. Brown "popped smoke"—set off yellow signal grenades—to bring in the American choppers, and while hovering Huey gunships laced the weeds with rockets and .50-cal. bullets, Team Two made its getaway, mission accomplished.

COMRADES: Clide Brown, left, shares a break with good friend Sergeant Arthur Silsby

Sergeant Brown, 24, is a Negro from the black belt of Alabama; in 16 sorties into Indian country he has not lost anyone on his five-man team, none of whom is a Negro. The cool professionalism of Clide Brown's patrol underscores in microcosm a major lesson of Vietnam—a hopeful and creative development in a dirty, hard-fought war. For the first time in the nation's military history, its Negro fighting men are fully integrated in combat, fruitfully employed in positions of leadership and fiercely proud of their performance. In Vietnam, the American Negro is winning—indeed has won—a black badge of courage that his nation must forever honor. That badge proclaims a truth that Americans had not learned about themselves before Vietnam: color has no place in war; merit is the only measure of the man.

Though Harry Truman ordered the military services desegregated in 1948, the Korean War found Negroes still serving in all-black outfits, or else in behind-the-lines non-combat roles. But in Vietnam, black-white relations in a slit trench or aboard a combat-bound Huey are years ahead of Denver and Darien, decades ahead of Birmingham and Biloxi. "The only color out here is olive drab," says a white sergeant. ∎

SHOWING OFF: On April 30, 1975, a North Vietnam army tank smashes through the fences around the presidential palace in Saigon, even though the gate had been left open

Endgame

In a final, humiliating bugout, the war ends in chaos as Americans and Vietnamese allies battle for space in the last helicopters out of Saigon

Most Americans wanted to believe the country's divisive commitment to the defense of South Vietnam had ended with the signing of the 1973 peace accords and the return of most of the U.S. troops. But the war's final chapter was not written until two years later, when South Vietnam's President, Nguyen Van Thieu, abruptly decided to cede control of vast areas of his land to the army of North Vietnam and the Viet Cong guerrillas. As hundreds of thousands of South Vietnamese clogged the highways into Saigon, President Gerald Ford ordered all Americans evacuated from the imperiled capital. The last days of the city's freedom represent one of the low points in 20th century U.S. history.

March 31, 1975

The Final Reckoning

Hué … Khe Sanh … An Loc … Quang Tri … The names stir bitter memories of battle sites drenched in blood, the blood of thousands of Vietnamese and Americans who fought to defend or retake those contested pieces of land. Once these places were proclaimed essential to the survival of South Vietnam and, in the view of successive U.S. Administrations, to the ultimate security of America. Now, in a stunning and unexpected move, the South Vietnamese were pulling out.

Abandoning a 20-year government policy of fighting for every inch of South Vietnamese territory, President Nguyen Van Thieu surrendered fully one-fourth of his country—seven provinces with an estimated population of more than 1.7 million people—to the attacking Communists. Thieu's decision to give up the apparently indefensible provinces caught almost everyone, including U.S. intelligence officials, by surprise.

Kontum, Pleiku and Darlac provinces in the Central Highlands were the first to go. Later, Quang Tri province in northernmost Military Region I was given up. Although not officially abandoned by Saigon, Thua Thien, containing the ancient imperial capital of Hué, was by week's end clearly in imminent danger of falling into North Vietnamese hands. In the South, only

50 miles north of Saigon, Binh Long province was relinquished.

The surrender of the provinces was unutterable tragedy for the true victims of the war, the South Vietnamese people. Helped by retreating ARVN soldiers, upwards of half a million refugees trekked by military convoy on motorcycle, buffalo cart, bicycle or foot toward areas still held by the government. It was the largest exodus since Vietnam was divided in 1954. ∎

April 14, 1975
Collapse in Vietnam

This is not the way a war should end. At least it was not the way in which many Americans had hoped it would end—by somehow fading away. As South Vietnam verged on collapse, the scenes of chaos inflamed anew America's frustration and horror over its most tragic foreign experience.

Even as President Gerald Ford pleaded for more military aid to South Vietnam, Saigon's troops fled from the north in a frenzy, abandoning an estimated $700 million worth of military equipment. Said a Pentagon officer: "We might just as well send the stuff directly to Hanoi—then it wouldn't get damaged."

At the Pentagon, some senior officers compared the South Vietnamese rout with other military disasters: Napoleon's debacle in Moscow in 1812, the fall of France in 1940, the Chinese Nationalist collapse in 1949. Yet the troops of President Nguyen Van Thieu were not retreating in the face of a massive Communist offensive; most were not in contact with the enemy at all. A full six South Vietnamese divisions had simply dissolved in a cascade of fright after Thieu abruptly ordered a massive retreat without giving his commanders time to lay the complex plans necessary to keep such a risky maneuver from turning into a rout.

While South Vietnamese troops fled in disarray, the Communists continued their relentless advance, mopping up with embarrassing ease the coastal cities that remained in government hands. By the end of the week four more provinces had fallen to Communist control—three-fourths of South Vietnam's territory. ∎

May 12, 1975
End of a War

The last images of the war: U.S. Marines with rifle butts pounding the fingers of Vietnamese who tried to claw their way into the American embassy compound to escape from their homeland. An apocalyptic carnival air—some looters wildly driving abandoned U.S. cars around the city until they ran out of gas; others ransacking Saigon's Newport PX, that transplanted dream of American suburbia, with one woman bearing off two cases of maraschino cherries on her head and another a case of Wrigley's Spearmint gum. Out in the South China Sea, millions of dollars' worth of helicopters profligately tossed overboard from U.S. rescue ships, discarded like pop-top beer cans to make room for later-arriving choppers.

In the end, the Viet Cong and North Vietnamese poured into Saigon and raised the flag of the Provisional Revolutionary Government. For many Americans, it was like a death that had long been expected, but was shocking

JETSAM: Sailors push a U.S. helicopter off the U.S.S. *Blue Ridge* and into the ocean to make room for incoming choppers during the evacuation of Saigon

FULL HOUSE: South Vietnamese civilians seeking refuge storm the barriers around the U.S. embassy in the last days before Saigon became Ho Chi Minh City

when it finally happened.

So the century's longest war was over, in an efficient but ignominious evacuation. It was nightmarish enough, but it could have been worse; only a few South Vietnamese soldiers fired at the departing Americans, and none were on target. At least the U.S. was spared the last awful spectacle of its people fighting a pitched battle with its late friends and allies. In fact, the Americans managed to bring about 120,000 South Vietnamese refugees out with them. Perhaps appropriately, the American goodbye to Vietnam was the one operation in all the years of the war that was utterly without illusion.

At about 4 a.m. on Tuesday, April 29, the Communists launched a massive rocket and artillery assault on already beleaguered Tan Son Nhut airbase just outside Saigon. Some 150 rockets and 130-mm shells whined in, forcing an immediate halt in the ongoing evacuation of Americans and Vietnamese. At the same time, Communist troops were reported pushing into some of the city's suburbs.

It was 4 p.m. Monday in Washington when the shelling of Tan Son Nhut began. Within hours, a series of meetings between President Ford and his top advisers led to the decision to evacuate all remaining Americans. By mid-afternoon in Saigon, dozens of American helicopters had begun arriving. By 7:52 the following morning, the last chopper had lifted off the roof of the American embassy.

Before noon Wednesday five Communist tanks, a dozen armored personnel carriers and truckloads of green-uniformed troops who wore helmets inscribed TIEN VI SAIGON—Onward to Saigon—swept down Unity Boulevard to the presidential palace. The gates had been left ajar, but one tank, followed by several others, smashed through the fence nonetheless, then fired triumphal salvos. At 12:15 p.m. the Provisional Revolutionary Government flag was raised over the palace. Thursday, the first morning of "liberation," was also May Day, and huge parades involving thousands of soldiers and Saigonese citizens were held on the city's flag-festooned streets. Communist troops offered children rides on their tanks. ∎

May 12, 1975

Last Chopper Out

• •

Among the some 1,400 Americans and 5,600 South Vietnamese evacuated from Saigon just before the last escape routes from the city were cut off was TIME *correspondent Roy Rowan. From the U.S.S.* Mobile *in the South China Sea, he sent this report:*

• •

The emergency plan had called for the evacuation of the remaining Americans in three stages—on Tuesday morning, afternoon and evening. But by 10:30 a.m. Tuesday, with Tan Son Nhut airbase under pounding by rockets, mortars and artillery, word came from the American embassy: "This is it! Everybody out!" I glanced at my watch: it was 10:42. People peered through iron gates that had been pulled shut because of the 24-hour curfew. Their eyes were easy to read. "You're leaving us," they said.

Nobody knew what the plan was.

Would the "helos" pick us up from a pad on the roof? Or would buses take us to Tan Son Nhut, which had been under Communist attack for twelve hours? A few French civilians joined our group. Mme. Madeleine Morton, owner of the best restaurant in Saigon, the Guillaume Tell, greeted her customers. "I am trying to go to Bridgeport, Con-nec-ticut," she announced. At 12:20 two black buses finally arrived and were quickly boarded.

The buses headed toward Tan Son Nhut, right into the rocket belt. Guards at the gate were firing at the buses. Pillars of black smoke rose from the airbase. We heard our Marine escort ("Wagon Master") ask "Dodge City," "What's the situation at the gate?" "Bust it if necessary," came the reply.

We did not have to. Inside the surrounded airbase, a damaged American helicopter, one skid broken off, lay on the ground, its rotor still spinning. A tremendous explosion rocked our bus as a North Vietnamese 130-mm shell hit the Air America terminal just across the road. "Don't panic!" shouted our Marine escort.

Crouching and running, the passengers raced inside a reassuring structure with thick concrete walls. About 500 evacuees were already waiting in line. Word was passed down the line: one suitcase and one handbag per evacuee. Just as our group of 50 prepared to leave, that rule was changed to make way for more passengers: the Marine at the door shouted, "No baggage!" Suitcases and bags were ripped open as evacuees fished for their passports,

DESPERATE MEASURES: There's only so much room on board—and U.S. pilot Robert D. Hedrix knows everyone can't fit

papers and other valuables. I said goodbye to my faithful Olivetti, grabbed my tape recorder and camera and got ready to run like hell. The door opened. Outside I could see helmeted, flak-jacketed Marines—lots of them—crouched against the building, their M-16s, M-79 grenade launchers and mortars all at the ready.

Two Sikorsky C-53 Sea Stallions were sitting in the parking lot. I raced for it. Marines, lying prone, lined the area, but they were hard to see—their camouflaged uniforms blended with the tropical greenery. I almost stepped on a rifle barrel poking out from under a bush as I entered the lot.

The Sea Stallion was still 200 ft. away, its loading ramp down and its rotors slashing impatiently. Fifty people,

Americans and Vietnamese, some lugging heavy equipment despite the order to abandon all baggage, piled in, one atop another. The loadmaster raised the ramp, the two waist gunners gripped the handles of their M-16s, and, with about a dozen passengers still standing like subway straphangers, the helicopter lifted off. As the tail dipped, I could see towers of smoke rising from all over Tan Son Nhut.

Beside us was the second Sea Stallion. Tilting and swaying in unison, the two machines gained altitude. Saigon lay below, brown and smoky in the afternoon light, its serpentine river cutting a winding swath through the city. I glanced at my watch: 3:52, five hours and ten minutes since our evacuation had commenced. ∎

ESCAPE: Fleeing for their lives, refugees head for U.S. ships waiting offshore from South Vietnam

May 7, 2001

Bob Kerrey

Three decades later, the war haunts the career of a former U.S. Senator

H E WAS IN THE LAND OF NIGHTMARES, WHERE NOTHING counted but killing or being killed. Twenty-five and eager to do his duty, whatever that might be. He was supposed to kill, and as platoon leader he was also responsible for the lives of six men in a war with almost no rules. The enemy was all around, but he didn't know who or where they were. The dark, the confusion, the strain of listening for sounds that signaled death, the tension, the terror. Suddenly he had to make a choice, and he gave the order: Oh, God, what have I done?

For former Senator Bob Kerrey, that nightmare never goes away. He knows that one night 32 years ago in Vietnam, he and his squad of Navy SEALs (short for Sea, Air Land unit) killed nearly a score of unarmed civilians, mainly women and children. The shame and guilt and remorse have haunted him ever since. Kerrey, who received a Congressional Medal of Honor for a later incident when he lost half his right leg after a grenade hit his foot, did not want to make his personal anguish public. But because a fellow SEAL who lived through the same nightmare has come forward in the New York *Times* Magazine and on TV's *60 Minutes II* with an even more damning chain of events than Kerrey admits to, his private pain is erupting into hard questions about war, memory and guilt.

As Kerrey recalls it, the nighttime assault unfolded amid the confusion endemic to Vietnam. In-country for just a month, the young lieutenant had charge of a squad of élite SEALs trained to emerge from the dark, kidnap or kill local Viet Cong leaders, then melt back into the jungle. This night their target was a village secretary reportedly holding a party meeting in Thanh Phong, deep in the Mekong Delta "free-fire zone," where innocent civilians had—officially at last—been cleared out, and everyone left was deemed an enemy.

Kerrey's Raiders, as the squad called itself, had little experience but lots of enthusiasm. Toward 12 midnight on a moonless night, the men piled into a swift boat and headed for Thanh Phong. Darkness gave cover but heightened the confu-

GHOSTS: Bob Kerrey at the Vietnam Memorial in 2001, above, and in Vietnam in 1965, right

sion. As the men left the boat and crept toward the village, they bumped into an outlying hooch they thought was a warning outpost. Kerrey says his men, wielding knives, told him they would "take care" of the people inside to prevent them from alerting the village. But Kerrey says he did not join in the killings or examine the victims. Some minutes later, Kerrey recalls, the squad spotted four or five huts by the faint flicker of candles inside. Then out of the night came the whine of gunfire. "We returned it," says Kerrey, who gave the order for his men to unleash a ferocious barrage of automatic rifle rounds, grenades and armor-piercing rockets. In the flashing tracer light, no one could see who was being hit. When the men in the unit spotted several people running way, they shot them too. The assault lasted only a few minutes.

When the gunfire subsided, Kerrey's men discovered that half the dead were women and children. If the inadvertent killing of civilians was a grim commonplace in Vietnam, deliberate execution was a criminal violation of the laws of war. Yet Gerhard Klann, the veteran among Kerrey's tyros, told the *Times* Magazine and *60 Minutes II* that the five villagers knifed in the first hooch were, in fact, an old man, his wife, two young girls and a boy. Kerrey, he said, ordered the killing and helped him cut the old man's throat. Klann said he heard no incoming fire as the squad entered Thanh Phong. He said that when they failed to find the Viet Cong official, Kerrey ordered the SEALs to round up the unarmed women and children in the hooches. Then, Klann said, "an order was given" to shoot them. "We lined up, and we opened fire."

Responding to Klann's charges, Kerrey and the other five soldiers in the squad agreed on two points: they had been fired upon first, and no one had given or received an order to deliberately shoot civilians. Kerrey himself has insisted over and over that while the massacre was an "atrocity," it had been accidental. "It's come back to haunt me about every other day," he told TIME. "If you feel that shame, it's very hard to talk about it." It is still impossible to settle whose version is right and whose is wrong.

To know and understand what Kerrey's Raiders did that night in Thanh Phong can be cathartic. To condemn it is something else, requiring a clarity that was almost never available to young men shooting in the dark. It is a clarity our nation likewise never had at the time. When we judge Bob Kerrey, we judge our nation as well.

■

Notebook

The Allies

South Korea, Thailand, Australia, New Zealand and Canada all sent combat soldiers to assist the U.S. in Vietnam. In total, they numbered more than 30,000 troops. More than 5,000 of them were killed in action.

Heroes

American soldiers were awarded the Congressional Medal of Honor 239 times during the Vietnam War. The most decorated soldier was David Hackworth, who won more than 70 medals for valor in combat, including two Distinguished Service Crosses, one Distinguished Flying Cross, nine Silver Stars, eight Bronze Stars and eight Purple Hearts. In 1971 (when he resigned from the military in disgust over the conduct of the war), he was, at 40, the youngest colonel in the Army.

Casualties

In July 1959, military advisers Major Dale Buis and Master Sergeant Chester Ovnand were killed by machine gun fire in the village of Bien Hoa, becoming the first Americans to die in Vietnam. In April 1975, the day before the last Americans left Vietnam, Marine Corporal Charles McMahon, 19, and Lance Corporal Darwin Judge, 18—who had, between them, been in the country for a total of 20 days—became the last. McMahon and Judge had been guarding the American withdrawal from Saigon's Tan Son Nhut airport when a rocket attack claimed their lives.

The American death toll in Vietnam is 57,690 personnel, including 10,446 lost to accidents or disease. An unknown number of Vietnamese (thought to be in the neighborhood of 1 million) lost their lives.

Hardware

AP/WIDE WORLD

U.S. AIR FORCE

Rolling Thunder, Whirling Wonder

The B-52 bomber became the workhorse of the U.S. Air Force during Vietnam and remains so today. Its role in Vietnam was particularly terrifying—B-52s fly so high and so fast that they are almost impossible to see or hear from the ground. Each one carried up to 70,000 lbs. of bombs, which were often aerodynamically designed so that they made no noise while falling. Though the last new B-52 rolled off the production line in 1961, the planes have been updated and may remain in the air until at least 2040.

Time has been less kind to the the Bell UH-1 ("Huey") helicopter. More than 2,500 of the Army's first Utility Helicopters served in Vietnam. The advent of shoulder-fired missiles in the early '70s made Hueys obsolete in combat; the last few in military service will be retired by the end of 2002.

The Last Word

Text of the final cable to Washington from the U.S. embassy in Saigon, 2:10 a.m., April 30, 1975: "… wish to advise that this will be final message from Saigon Station. It will take us about 20 minutes to destroy equipment … It has been a long hard fight and we lost … Let us hope that we will not have another Vietnam experience and that we have learned our lesson. Saigon signing off."

> **"You let a bully come into your yard, next day he'll be on your front porch."**
> **—Lyndon B. Johnson**

Theaters of War

When the stars of stage and screen turn up in some of the world's more remote locations to put on a show, it's hard to say who enjoys it more—the troops or the troupers. Bob Hope is the grand old man in this role, an ongoing inspiration to Mariah, Arnold and Shaggy

▲ **Bombshell**
Marilyn Monroe, a pinup favorite in the Korean War, gives the boys an eyeful in 1954.

◀ Homecoming Queens
September 1945: The Andrews
Sisters—from left, LaVerne,
Maxene and Patti—perform an
impromptu number for U.S. G.I.s
who have disembarked from the
Queen Mary ocean liner at a
New York City pier.

▲ Showtime
Songwriter turned
performer Irving
Berlin applies makeup
before a performance
of his revue *This Is the
Army* in Italy, 1944.

▶ Taps
Playing the palace,
Fred Astaire dances
for U.S. soldiers at
Versailles in Septem-
ber 1944, a month
after Paris was freed.

◀ Sailors' Delight
It's safe to say that few
eyes are on Bob Hope as he
escorts actress Carroll
Baker across a stage on the
flight deck of the aircraft
carrier U.S.S. *Ticonderoga*.
Location: off the coast of
Vietnam, December 1967.

► **¡Muy Caliente!**
April 2002: Members of the Cheerleaders of America, a troupe of former N.F.L. cheerleaders, shake their maracas at an outdoor show for soldiers stationed at Guantánamo Bay Naval Base in Cuba.

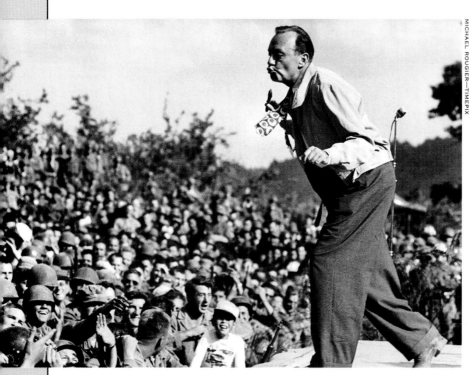

▲ **Brush Up Your Wordsworth**
The USO was never this frisky—Australian troops in Vietnam ogle showgirl Pat Wordsworth of Aussie favorite *The Bobby Lime Show.*

▲ **Festive Fourth**
Jack Benny seems to be blowing a kiss to a soldier at an outdoor show in Germany. The date: July 4, 1945.

► **Pumped!**
In today's Army, female soldiers get to take their turn with Hollywood stars. Here Arnold Schwarzenegger visits with fans in Bosnia in 2002.

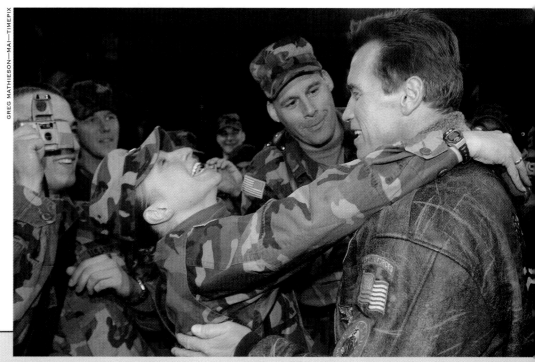

▲ Where There's Life ...

Touring tirelessly, putting himself in danger and taking time to visit with common soldiers, Bob Hope was the favorite of U.S. troops for decades. Here he's visiting Korea in 1950.

▶ Me and My Big Mouth

Comedian Martha Raye sings for an audience of U.S. soldiers still stationed in North Africa in December 1947. Does anyone doubt that she sang *White Christmas?*

▲ Grand Dame
A refugee from Hitler's Nazi regime, Marlene Dietrich became a favorite of Allied soldiers in World War II. She celebrates with troops in liberated France, 1944.

◄ Sitting Pretty
Pop diva Mariah Carey displays new ways to accessorize the camouflage jumpsuit to appreciative soldiers before a holiday show in Kosovo in 2001.

▲ Whatever Lola Wants
A splash of orange in a sea of khaki, Lola Fallana leaves the stage to fraternize with the troops during this 1970 Bob Hope USO tour in Vietnam.

▲ Big Finish
Top right, Al Jolson belts out a number for troops in Pusan, South Korea, on a happy occasion: the invasion of Inchon was two days before.

▲ Tonight: The First Lady Five
Or … One Pro and Four Rookies. From left, singer Sheryl Crow, Secretary of the Army Togo West, Hillary Clinton, Chelsea Clinton and Admiral Leighton Smith harmonize in Bosnia in 1996.

◄ Keep Your Chin Up
Comedian Jay Leno shows his patriotic side aboard an Air Force jet en route to Afghanistan in December 2001. Country singer Dwight Yoakam, far left, seems more interested in gear.

PETER STACKPOLE—TIMEPIX

▲There Is Nothing ...

… Like a dame. A trio of USO chorus girls do a song-and-dance number on a beach in Guam in 1945. Top that, Rodgers and Hammerstein!

▶ Testifying

Times change, styles change—and even the Army changes. American soldiers, male and female alike, love Shaggy's blend of reggae and rap in the Balkans in 2001.

GREG MATHIESON—MAI—TIMEPIX

◀ **There She Is**
Miss America
Jane Anne Jayroe
entertains U.S.
soldiers in South
Vietnam in 1967.
We can't help
wondering if the
troops might not
have preferred a
rerun of the
swimsuit contest
to a review of the
talent competition.

▲ **On the Air**
A group of natives prepares to
perform on the Army's "Mosquito
Network," which broadcast live
radio from Guadalcanal across
the South Pacific theater.

◀ **Stylin'**
Vietnam, 1967: Raquel Welch
shows the troops what they're
missing in homeland fashion—
miniskirts and white go-go boots.

ON THE WARPATH: U.S. soldiers drive a humvee across the desert as oil wells, torched by retreating Iraqi troops, blacken the sky

War of Restoration

As the U.S. leads an allied coalition to victory over Iraq and returns Kuwait to freedom, America's armed forces regain the world's respect

THE GULF WAR SOUNDED TAPS TO 40 YEARS OF FRUStration for the U.S. military. Like World War II, it united Americans in a common, clearly humane cause, as leader of a great worldwide coalition of allies. Like World War II, it offered a clear-cut villain: no one doubted that Iraq's Saddam Hussein was a tyrant and that his invasion of neighboring Kuwait was a violation of national sovereignty. In quickly defeating Saddam, Americans slammed the door on four decades of division and indecisiveness. And men and women in uniform again walked tall.

Linking the two conflicts was President George Bush, a former Navy pilot who had been shot down over the Pacific in World War II. In the first weeks of 1991, all Americans seemed to share his determination to prove that even if we had sometimes lost our way in the years since 1945, we were still able to lead the world in an armed struggle against naked aggression.

And if it was fitting that this war should begin 50 years after the U.S. entry into World War II, then it was equally fitting that it should come within months of the close of another epic struggle, the cold war. The Berlin Wall had fallen, and the Soviet Union was disintegrating. The long twilight struggle that had given us "red scares" and mutually assured destruction, U-2 planes and bomb shelters, was over. When Russia, Saudi Arabia and even Syria joined Israel in the U.S.-led coalition against Iraq, Bush's new world order seemed very real.

The Gulf War put to rest America's long military malaise. All at once, we seemed to reap the good fortune that had eluded us for years in the swamps and jungles of Vietnam and at a gazetteer's worth of other tragic, woebegone places like the the Desert One landing site in Iran and the Marine barracks near Beirut—places where American blood was shed, yet America seemed to get little or nothing in return.

This time, it seemed almost effortless: thousands of air strikes in the course of a few weeks, a ground war that was over so quickly that TIME ran a cover story about its beginning one week and its victorious conclusion the next, and a tally of the honored dead (fewer than 400) in which more Americans were lost to accidents and illness than were killed in combat.

After decades of disinterest, the vast majority of Americans took pride in their armed forces. General "Stormin' Norman" Schwarzkopf and Chairman of the Joint Chiefs of Staff Colin Powell were the first universally admired military heroes to appear on the American stage since the days of Matt Ridgway and Omar Bradley. And for the first time we saw America's modern military machine in action, deploying a dazzling new arsenal of high-tech weapons—Stealth fighters and bombers, smart bombs, night-vision capability—and profiting from the participation of women, who, as blacks had done in Vietnam,

TROOPERS: Women served in the regular Army for the first time in the Gulf War

proved in the gulf their right to be regarded as equals.

In the decade since our easy victory over Saddam, we have learned two things. First, that the post–cold war world can be as troubling and dangerous as the world it replaced. And second, that even a decisive military victory can be compromised by indecisive diplomacy. To wit: Saddam himself. In the most controversial act of the war, his regime was spared by the allied coalition. As of this writing, there is a real possibility that he may yet find himself facing a new generation of Americans in uniform, led by a President with a familiar name. ∎

The Gulf War

The Gulf War was so brief that one photographer's work cannot fully represent it. Here we profile Christopher Morris, who took the picture on these pages—and was taken captive by Iraqi troops during the war. The following pages feature the work of other photojournalists who covered the conflict.

Fight at the Airport

In one of the Gulf War's few pitched battles, members of the U.S. 1st Marine Division's Task Force Ripper lay siege to Kuwait International Airport. The task force overcame an Iraqi phalanx equipped with more than 100 Soviet-made tanks—without suffering a single casualty.

I t's hard to talk about it," says veteran TIME photographer Christopher Morris when asked about some of his more intense experiences documenting warfare around the globe. "People don't realize what photographers have to go through. It's the kind of thing you see in films." Indeed, Morris' curriculum vitae reads like the script from a thriller: he has been fired upon by snipers in the Balkans; beaten for hours by Russian thugs; and kidnapped in Panama, Yugoslavia and Iraq.

In Iraq, Morris got into trouble just as the war was winding down. "When they finished the peace talks and the Iraqi generals came back, they drove toward Basra," Morris recalls. He and some 30 journalists (including fellow TIME photographer Anthony Suau) followed, hoping to cover a battle there between Saddam's Republican Guard and Shi'ite rebels. "The Iraqis never waved us off or anything … they were very friendly with us. And we met some resistance people along the road who said that they controlled Basra."

But when Morris and his group arrived at the outskirts of the town, "a bridge was blown up so there was a choke point with all the tanks and the Republican Guard. And when our convoy's vehicles showed up there, we were trapped. We couldn't back up and turn around. They just basically pulled us out of the cars and then stole everything—money, cameras, food, clothing, anything you had."

For the next six days, the group seemed to have dropped off the face of the earth. They were moved continually—from a university campus in Basra to a military barracks—and always kept in sealed rooms while pitched battles between Iraqi government forces and rebels raged all around them.

Finally, the entire group was brought to Baghdad, given a decent meal and turned over to the Red Cross. About his time in captivity, Morris has one regret ("We went from Dhahran to Kuwait City to Basra to Baghdad to Amman, and not one roll of film to show for it") and one philosophic observation: "When there's a really close call, you can feel life more."

DIANA WALKER

▲ Pitchman

At Thanksgiving, George Bush tosses souvenir tie clips to Marines at a base in Saudi Arabia. Bush gave them a set of horseshoes and challenged them to send their best team to the White House. The next summer, the President whupped the veterans.

▲ Farewell to a Friend

Army Sergeant Ken Kozakiewicz grieves upon learning that his friend and comrade, Andy Alaniz, is in the body bag on the right. Like almost one-fourth of all American combat fatalities in the Gulf War, Alaniz was killed by friendly fire.

▼ A Brief, Tragic Life

After the war Saddam renewed his purge of ethnic Kurds in Iraq's north. Here, Kurds bury an infant in a makeshift cemetery in a refugee camp.

ELI REED—MAGNUM

STEPHANIE COMPOINT—CORBIS SYGMA

▲ Conquering Heroes
Gulf War veterans escort Old Glory in a traditional New York City ticker-tape parade. Some 4 million people hailed 24,000 marchers from 17 nations—a far cry from the neglect, even scorn, endured by returning Vietnam vets.

▲ Still Life with Gusher
A crew of Canadian oil-well fire fighters struggles to control a well sabotaged by retreating Iraqi troops. More than 600 Kuwaiti wells were set on fire, unleashing a torrent of up to 7 million wasted barrels of oil per day.

▶ Making Tracks
A column of the First Armored Division's self-propelled 155-mm howitzers traverses the desert. This gun can toss a 95-lb. shell more than 15 miles once every 60 seconds. The Iraqis had a similar weapon, but it wasn't mobile.

WIN MCNAMEE—DOD

Blowout

SPECTACLE: For the first time, we watched a war begin live on television as U.S. bombs hit Baghdad on the night of Jan. 16, 1991

Reinventing the face of war with high-tech weapons, the U.S. and its allies score a fast victory over the disheartened troops of Iraq's dictator

When Saddam Hussein sent his troops to take over Kuwait, he apparently thought his act would be unopposed. But U.S. President George Bush assembled and led an allied coalition whose military forces boasted an overwhelming advantage in the sophisticated weaponry of high-tech warfare, from cruise missiles to unmanned reconnaissance drones. General Norman Schwarzkopf's masterly ground-war strategy, an unexpected flank attack, gave the U.S. and its allies an easy victory. But did we end the one-sided conflict too soon? Critics then and now believe the allies should have driven Saddam out of power while they had a massive army deployed in the region.

August 13, 1990

Iraq's Power Grab

With the benefit of hindsight it looks so obvious, so wickedly brilliant. There sat Kuwait, fat and ripe, bulging with enormous reserves of oil and cash, boasting an excellent port on the Persian Gulf—and utterly incapable of defending itself against Iraq's proficient war machine. Saddam Hussein, hungry for money but greedier still for regional dominance, knew before the first of his soldiers crossed the border that it would be a walkover. And it was. In 12 hours, Kuwait was his.

With his brief romp through the desert, the imperious Iraqi President doubled the oil under his control to some 20% of the world's known reserves; only Saudi Arabia, with 25%, has more. He strengthened his claim to the position he has long coveted: overlord of the Arab world. And he made the entire world quake, weak-kneed, at his raw power. Not since the brilliant military leader Nebuchadnezzar ruled the Babylonian Empire more than two millenniums ago had Baghdad exercised such sway.

By provoking the first major military conflict of the post-cold war era, Saddam provided the maiden test of the proposition that the U.S. and the Soviet Union can create more peace working together than apart. The Iraqi blitz prompted Washington and Moscow to act in stunning unanimity, demanding, in an unprecedented joint statement, that the invaders retreat. That position was also endorsed by the United Nations Security Council. While all parties were clearly loath to take on the mightiest army in the Arab world—a force of 1 million fighting men—the rare convergence of views raised the possibility that Iraq's expansionism can somehow be contained.

All the points of discord between Iraq and Kuwait—money from oil revenues, the disputed provinces and islands—were on the agenda of talks between the two countries at last Wednesday's meeting. From the outset the Kuwaitis made it clear that they were willing to pay Baghdad a sizable sum for peace. But the Iraqis, who demanded Kuwait's total capitulation on every count, were determined to see the negotiations break down. After a fruitless two hours, they did. At exactly 2 the next morning, the 100,000 Iraqi soldiers massed on the border—a force nearly five times as great as the entire Kuwaiti military—spilled south. Two additional commando units swarmed in by air and sea.

Rolling unchallenged down the empty superhighway Kuwait had built —as a token of friendship with Iraq—to link the two countries, the troops made the 37 miles to the capital, Kuwait City, in just four hours. While an estimated 300 Iraqi tanks prowled the city, an additional 50 surrounded the Emir's palace and the nearby U.S. embassy. But the Emir, Sheik Jaber al-Ahmed al-Sabah, and his family were able to flee to Saudi Arabia by helicopter. Though the invaders had quickly seized Kuwait's radio and television station, a hidden transmitter continued to broadcast exhortations to resist the raiding foreigners and pleas for help from other Arab states.

Though help never came, Kuwaiti troops put up small pockets of resistance. At the palace, the country's symbolic heart, the Kuwaitis held their own through a two-hour artillery barrage. During the battle, the Emir's younger brother Fahd was killed. The Iraqi force assigned to secure the oil rigs off Kuwait's shores saw the most action. Kuwaiti troops and missile boats managed to sink and burn an unknown number of Iraqi landing craft and escort ships. By early afternoon, however, nearly all Kuwait's guns had been silenced. In all, it is estimated that 200 Kuwaitis were killed in the assault. No figure for Iraqi casualties was available. ∎

December 3, 1990
Turkey in the Desert

There were 350 journalists accompanying President Bush on his Thanksgiving stop in Saudi Arabia, and most of them seemed to approve of his performance. The network anchors rushed for their desert tunics and created as much stir among the troops as the President himself. At the end of the stage show, elaborate broadcasting facilities in the middle of the desolate sand beamed back live reports from the media superstars.

Bush walked among the G.I.s more as a comrade-in-arms than as a Commander in Chief, never short of a quip: "If push comes to shove, we're going to get Roseanne Barr to go to Iraq and sing the national anthem," he joked to troops. He signed T shirts and caps, and posed for snapshots. He had turkey ("pretty good") with the Army and Marines on land and attended Thanksgiving services aboard the Navy's U.S.S. *Nassau,* a helicopter-landing ship. Bush was plainly heartened by the enthusiasm of the troops.

Bush came within 70 miles of the Kuwaiti border, his chopper escorted by menacing gunships. Fighter planes ranged high overhead. "Security good?" somebody asked Desert Shield commander General Norman Schwarzkopf. "It had better be, or I'm in trouble," he replied. Bush wore one of those camouflaged barracks hats that have become the symbol of the waiting game in the desert. The President also had a gas mask handy; aboard Air Force One he had been shown how to use it.

Bush left horseshoe-pitching gear with the land forces, suggesting they practice up, then come by the White House when the crisis is over to challenge him and one of his sons. Four other political luminaries were at Bush's side during his Thanksgiving pilgrimage. He had shrewdly asked the top congressional leaders—Senators George Mitchell and Robert Dole and Speaker Thomas Foley and House minority leader Robert Michel—to come take turkey in the desert, an offer that could not be refused. They looked like hired extras swept unexpectedly into the Bush spectacle. ∎

CORBIS SABA

BIG BROTHER: A billboard hailing Saddam—one of many to be found in Iraq—portrays the dictator in battle garb

SKYLIGHT: An Iraqi civilian examines the damage created by an allied smart bomb in Baghdad

January 28, 1991

Bombs in the Dark

Previous generations of pilots had spoken of a "bomber's moon." But that was in an era of what would now be considered low-tech conflict. Today the ideal condition for an air raid is a pitch-black night. Infra-red devices and laser-guided bombs enable pilots to see and hit their targets through inky darkness; moonlight would serve only to make their planes more visible to antiaircraft gunners. Jan. 15 was the first of three moonless nights in Iraq, but the U.S. had set a deadline of Jan. 16 for Saddam to pull out of Kuwait; the night of the 16th was the earliest time when both political and astronomical conditions would be ripe for war.

Just before 1 a.m. in the Middle East, pool reporters at U.S. air bases in Saudi Arabia heard and felt the ground-shaking thunder of wave after wave of jets taking off. The planes headed north toward Kuwait and Iraq. At about the same time, more jets were winging off six U.S. carriers in the Persian Gulf and Red Sea. Eventually, about 2,000 planes of the U.S. and six allied nations—Britain, France, Italy, Canada, Saudi Arabia and the Kuwaiti government-in-exile—hit a host of targets throughout Iraq and Kuwait. The outside world got the first news from Western television correspondents at Al Rasheed Hotel in downtown Baghdad, who told of hearing air-raid sirens and seeing tracer bullets and antiaircraft bursts lighting up the black skies. In Washington, Presidential spokesman Marlin Fitzwater declared to reporters, "The liberation of Kuwait has begun."

By that time, the destruction was well under way. Pilots returning from the first attack described an awesome pattern of flashing multicolored lights—some antiaircraft bursts, some bombs—brightening the dark ground and skies. One after another of them likened it to a Fourth of July fireworks display or a Christmas tree.

The pinpoint accuracy of the attacks was spectacular. At a Friday briefing in Saudi Arabia, Air Force Lieut. General Charles Horner showed videotapes of two laser-guided bombs sailing through the open doors of a bunker in which an Iraqi Scud missile was stored, and a

FIRE! Sailors watch a cruise missile launched at Iraq from the U.S.S. *Wisconsin* in the Persian Gulf

third plopping down the rooftop air shaft of a tall building in Baghdad and then blowing up the top floors. Bombs and missiles also hit other targets around and even in the heart of Baghdad—Saddam Hussein's presidential palace, for one—while apparently doing little damage to civilian lives or property.

A British television correspondent standing on a sixth-floor balcony of Al Rasheed Hotel reported a weird sight: a U.S. cruise missile whizzing past at eye level and slamming into the Iraqi Defense Ministry nearby.

After the first raids, U.S. and allied planes pounded targets throughout Kuwait and Iraq around the clock, not so much in waves as in a steady stream. They hit Baghdad again before dawn Saturday, knocking out the city's electricity, water and central telecommunications facility. By Sunday they had flown more than 4,000 sorties (one plane flying one mission). About 80% were said to have been effective. Yet casualties among the Allied airmen were phenomenally light: six U.S., two British, one Italian and one Kuwaiti plane downed as of early Sunday. Iraqi antiaircraft fire was in some cases heavy, but inaccurate. ∎

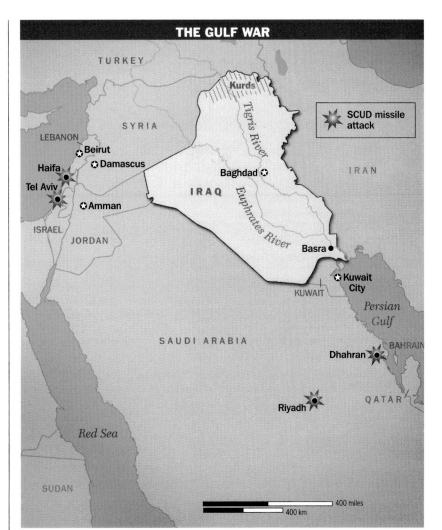

THE GULF WAR

PRECAUTIONS: As Iraq launched Scud missile attacks, civilians and soldiers alike donned gas masks in Tel Aviv and in both a hotel and a bunker in Saudi Arabia

January 28, 1991

Popgun Retaliation

From the very first, Saddam Hussein had loudly proclaimed that an important strategy for winning a war was to strike Israel, probably with missiles releasing clouds of poison gas. The idea was to goad Jerusalem into striking back, thus enabling Saddam to claim that the war now pitted his Arab nation against Israel, its American ally and Arab stooges.

As the first 24 hours of the war ticked by without an assault, hope grew that Saddam had been prevented from trying his cynical gambit. No such luck. Early Friday morning, air-raid sirens went off throughout much of Israel. The government radio ordered all citizens to don the gas masks that had been distributed earlier and move into the sealed rooms that every household had been urged to prepare. Then blasts began rocking Tel Aviv and Haifa. Early reports said at least one missile had released nerve gas.

Not so. By Israeli count eight Scuds hit Tel Aviv, Haifa and the Ramallah area on Friday, but none released gas. They injured about a dozen people but killed no one. Within hours, American planes had destroyed six of Iraq's Scud truck launchers, three with missiles inside. One other Scud missile had been launched earlier against Saudi Arabia, but was blown up in midair by a Patriot antimissile missile. That was a technological triumph, the first known time that an attack missile had been destroyed by a defensive missile in combat.

On Saturday morning three more Scud missiles fell on Tel Aviv. This time 10 people were injured, but again no one was killed. After the Israeli Cabinet met in a concrete bunker on Saturday, the nation's government once more assured Washington that it would not retaliate now. ∎

MOVING IN: A Marine in Task Force Ripper hits the sand as U.S. troops reach the outskirts of Kuwait City

March 11, 1991

The 100 Hours

Among Americans, victory in the gulf has finally laid to rest all the ghosts of Vietnam. Self-doubt, deep divisions, suspicions of national decline—the very words suddenly seem quaint. The problem now may be to contain the surge of pride and unity before it bursts the bounds of reason and passes into jingoism, even hubris. None of that, however, can detract from the awesome speed, power and totality of the allies' military victory. The war, particularly its climactic 100-hour campaign, bids fair to be enshrined in military textbooks for as long as the annihilation of a Roman army by Hannibal at Cannae in 216 B.C, still a model for a strategy of encirclement, like the one followed by General H. Norman Schwarzkopf, the allied commander in the gulf blowout.

The war as a whole might be the most one-sided in all history. Latest casualty count for the full 43 days: 149 killed and 513 wounded among the allies, vs. perhaps more than 100,000 deaths and injuries among the Iraqis, though an accurate total may never be known. Allied forces routed and slaughtered, by a combination of firepower, speed and deception, Iraqi troops that outnumbered them at least 3 to 2 and were extremely well dug in.

Five weeks of bombing had destroyed much of the Iraqis' armor and artillery. But not until coalition soldiers could see the corpses piled in Iraqi trenches and hear surrendering soldiers' tales of starvation and terror did it become obvious how bloodily effective the air campaign had been. The bombing completely disrupted Iraqi command and communications; troops could not communicate, even with adjoining units. One unit of the Republican Guard was devastated on the war's last day while its members were taking a cigarette break; comrades in nearby units had been unable to warn them that onrushing U.S. forces were almost on top of them.

Bereft of satellites or even aerial reconnaissance, Saddam's commanders could not see what was going on behind allied lines. Thus Schwarzkopf was able to hoodwink Baghdad into concentrating its forces in the wrong places until the very end. Six of Iraq's 42 divisions were massed along the Kuwaiti coast, guarding against a seaborne invasion. As zero hour approached, an armada of 31 ships swung into position to put them ashore near Kuwait City. The battleships *Missouri* and *Wisconsin* took turns, an hour at a time, firing their 16-in. guns at Iraqi shore defenses. It was all a feint; the war ended with 17,000 Marines still aboard their ships.

Most of Iraq's front-line troops hunkered down behind minefields and barbed wire along the 138-mile Saudi-Kuwait border, awaiting what Baghdad obviously expected to be the main allied thrust. Coalition troops did in fact initially concentrate in front of them. But in the last 16 days before the attack, more than 150,000 American, British and French troops moved to the west, as far as 300 miles inland from the gulf, setting up bases across the border from

JOY: U.S. soldiers celebrate Kuwait City's liberation only days after the ground attack was launched

an area of southern Iraq that was mostly empty desert. Part of that allied force was to drive straight to the Euphrates River, cutting off retreat routes for the Iraqi forces in Kuwait; another part was to turn east and hit Republican Guard divisions along the Kuwait-Iraq border, taking them by surprise on their right flank.

During the night, American B-52s pounded Iraqi positions and helicopter gunships swept the defense lines, firing rockets at tanks and artillery pieces and machine-gunning soldiers in the trenches. Allied artillery opened an intense bombardment from howitzers and multiple-launch rocket systems that released thousands of shrapnel-like bomblets over the trenches. Everything was ready for the ground troops to begin moving in the last hours of darkness, taking advantage of the allies' superior night-vision equipment.

On Sunday, between 4 a.m. and 6 a.m., allied forces jumped off at selected points all along the 300-mile line. Though Hollywood has long pictured the desert as a place of eternal burning sunshine and total aridity, the attack began in a lashing rain that turned the sand into muddy goo. The first troops through were wearing bulky chemical-protective garb, in keeping with the allied conviction that Saddam would use poison gas right from the beginning. In fact, the Iraqis never fired their chemical weapons.

Saudi and other Arab troops hit the strongest Iraqi fortifications near the coast. To their left were the U.S. 1st and 2nd Marine Divisions, which had moved inland. The Marines attacked at points known to allied commanders as the "elbow" of Kuwait, where the border with Saudi Arabia turns sharply to the north, and the "armpit," where it abruptly sweeps west again.

At the far western reach of the allied line, the French 6th Light Armored Division jumped off before dawn Sunday, attacking across the Iraqi border with the U.S. 82nd Airborne Division toward a fort and airfield named As Salman, 105 miles inside Iraq. On the way, American artillery and French Gazelle helicopter gunships firing antitank missiles subdued a force of Iraqi tanks and infantry, many of whom surrendered. To the right of the French, the U.S. 101st Airborne Division mounted a deep-penetration helicopter assault into southeastern Iraq. Chinook helicopters, some skimming only 50 feet above the sand, others slinging humvees, modern versions of the old jeeps, below their fuselages, ferried 4,000 men with their vehicles and equipment into the desert. The force established a huge refueling and resupply base, then jumped off again from there deeper into Iraq and struck out for the Euphrates River. Other units—the British 1st Armored

PRISONERS: Marines guard some of the tens of thousands of Iraqi troops who surrendered to allied forces in the first days of the ground war

SMOKIN' CAMELS: In a last gesture of defiance, Saddam's troops set Kuwait's oil wells ablaze as they hurried to retreat to Iraq

Division, seven U.S. Army divisions, and Egyptian, Saudi and Syrian units—attacked at various times throughout the morning and early afternoon at points along the Saudi-Iraq border into the western tip of Kuwait. All moved fast and attained their most ambitious objectives. The 1st Marine Division, for example, by Sunday night had reached al-

EXODUS: After the war, Saddam vented his rage on the ethnic Kurds in the north of Iraq, attacking villages, gassing thousands and creating a vast refugee crisis

Jaber airport, half the 40-mile distance from the Saudi border to Kuwait City.

On Monday, nearly all units continued moving at rapid rates. Mass surrenders began almost with the first breaches of the Iraqi lines Sunday and by Tuesday had reached 30,000; by war's end the number had easily passed 100,000. They came out of col-

lapsed bunkers, waving handkerchiefs, underwear, anything white. About 40 Iraqis tried to surrender to a reconnaissance drone, turning round and round, waving their arms as the pilotless drone circled above.

Oddly, though, this day of burgeoning victory, brought the one U.S. tragedy of the war. An Iraqi Scud missile heading for Saudi Arabia broke up in flight: the warhead plunged onto an American barracks near the huge base at Dhahran. The blast killed 28 soldiers, causing in an eye blink almost a third of all American battle deaths in the entire war. An additional 90 soldiers were injured, many seriously.

On Tuesday, residents of Kuwait City awoke to the sound of tanks revving up. The Iraqis were pulling out, sparing the city, its inhabitants and the allied forces closing in the agonies of house-to-house fighting. By afternoon Kuwaiti resistance fighters said they were in control of the city.

Outside the city, said a U.S. briefing officer, "the whole country is full of people escaping and evading." Though some allied commanders described the Iraqi pullback as an orderly fighting retreat, at times it looked like a pell-mell bugout. Roads leading north toward the Iraqi city of Basra, military headquarters for the Kuwait theater, were so jammed with vehicles and troops that a pilot from the carrier U.S.S. *Ranger* in the gulf said it looked like "the road to Daytona Beach at spring break." Correspondents touring the road at week's end found mile after mile of blasted, twisted, burned, shattered tanks, trucks and other vehicles, many still incongruously carrying loot from Kuwait City: children's toys, carpets, television sets.

Some allied units had reached the Euphrates as early as Monday; by Wednesday morning they were established in enough force to prevent further crossings. British units cut the main Kuwait City–Basra highway early in the day; American Marines had reached it farther to the south the previous afternoon. The gate had slammed shut on Saddam's forces in Kuwait. Their escape routes were broken. Encirclement was complete.

The day was dominated by the two big tank battles of the war. U.S. Marines ran into a major Iraqi armored force at Kuwait International Airport. The sky was so dark because of the heavy smoke from oil wells set afire by the Iraqis that Marine Major General Michael Myatt had to read a map by flashlight. The Marines nonetheless resumed the battle by what light there was, and late in the day reported having destroyed all 100 Iraqi tanks they had engaged.

In a far bigger clash along the Kuwait-Iraq border, American and British troops pushing eastward after their flanking maneuver through the desert finally broke the Republican Guard. British troops encountered some guard units as early as Monday night, destroying a third of their armor at the first blow with long-range artillery fire and aerial attack. Fighting between American troops and guard units also began Monday and steadily intensified; by nightfall Monday a briefer reported one of the guard's seven divisions in the area rendered "basically ineffective." The big battle raged all day Wednesday. U.S. M1A1 tanks proved superior in maneuverability and firepower to Iraq's best, the Soviet-built T-72s. One U.S. officer said: "basically we are chasing them across the plains, shooting as we go."

In a few more hours, the shooting officially ended. At 5 a.m. (9 p.m. Wednesday in Washington) Bush went on TV to announce that he was ordering a suspension of all offensive action, to take effect three hours later. Since it was a unilateral action, it was not officially a cease-fire, but it had the same result. Shooting stopped at 8 a.m., and only sporadic incidents broke the silence as the weekend began.

Such overwhelming success may be unrepeatable. The U.S. and its partners are unlikely to face soon, or ever, another combination of a cause so clear that it unites a mighty coalition; ideal terrain for high-tech warfare; a dispirited and war-weary enemy army; an almost total lack of opposition in the air; and an adversary, Saddam, who made nearly every blunder in the book. ∎

DEVASTATION: In the last hours of the war, Iraqis fleeing Kuwait City on the highway to Basra were easy prey for superior allied air power

February 4, 1991

Norman Schwarzkopf

Proud, petulant—and prescient—he heads up Operation Desert Shield

THE MAN WHO COMMANDS THE VAST MILITARY MIGHT of the allied coalition in the gulf is a passionately engaged leader of considerable talents and, what's more, possessed of a startling, prophetic mind. As long ago as 1983, General Norman Schwarzkopf foresaw the possibility that the U.S. might one day find itself at war in the Middle East. Five days before Saddam Hussein launched his invasion, Schwarzkopf's staff happened to be running an exercise predicated on the possibility that Iraq might overrun Kuwait. All that was necessary after that was for Schwarzkopf to polish his plan. It became Operation Desert Shield.

OLD HAND: An Army brat, Schwarzkopf first went to the Middle East at age 12

DENNIS BRACK—BLACK STAR

After directing—on perilously short notice—the biggest buildup of U.S. forces since Vietnam, Schwarzkopf is orchestrating a complex war machine comprising forces from 28 allied nations totaling 675,000 troops, hundreds of ships and thousands of airplanes and tanks, all fully equipped and operating, says the Pentagon, right on schedule. At the same time, Schwarzkopf has demonstrated the talents of a first-rate diplomat, achieving cohesion not only among the traditionally rivalrous U.S. military services but also among the Arab and Western allies with all their conflicting interests.

"Initially," says a British commander, "we were taken aback by his gung-ho appearance, but in a very short time we came to realize that here was a highly intelligent soldier—a skilled planner, administrator and battlefield commander." Schwarzkopf's old friends regard him with unalloyed admiration if not

outright idolatry. Retired Army General Ward LeHardy, who was Schwarzkopf's West Point roommate, insists that "Norm is this generation's Doug MacArthur. He's got the tactical brilliance of Patton, the strategic insight of Eisenhower and the modesty of Bradley." Many people might quarrel with the modesty part. Schwarzkopf can be charming, but he also possesses the ego—and petulance—of a field marshal. He has been known to pore over his press clippings, underlining criticisms. He has epic temper tantrums. What is most striking about Schwarzkopf, however, is his abiding certitude, a bristling self-assurance, the kind that many Army brats acquire with their first pair of long pants.

Schwarzkopf's father H. Norman Sr. was also a West Pointer; from 1942 to '48, he led a mission to Iran. Norm Jr.'s first overseas posting, at 12, was to Tehran with his father, and the exposure to the exotic ways of the Middle East was to have a lasting impact on his sensibilities. After a year, he was packed off to European schools, where he dreamed all the while of a military career. At West Point, the young plebe was known variously as Norm, Schwarzie, Bear and, in recognition of his notorious temper, Stormin' Norman.

After graduating in 1956, Schwarzkopf took on various Army assignments and later served two tours in Vietnam, first as a paratrooper advising Vietnamese airborne troops, then as commander of an infantry battalion. Twice he was wounded in action; three times he won a Silver Star. On one occasion, he tiptoed into a minefield to rescue a wounded soldier; it scared him to death, he told a reporter later.

What he gained was the conviction that the Vietnam debacle resulted from a failure of public and political support for the military. Bitterly, he determined that the U.S. should never again engage in a limited war with ill-defined aims.

He has no such reservations about the Gulf War; he wants only to win it fast and suffer the fewest casualties possible. In the war room as in the field, noncoms and enlisted soldiers are as devoted to Schwarzkopf as his officers. None seem overly intimidated by his gruffness, his size (6 ft. 3 in., 240 lbs.) or even his flare-ups. He is, after all, the Bear, whom some describe as only part grizzly and the rest Teddy. His wife Brenda and their three children know him as a pussycat: an outdoorsman, an amateur magician, a cookie muncher, a fellow who lulls himself to sleep listening to tapes of Pavarotti or the sounds of honking geese and mountain streams. So what if he likes Charles Bronson movies?

Schwarzkopf is concerned that his long hours in the Riyadh war room prevent him from visiting his troops as often as he would like. When he does venture out, he is always accompanied by four military bodyguards in civilian clothes. On a recent tour, Schwarzkopf gazed across the Saudi border into Kuwait and declared that it was the most peaceful moment he had had in weeks. Then it was the general speaking: surveying the vast expanse of desert, Stormin' Norman pronounced it perfect for tank warfare. ∎

The First and the Last

Lieut. Commander Michael Scott Speicher was the first American to die in the Gulf War—if he is dead. On Jan. 16, 1991, Speicher's F/A-18 Hornet was shot down over Iraq. Pentagon officials assumed—and Iraq claimed—that Speicher was killed. But a 1995 U.S. inspection of the crash site found no trace of human remains and some evidence that Speicher had ejected before the crash. In 2001 his status was changed to Missing in Action. The last man killed in combat during the Gulf War was either Chief Warrant Officer Robert Godfrey, 28, or Staff Sergeant Tony Applegate, 32. Both died in the last two hours before the Feb. 28, 1991, cease-fire.

Female Casualties

Fifteen American women in uniform died in the Gulf War. Both as a percentage of the overall size of deployed forces and the length of time over which they served—only a few short weeks—more women died at a much faster pace in the gulf than in any other U.S. war. Seven women died in Vietnam, 18 in Korea and just more than 400 in World War II; each of those wars lasted for years.

Clipped Wings

Early in the war, Iraq flew more than 130 of its best airplanes to Iran for safekeeping. They are indeed safe: Iran has refused to return them, claiming that Baghdad owes Tehran billions of dollars in reparations from the Iran-Iraq war in the '80s.

> **"Travel light, freeze at night."**
> **—Soldiers' motto in the Gulf War**

Hardware

RAYTHEON

DEPARTMENT OF DEFENSE

Antimissile Missiles, Antiradar Planes

The Patriot missile system may have a disputed record at shooting down incoming Scuds, but it scored a direct hit in terms of public relations. Originally designed in the late 1970s to strike enemy aircraft, the Patriot was retooled in the mid-1980s to shoot down missiles. The Pentagon initially claimed that the Patriot was stopping 80% of the incoming missiles against which it was launched, then 70%, then 50%, then 40%. A congressional investigation later concluded that the true figure was more like 9%—a figure still hotly disputed by the Department of Defense and the Patriot's manufacturer.

The Air Force was flying the F-117A Stealth fighter for almost a decade before admitting it existed. Made of high-tech composite materials, shaped like an arrowhead and designed without any radar-friendly right angles, the plane is nearly invisible to electronic tracking and difficult to spot visually. During the Gulf War, Stealth fighters flew more than 1,300 sorties and scored direct hits on more than 1,600 targets in Iraq.

RALPH CRANE—TIMEPIX

The Home Front

The tentacles of war spread far beyond the battlefield to touch our lives—and change our society. World War II found Americans pitching in as one. Vietnam left us frayed and bitter. And the terrorist attacks of 2001 made us one nation under a motto: United We Stand

▲ **Safe Home!**
Mrs. Earl Godfrey, left, bids farewell to (we suspect) her husband. Young Godfrey isn't happy.

◄ A Woman's Place
Women streamed into the work force in World War II. Here Mary Farley, 20, works on a Wright Whirlwind airplane motor.

▼ A Run on These Colors
Workers at the Flag Center in Miami's Little Havana neighborhood struggle to meet the huge demand after the terrorist attacks of 2001.

WELCOME HOME SOLDIER
USA IS PROUD OF YOU

▲ Sign of the Times
Vietnam veterans, like this one in 1971, came back to a country that only wanted to forget them.

► Guess Who Won?
New Yorkers gathered in Times Square to cheer victory over Japan, August 17, 1945.

▶ **Peace Corps**

A young girl flashes the peace sign to police who have detained her at an antiwar gathering in the Vietnam era. Despite his official headgear, the gent on the left is perhaps not a police officer.

▲ **The Last Kiss**

Famed photographer Alfred Eisenstaedt shot a soldier saying farewell to his lady friend at New York City's Pennsylvania Station.

▲ **Joy**

The family of former Vietnam POW Robert Stirm greets him at Travis Air Force Base, California.

▶ **Grow Your Own**

Harry Ducote tends the victory garden he planted at his center-city parking lot in New Orleans. His crops: corn, radishes, tomatoes, lettuce.

WAR GARDENS FOR VICTORY

GROW VITAMINS AT YOUR KITCHEN DOOR

Enter VICTORY GARDEN CONTEST

PARKING *and* WASHING 60¢

▲ This Train Ain't Bound for Glory

While U.S. soldiers fought for freedom abroad in World War II, many Japanese Americans were sent to detention camps at home. Here a group awaits the ride to a camp, circa 1944.

▶ Steady, Old Paint

Newberry, Fla., residents Renee Linzalone, right, and daughter Tara join thousands of Americans in showing their patriotic colors after the terrorist attacks of Sept. 11, 2001.

KEEP THESE HANDS OFF!

BUY the Now VICTORY BONDS

▲**All Together Now**
Back from the Gulf War, an infantryman from the 24th Mechanized Divison greets his family, March 8, 1991.

▼**Hawk—or Eagle?**
The taxonomy may be tough, but the message is clear: Lyndon Johnson is a ferocious American raptor at this 1967 antiwar rally in New York City's Central Park.

▲**Buy Bonds!**
Lena Horne and pianist Silky Hendricks, with other members of the Jungleers band at rear, perform at a war bond show after touring the Pacific, 1945.

▶ **Old Yeller**
Yellow ribbon, a symbol of remembrance since the days of the frontier West, was still popular during the Gulf War in 1991.

In Support of American Troops in The Persian Gulf
Yellow Ribbon 1/2 Price

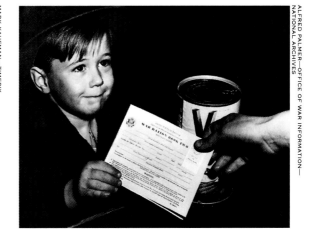

▲ This Just In …
Bacon, eggs and Tomahawk missiles are on the menu at a coffee shop in Rock Falls, Ill., the day after the allied bombing of Baghdad began.

▲ Shopping by the Book
Food shortages forced rationing during World War II. This boy—wearing Dad's hat?—proffers a War Ration certificate at a grocery store.

◄ An Old Soldier Fades Away—Not!
After he was fired by President Truman, General Douglas MacArthur was fêted coast to coast. Here he inhales ticker tape in New York City.

WHEN WAR COMES HOME: Photographer James Nachtwey has traveled around the world to document conflicts. On Sept. 11, 2001, he ran a few short blocks from his apartment to shoot this picture of fire fighters amid the ruins of the World Trade Center.

Other Soldiers, Other Fronts

Not all conflicts are wars, and as we learned in the deadly 2001 terrorist attacks on New York City and Washington, not all soldiers wear uniforms

IN JANUARY 1961, JOHN F. KENNEDY PROMISED THAT THE U.S. would "pay any price, bear any burden, meet any hardship, support any friend, oppose any foe" in its mission to safeguard not only American interests but also to "to assure the survival and the success of liberty."

Both the price and the burden turned out to be greater than even a cold warrior like Kennedy might have imagined. When the new President uttered those words in his Inaugural Address—11 years after Harry Truman sent U.S. troops to defend South Korea—the public was still struggling with the idea that U.S. foreign policy now demanded that Americans in uniform might be called upon at any time to risk their lives in faraway parts of the world, in hamlets whose names they couldn't spell.

When the U.S. embassy in Iran was stormed in 1979 and U.S. soldiers and diplomatic workers were taken hostage, the events horrified us, but they still seemed remote. The terrorist attacks on New York City and Washington in September 2001 ushered in a new, more frightening era. Suddenly we were forced to accept that the risks might appear on our own streets, in the buildings in which we live and work—and that the uniforms of our protectors might be worn by fire fighters and police officers as well as soldiers, sailors and airmen.

The earlier chapters of this book recall the full-scale wars in which U.S. soldiers were asked to spill their blood and perhaps sacrifice their lives. This chapter remembers that Americans of all kinds have struggled and died in places and in ways that not so long ago would have been difficult to imagine.

If anyone had predicted during the first half of this century that American soldiers would someday lay down their lives in Beirut or Somalia (in peacetime, no less), they might have been laughed at. If someone had imagined in 1970 that within a decade dozens of American embassy workers might be taken hostage by a Third World country and held for more than a year, with the U.S. military unable to free them, the idea might have been deemed fantasy. And if anybody had entertained the thought, as recently as the summer of 2001, that a conspiracy of suicidal religious zealots would succeed in infiltrating the U.S. to turn civilian airliners into weapons of mass destruction and kill thousands of innocent American civilians … well, who among us would have believed that?

Kennedy understood that America could not lead the free world and remain free from sacrifice. The numerous military and civilian engagements recounted in the following chapter tote up leadership's price. And they suggest that power and peril are linked almost inextricably. It is perhaps not a coincidence that the most grievous attack Americans have ever suffered on our own soil came at the moment of our nation's greatest ascendancy, after the cold war had been won and the U.S.

BACK AT YOU: A U.S. soldier in Afghanistan, where the Taliban regime that harbored Islamist terrorists was toppled

appeared to lack a serious political, military or economic rival.

The events of Sept. 11, 2001, taught us two things. First, that safeguarding America's interests requires more vigilance, not less—a greater readiness and a higher degree of sacrifice than we had ever imagined. And second, that the civilian heroes who died at ground zero and on Flight 93 prove that Americans will answer this call. As Kennedy put it in 1961, "This much we pledge, and more." Forty years later, New York City Mayor Rudolph Giuliani seemed to echo Kennedy when he described the toll of lives at the World Trade Center as: "More than any of us can bear." The "more" turns out to be the hard part. ∎

James Nachtwey

Don't call James Nachtwey a war photographer. "I'm an antiwar photographer," he insists. Indeed, Nachtwey's pictures are desolate, eloquent portraits of the human suffering that war leaves in its wake. "I want to wake people up," he explains, "to see war through the eyes of those suffering it."

In the cause of waking people up, Nachtwey has been gassed in South Korea, reported dead in Sri Lanka and infected with dengue fever in Central Africa. He has also endured a series of perilous close calls. In Bosnia, a bullet hit his car and pierced the headrest of his seat. In South Africa, as Nachtwey struggled to rescue a fatally wounded colleague, a bullet passed so close to his skull that it parted his hair. Along the way, he has won the Robert Capa Gold Medal for photojournalism of "exceptional courage" five times and been named the Magazine Photographer of the Year six times.

Attending Dartmouth during the Vietnam War, the young James Nachtwey knew instinctively that he wanted to be a photographer. "It was a time of revolution in the U.S., and I was interested in this drama," he says. "To experience danger, to tax myself in extreme situations. To go to war, but not to kill anyone." After studying art

EUGENE PIERCE

history and political science (both of which would later inform his work), Nachtwey taught himself photography and in 1981 headed for Northern Ireland. Since then he has been drawn to locations where tensions and body counts have risen: Lebanon, El Salvador, Nicaragua, Romania, Zaïre, Rwanda, Somalia, Bosnia, Kosovo, Sudan, Chechnya, Afghanistan —and, on the morning of Sept. 11, 2001—New York City's World Trade Center, only blocks from his apartment. Having returned from overseas the night before, he ran to the site that morning and was nearly killed when the towers collapsed in front of him.

"The strength of photography lies in its ability to evoke a sense of humanity," Nachtwey says. "If war is an attempt to negate humanity, then photography can be perceived as the opposite of war. And if it's used well, it can be a powerful ingredient in the antidote to war."

Playground

In 1982 a Nicaraguan boy twirls himself around the turret gun of a tank, which had been placed in a park to celebrate the overthrow of the Somoza regime. "I am a witness to history," the photographer says. "It is a job full of sadness, but it is something I am driven, compelled, to do."

▲Over the Barriers

A Palestinian youth jumps over a roadblock of flaming tires during a 1988 uprising in the West Bank. Says Nachtwey: "If I can upset people, if I can ruin their day, if I can make them see that something unacceptable is going on, then I have done my job."

▶A Brother Lost

At a cemetary in Afghanistan, a burka-clad woman mourns her brother, slain in 1996 during the nation's long civil war.

▶Wounded

Comrades cradle a Nicaraguan rebel in 1984. Nachtwey's images have been compared with classical paintings, but he claims the resonance is not intended. "If there's a similarity," he says, "it's because those paintings were taken from life as well."

▶ War in Our House

Survivors of the attack on New York City's
World Trade Center make their way north to
safety after the collapse of the Twin Towers.
Nachtwey, who has shot battles all around the
world, woke up on September 11, 2001, to
find a war zone only blocks from his home.

▲Up There!
A member of an anti-Taliban tank crew points out an American jet attacking al-Qaeda positions in 2001. The blast from the American plane's bombing run can be seen in the background.

◄The Mourners
Women grieve for family members in Kosovo. Black-and-white film, Nachtwey believes, "allows me to say more, to be more graphic, to get to the essence of emotion. Color is more limiting."

▲ In the Bedroom

A Croatian militiaman takes aim. "What makes this picture poignant for me," Nachtwey says, "is that it's taking place in a bedroom, where people share love and their most intimate moments, where life itself is conceived. And now it's become a killing ground."

▶ Intifadeh, 2001

Palestinians hurl Molotov cocktails at Israeli troops. Photographing warfare puts Nachtwey, in his words, "on the stage, along with the actors. And the script is being written as you go."

UNDER FIRE: A U.S.
soldier bolts for cover
in Santo Domingo

ARTHUR SCHATZ—TIMEPIX

Skirmishes

When trouble erupts—from Africa to the Caribbean to the Middle East—
America deploys troops to keep the peace. Too often, that means war

It's a cry almost as old as the Republic: "Send in the Marines!" More than 200 years ago, in 1801, President Thomas Jefferson sent a handful of Marines to Tripoli to punish the Barbary pirates, and a century later some 2,500 U.S. servicemen were rushed to China to help put down the Boxers, who had been attacking diplomatic missions in Beijing. When the U.S. became a global superpower after World War II, the need to send young Americans overseas to protect the interests of the U.S. arose more frequently. These can be demanding, difficult operations— and some of them are far from pretty. The following dispatches report on five U.S. actions in foreign lands; more could be added, from the deployment of Marines to Lebanon in 1958 to the invasion of Grenada in 1983 to the significant (and successful) NATO *bombing and peace-keeping operations in the Balkans in the 1990s.*

May 7, 1965

From Coup to War

Led by tanks with 90-mm cannon and armored troop carriers, the 2nd Battalion of the 6th U.S. Marines rolled across the red dust of a once trim polo field on the western outskirts of Santo Domingo and moved cautiously into the war-torn capital of the Dominican Republic. As the columns churned down Avenida Independencia, past the empty side streets, people appeared in windows and doorways. Some waved. Others stared. A few spoke. "I wish the Americans would take us over," muttered a woman.

In counterpoint to those desperate words of welcome, the rattle and burp of rebel gunfire echoed from the smoking city center barely a mile up the road. Down the street went the Marines, most of them green, all of them

scared, grimly clutching M-14 rifles, M-60 machine guns and 3.5-in. bazookas. Now the firing grew in intensity, and rebel bullets whined past the U.S. troops. Near the U.S. embassy, two Marines caught the full blast from a hidden machine-gun nest in an unfinished building a short distance away. Nine more were wounded before the bazooka men came up to blast the nest to shreds.

At approximately the same time, a battalion of the U.S. 82nd Airborne Division rolled out of San Isidro airbase, 14 miles away on the other side of the city. Linking up with loyal Dominican troops, the G.I.s drove up to the bridge spanning the Ozama River—and into another volley of rebel fire. Three hours passed and the casualty toll mounted to 20 wounded before the U.S. forces could declare their objectives secured: the paratroopers to clear the approaches to the Duarte Bridge into Santo

Domingo, the Marines to carve a 3.5-sq.-mi. "international zone" out of the city as a refuge for U.S. nationals and anyone else who hoped to remain alive in a city gone berserk in the bloodiest civil war in recent Latin American history. It was the first time that U.S. troops had gone ashore on business in the Caribbean since 1916, the first time since 1927, when Marines landed in Nicaragua, that U.S. forces had intervened in any Latin American nation. ■

October 31, 1983

Carnage in Lebanon

It was early Sunday morning in Lebanon, the beginning of an October day that promised even in that strife-riven country to draw crowds to the beaches and strollers to the corniches. Only the cooks were up and about in the reinforced-concrete Aviation Safety Building on the edge of the Beirut International Airport, used as headquarters by the Eighth Marine Battalion, the U.S. element of an international peace-keeping force.

Built around a courtyard, the structure contained a gymnasium, a reading room and the administrative offices for the battalion. It was also sleeping quarters for some 200 Marines; most were still in their cots, enjoying the luxury of Sunday, the one day of the week when they were free from reveille. Suddenly a truck, laden with dynamite, on a fanatical suicide mission, exploded with such force that the structure collapsed in seconds, killing or wounding most of the Marines inside. By evening the toll, still incomplete as rescuers picked through the rubble, stood at 147 dead, 60 wounded. [Note: TIME's story was written the day of the incident; the final death toll was higher: 241.—ED.]

For the U.S. armed forces, it was the worst disaster since the end of the Vietnam War a decade ago. The terrorist attack illustrated in the most grisly fashion possible just how risky it is for the U.S. to venture into a region that has been plagued for centuries by factionalism and hatred.

The attack began at exactly 6:20 a.m., when a red pickup truck approached the airport, where most of the 1,600-man Marine contingent in Lebanon is based. As the vehicle turned left into the parking lot, a Marine guard reported with alarm that it was gathering speed. Then, in a lightning move, the truck charged toward the entrance of the four-story building, hit the sandbagged guard post, burst through a barrier and vaulted another wall of sandbags into the lobby. It exploded with a deafening roar, destroying the building. A cloud of acrid smoke hung over a scene of utter desolation.

All across the nation on Sunday night, Marine Corps officers walked up to homes and apartments to inform Americans that their sons or brothers or fathers or husbands had died under the twisted, smoking debris in Beirut. ■

AFTERMATH: Marines evacuate a comrade after the Beirut bombing. A building housing French soldiers was also bombed, killing 58.

TAKE COVER! Amid a firefight, a U.S. soldier shields Panamanian civilians while shouting orders

January 1, 1990

Showing Muscle

The invasion of Panama—the biggest American military operation since the Vietnam War—was supposed to accomplish three goals: 1) swiftly rout resistance; 2) capture the country's dictator, Manuel Antonio Noriega, and bring him to trial in the U.S. on drug-running charges; 3) install a stable, democratic government headed by politicians who had apparently won May elections, which Noriega later overruled.

It was impossible to tell whether the invasion would end up more like Vietnam or Grenada. Some 24,000 U.S. troops had quickly taken command of most of Panama and overwhelmed organized resistance by the Panama Defense Forces, Noriega's combination army and police. But Noriega got away and was thought to be hiding in the forests or even in the sprawling capital city itself.

American troops faced a tough battle to restore order in Panama City, where Noriega's misnamed Dignity Battalions, a paramilitary force, were putting up a street-to-street fight. Noriega's loyalists staged hit-and-run attacks. On Friday, two days after American military commanders began declaring victory, they fired shells at the headquarters of the U.S. Southern Command. The Pentagon admitted that its forces had encountered stiffer resistance than expected, and Bush ordered an additional 2,000 troops to Panama as reinforcements. ∎

October 18, 1993

Anatomy of a Disaster

For Carlos Rodriguez the battle was a few seconds of terror, hours of agonized waiting. While his comrades stormed the building near the Olympic Hotel in Mogadishu to try to snatch Somali warlord Mohammed Farrah Aidid, Rodriguez and the rest of his squad swarmed down ropes from a helicopter and began a security patrol through a nearby street. "It was bright daylight; there were windows and doors all around us, and you can't watch all of them all the time," said Rodriguez, an Army Ranger specialist four. "All of a sudden the Somalis just opened up on us, small arms and grenades. There was shooting from all directions, and we couldn't see who was shooting at us. I saw a muzzle once, sticking around a corner, and I shot at it." Almost instantly, though, Rodriguez himself "got shot in the right hip. Then I got some shrapnel in my left foot and a little bit in my face. It broke some bones, and I was down. Our squad leader got hit too. It got pretty confusing."

The confusion only grew worse. "Some of our buddies pulled us into a room" in a nearby house," recalled Rodriguez. "There were four of us in there wounded … I was bleeding pretty good but [a unit medic] came and put pressure pants on me." (These are inflatable sleeves used to immobilize limbs and stop bleeding.) Then "we

INFAMY: Somalis parade a fallen American's body through the streets of Mogadishu

just sat and waited"—for almost eight hours, until rescuers arrived. "We couldn't get medevacked [taken out by helicopter]. I don't know exactly why."

By the time Rodriguez gave TIME this account from a hospital bed in Landstuhl, Germany—in an interview cut short by a general who arrived to pin a Purple Heart on him—the rest of the world knew why the rescue had been so delayed. Just as his unit was being shot at, the Rangers storming the building near the Olympic Hotel looking for Aidid were also being hit by murderous fire. Helicopter troops nonetheless captured the hotel and environs and bagged more than 19 Aidid supporters. But as they tried to lead the prisoners away, the streets erupted with gunfire. Somali fighters from all over Mogadishu ran to join the action; in the Bakahara market near the hotel, they set up barricades of burning tires and anything else flammable to block the Rangers' retreat. Rescue helicopters could not land in the narrow streets. With three U.S. helicopters down, the only way out was by ground.

From that point on, Ranger Major David Stockwell, the U.N. military spokesman, said, "it sounded like the air was filled with angry hornets. The buzz and crack of small-arms fire was all around" the pinned-down Rangers, as two rescue columns fought to reach them. One, a Quick Reaction Force riding unarmored trucks and humvees, could not get through. Pakistani, Malaysian and U.S. troops—some, ironically, aboard Soviet-made armored personnel carriers—finally made it to the scene 10 hours after the Rangers came under attack.

By then, though, the Rangers had suffered a shocking toll: 14 dead, plus one who died four days later, and 77 wounded, including Rodriguez. Known to be taken prisoner: one. A mortar attack by Aidid's men on Ranger forces at the Mogadishu airport Wednesday night killed another American and wounded 12 more. ∎

Walking a Thin Line

Despite the chaos in Haiti's streets, U.S. troops secured one objective after another with clocklike precision. On Monday, American MPs moved into five of Port-au-Prince's most notorious police precincts. Then on Tuesday, U.S. forces secured Haiti's simple white parliament building.

Meanwhile, out in the countryside the disintegration of the Haitian military left a yawning power vacuum. In the north, civil authority virtually collapsed following the fire fight on Sept. 24 in which a company of Marines cut down 10 Haitian police officers. Since then, the army and police have evaporated throughout the region.

The total number of U.S. troops serving in the Haitian campaign—some 28,800—eclipses the 26,000 Americans who invaded Panama in 1989 and the 25,800 sent to Somalia. ∎

PEDRO UGARTE—AFP

YANKEE STAY HERE: Most Haitians—like those watching from a boat in Port-au-Prince Harbor— hailed the arrival of U.S. troops to end the unrest in their nation

Hostages

IDOL: In the holy city of Qum, fervent believers hail the Ayatullah on his return to Iran in 1979

After a religious revolution topples Iran's government, its leader brands the U.S. "the Great Satan"—and ordinary Americans are held in captivity

When Iran's foremost Islamic cleric, the Ayatullah Ruhollah Khomeini, returned to his nation in triumph after 15 years in exile, the days of the pro-U.S. regime of Shah Reza Pahlavi were clearly numbered. After the Shah's government fell, the religious uprising raged out of control: within months, anti-Western radicals took over the U.S. embassy in Tehran, seizing 52 Americans as hostages—not only Marines, but also code clerks, secretaries and political officers. After five months, with America's patience dwindling, President Jimmy Carter dispatched a rescue mission that failed miserably. The Iranians held the hostages in their grasp for another nine months, releasing them the day Ronald Reagan was inaugurated and Carter was no longer President.

February 12, 1979

Khomeini Returns

The chartered Air France 747 circled over the city and passed the nearby Elburz Mountains three times before settling down gently on the tarmac of Tehran's Mehrabad Airport. A frail old man, wearing a black turban and ankle-length robes, stepped out of the aircraft's door into the chill February morning. His back hunched, he clutched the arm of an Air France purser as he walked down the portable ramp to touch Iranian soil. After 15 years in exile, Ayatullah Ruhollah Khomeini, 78, spiritual leader of a revolution that has been building to a frightening climax, had come home at last. The moment was, conceivably, the

start of a new era for a country that has seemed dangerously out of control.

Iran went wild with joy. From all across the country, millions of people thronged into the capital; they lined the 20-mile route out to Behesht Zahra Cemetery, where many of the martyrs of the revolution are buried, to catch a glimpse of the Ayatullah. There, in Lot 17, he prayed and delivered a 30-minute funeral oration for the dead.

From his bungalow outside Paris, the Ayatullah had been sending home a steady stream of *Elamiehs*, messages summoning the faithful to bring down the monarchy in favor of what he has somewhat vaguely termed an Islamic republic. Much of the population heeded Khomeini. It was popular uprising in his name that forced the hated Shah Reza Pahlavi to take a vacation that might well extend to exile, and left the government in the uncertain hands of Prime Minister Shahpour Bakhtiar. Iron-willed, giving little hint of compromise, Khomeini has rejected the government because it was appointed by the Shah.

Despite unconfirmed reports that Iran was being flooded with weapons, including some purportedly provided by the Palestine Liberation Organization, pro-Khomeini demonstrations have been remarkably peaceful and well disciplined. ∎

November 19, 1979

Blackmailing the U.S

It was an ugly, shocking image of innocence and impotence, of tyranny and terror, of madness and mob rule. Blindfolded and bound, employees of the U.S. embassy in Tehran were paraded last week before vengeful crowds while their youthful captors gloated and jeered. On a gray Sunday morning, students invoking the name of Iran's Ayatullah Ruhollah Khomeini invaded the embassy, overwhelmed its Marine Corps guards and took some 60 Americans as hostages. Their demand: surrender the deposed Shah of Iran, currently under treatment in Manhattan for cancer, as the price of the Americans' release.

While flatly refusing to submit to such outrageous blackmail, the U.S. was all but powerless to free the victims. As the days passed, nerves became more frayed. A wave of anger spread across the U.S. On campuses, Iranian flags were torched and the Ayatullah Khomeini was burned in effigy.

The crisis began on Sunday, Nov. 4. Hundreds of protesters gathered in downtown Tehran outside the U.S. embassy, a 27-acre compound surrounded by ten- and twelve-foot brick walls and secured with metal gates. The students, most of whom were unarmed, chanted anti-American slogans and carried banners: DEATH TO AMERICA IS A BEAUTIFUL THOUGHT and GIVE US THE SHAH. At the very same hour, the Ayatullah Khomeini was telling a student in the holy city of Qum, some 80 miles to the south, that the American embassy in his country's capital was "a nest of spies" and "a center of intrigue."

That was all the inspiration the students needed. Just before 11 a.m., someone with a pair of powerful shears managed to break the chain that held together the gates on Taleghani Street, and the crowd surged through. Once inside the compound, some headed for the ambassador's residence, where the servants offered no resistance (there has been no U.S. Ambassador in Tehran since William Sullivan left in April). Others tried to take over the chancellery but found it protected with armor plating and grillwork. Using bullhorns, they shouted at the occupants: "Give up and you won't be harmed! If you don't give up, you will be killed!" As the attackers struggled to get inside, other protesters and a crowd of curiosity seekers clambered over the embassy walls and swarmed through the compound.

Inside the two-story brick chancellery building, known to Americans as "Fort Apache" for its special security reinforcements, Marine guards donned flak jackets and gas masks and ordered everyone to the top floor. There, in the ambassador's office, Political Officer Victor Romseth was on the phone to the embassy's ranking officer, Chargé d'Affaires L. Bruce Laingen, who was at the Foreign Ministry. Just before 1 p.m., Laingen ordered: "Final destruction." Embassy officers grabbed files from safes and began shredding and burning classified documents.

Finally, after stalling as long as possible, a Marine opened the door, and students rushed in, their eyes moist from tear gas. The students grabbed the

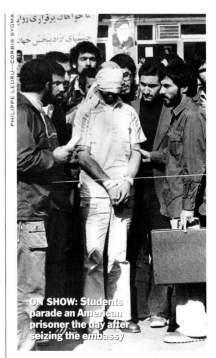

ON SHOW: Students parade an American prisoner the day after seizing the embassy

masks of the Americans. Said one attacker: "We had the gas for three hours. You can taste it for a while." Then they blindfolded the embassy staff, bound their hands and made them sit on a corridor floor. Soon the students put one of their prisoners on parade, draping his body with a Khomeini poster.

No shots were fired inside the chancellery, which may have disappointed the students. Said one: "If the Marines don't shoot, we take over. If they do, we have our martyr. Either way, we win." Any hopes that embassy officials once had of preventing attackers from scaling the walls of the compound were

INFLAMED: An effigy of the Shah is burned by demonstrators outside the embassy walls

SURROUNDED: Protesters gather outside the 27-acre grounds of the U.S. embassy in the second week of its occupation by religious militants

abandoned after an assault last February, when Muslim guerrillas easily overpowered a handful of Iranian police guards and the embassy's Marines. As a result, the basic defense plan of the embassy was simply to have the Marines hold off any assault long enough for sensitive material to be destroyed.

By 4 p.m. the compound was completely in the hands of the students, who now numbered about 600. By Monday the streets outside were jammed with thousands of people.

What could Washington do? An increasing number of Americans began raising an old familiar cry: send in the Marines. Would it not be natural, if the Americans continued to be held hostage, for Washington to dispatch commandos to rescue them? TIME put this question to nearly two dozen experts. Their near unanimous negative conclusion was summed up by Elmo Zumwalt Jr., the former Chief of Naval Operations: "I think it's pretty much out of the question." Added Robert Cushman Jr., the retired Marine Corps Commandant: "You could kill a lot of Iranians, but you wouldn't save the Americans." ∎

May 5, 1980

Debacle in the Desert

Two lines of blue lights etched the outlines of the remote landing strip. Suddenly flames illuminated the night sky, then gradually flickered out. On the powdery sands of Dasht-e-Kavir, Iran's Great Salt Desert, lay the burned-out hulk of a lumbering U.S. Air Force C-130 Hercules aircraft. Nearby rested the scorched skeleton of a U.S. Navy RH-53 Sea Stallion helicopter. And in the wreckage were the burned bodies of eight American military air crewmen.

In a startlingly bold but tragic gamble, President Jimmy Carter had ordered a courageous, specially trained team of American military commandos to try to pluck the hostages out of the heavily guarded U.S. embassy in Tehran. The supersecret operation failed dismally. It ended in the desert staging site, some 250 miles short of its target in the capital city. And for the world's most technologically sophisticated nation, the reason for aborting the rescue effort was particularly

painful: three of the eight helicopters assigned to the mission developed electrical or hydraulic malfunctions that rendered them useless. For Carter in particular, and for the U.S. in general, the desert debacle was a military, diplomatic and political fiasco.

The time to move had seemed ripe. An International Red Cross visit had determined that all 50 hostages seized at the embassy were still being held in the compound. U.S. planners had learned that the number of militants guarding the captives had declined. On Thursday, April 24, the President gave the word: Go.

On Thursday afternoon, six of the team's C-130s rose from an undisclosed airfield in Egypt. The transport planes carried about 90 commandos in camouflage garb and another 90 crew members. Following an undisclosed route, the small air fleet droned along as low as 150 ft. to foil Iranian radar as it approached its first staging site in the desert near the isolated village of Poshte-Badam. Other planes are reported to have helped by jamming Iranian detection systems.

One by one, the cumbersome C-130s

roared in over the desert and landed on the strip marked out on the salt flats. Meanwhile, eight RH-53 helicopters flying in from an aircraft carrier, the U.S.S. *Nimitz,* in the Arabian Sea were finding the going much more difficult. As they emerged over land from the Gulf of Oman, flying without lights in the moonlight night, two of the choppers ran into a fierce desert sandstorm. Both developed crippling problems. One could not stay aloft because of hydraulic troubles and settled down in the bleak desert. Another helicopter crew found the disabled craft, picked up its occupants and completed the five-hour, 500-nautical-mile flight to the landing strip. The second laboring chopper discovered a faulty gyro and turned back to the *Nimitz.* Finally, six of the eight RH-53s reached their destination.

Then came a critical accident. After landing, one of the helicopters had its entire hydraulic system knocked out; the aircraft could not fly. The commanders debated whether the mission could fulfill its task with just five choppers. The plan had called for a minimum of six. Two extra had seemed a sufficient backup. Now three were out of action.

The on-site commander, an Army paratroop colonel, concluded that the diminished passenger capacity of the fleet would mean that if the later stages of the raid were not entirely successful, some of the hostages or commandos might have to be left behind in Tehran. He radioed his recommendation that the odyssey be ended to his superiors. The final decision was bucked up to President Carter at the White House.

At 4:50 p.m. in Washington, after the would-be rescuers had been on the ground in the Iranian desert for nearly four hours without being discovered, the very disappointed President agreed that the team should be recalled. Carter found one consolation. "At least there were no casualties," he said. "And there was no detection. It could have been worse."

But matters were about to get much worse. Around midnight (local time) a bus carrying some 40 Iranians had rolled along a dirt road that ran right through the landing area. Both the travelers and the Americans were startled to see each other. More radio messages were flashed across the 8,000 miles from the desert to the Pentagon. What should be done with the unexpected visitors? The final decision: put them all on a C-130 Hercules and fly them temporarily out of Iran.

The mission's most tragic moment intervened. One of the helicopters had refueled on the ground from a C-130. When the large plane's tank ran dry, the chopper lifted slightly to move toward another C-130 to pick up more fuel. But in doing so, the pilot turned his RH-53 too abruptly; its rotary blade ripped into the transport's fuselage. Instantly, flames roared through the two aircraft. Ammunition began exploding, striking other aircraft. Three Americans in the Hercules were killed. Five died in the Sea Stallion. Four others sustained severe burns, one of them hauled to safety out of the blazing C-130 by heroic efforts.

Meanwhile, a truck had come down the road and the driver escaped after a headlight was shot out by the U.S. troops. The unexpected traffic along the remote road, the certainty of discovery, the deaths of their comrades and the need to get the burn victims to hospitals all forced a difficult decision: the Americans had to leave the desert immediately. There was no time to let the wreckage cool to recover the bodies. Instead, the rescuers had to rescue themselves. They climbed into the remaining C-130s and took off. ∎

DISASTER: The severely burned body of a U.S. Marine lies amid the wreckage of a C-130 transport plane and an RH-53 helicopter in Iran

FREE AT LAST: The former hostages rejoice on their landing in Algeria en route to West Germany

February 2, 1981

The Ordeal Ends

America's joy pealed from church belfries, rippled from flag staffs and wrapped itself in a million miles of yellow ribbon, tied around trees, car antennas and even the 32-story Foshay Tower in Minneapolis. Barbara Deffley, wife of the Methodist minister in Holmer, Ill., rang the church bell 444 times, once for each day of captivity. "At about 200 pulls, I thought I'd never make it," she gasped. "Then at about 300 pulls, I got my second wind and kept going all the way."

Massachusetts House Speaker Thomas W. McGee, 56, was too impatient to wait for a ladder, so he shinnied ten feet up a pole to reach the halyard and hoist the U.S. flag over the statehouse in Boston. Patrolman Joseph McDermott coasted his cruiser to the side of a street in Rochester, N.H., fighting back tears. Said he: "I am overjoyed. I feel proud again."

Joy at the restoration of pride to a nation that had been humbled for too long by a puny tormentor was but one of the many reactions of Americans to Iran's final release of the 52 U.S. hostages last week. The mood was one of continuing celebration, from the moment the first plane carrying the former captives cleared Iranian airspace to the climactic touchdown on U.S. soil of *Freedom One* just before 3 p.m. on Jan. 25 at Stewart Airport, 50 miles north of New York City.

Before their release, the Americans endured a final episode of psychological abuse. They had been divided by their captors into at least two groups for transportation to the airport in buses with blackened windows. The Americans then were run through a gauntlet of chanting militants. While some of the hostages thought the dozens of militants forming a corridor to shout "Death to America!" at them were just performing for propaganda effect, others were genuinely frightened and reported that they had been kicked and shoved during their last steps on Iranian soil.

Champagne corks popped aboard the Air Algérie 727 as it headed west over Iran. Now the Americans were all together for the first time since their imprisonment. They embraced emotionally. They excitedly roamed the plane's aisle, comparing experiences in captivity and wondering what had been happening in the outside world during those 14⅝ months.

Americans got their first glimpse of the released hostages when the plane, after a refueling stop in Athens, landed in Algiers in a rainstorm. In the glare of television lights, Bruce Laingen, the chargé d'affaires at the Tehran embassy, led Kathryn Koob and Elizabeth Ann Swift, who wore the familiar yellow ribbons in their hair, down a ramp.

Despite beards, the faces of some of the men that followed reflected their exuberance. They flashed victory signs and clenched fists and shouted to throngs of spectators: "Thank you! Thank you! We made it!" Now the rain stopped, stars became visible and some of the Marines broke into a sprint for the waiting U.S. planes. The winner thrust his arms in the air and shouted: "God Bless America!"

Landing at Rhein-Main Air Base in Frankfurt, West Germany, before dawn on Wednesday, the Americans were rushed toward two blue buses for the 25-mile ride to a hospital in Weisbaden, where they were met by a banner proclaiming WELCOME TO THE FREEDOM HOTEL.

When the nine Marines who had been held captive first reported to the senior Marine colonel, their disheveled leader snapped off a salute and said: 'The Marine squadron from Tehran reporting for duty, sir.' Returning the salute, the smartly uniformed officer ordered them to march off to the barbershop and get rid of the beards and long hair. They did. ∎

February 9, 1981

Michael Metrinko

A former hostage looks back in anger on his days in solitary confinement

AFTER SPENDING HIS FIRST NIGHT AT HOME, ABOVE HIS family's tavern in Olyphant, Pa. (pop. 5,138), Michael Metrinko looked out the window at the gently falling snow. "I knew at that moment that at last it was over," he says. "There I was, standing in the bedroom of my boyhood. Nobody was threatening me. No one was calling for my death. I was home." For Metrinko, a 1968 Georgetown University graduate who was a political officer at the U.S. embassy in Tehran, it was a particularly blessed moment. He was one of the hostages treated most harshly by the militants. He spent a total of 261 days in solitary confinement because of his constant defiance. His captors were convinced that their Farsi-speaking prisoner was a CIA agent. They interrogated him more than a dozen times, usually late at night and for up to seven hours at a time. Says Metrinko: "They had broken into my office safe, and they had the names and phone numbers of all my Iranian friends. So they would say, 'How do you know Mr. So-and-So?' and I'd say, 'He's a friend.' But they found it hard to believe. They thought that anyone I knew had to be part of a spy network. They didn't like my attitude or my answers."

After two weeks, the militants put Metrinko into a 6-ft. by 8-ft. basement storage room that was furnished with only a mattress. Says Metrinko: "When I was awake, I'd lean it against the wall because you couldn't move around with it on the floor." He spent four months there, volunteering to scrub toilets, mop floors, "do anything that got me out of that hole." He spent many of the hours reading, including *The Gulag Archipelago,* Alexander Solzhenitsyn's grim portrait of Soviet prison life. Says Metrinko dryly: "I can't imagine a better place to read it."

In April, Metrinko was suddenly moved to a large embassy office with two windows overlooking the main street. The reason quickly became apparent: within an hour a Red Cross representative came to visit him. A day later, he was moved into a smaller office. Says Metrinko: "The new room was at least large enough to exercise in, and it had a chair, a table and a mattress." To pass the time, he drew geometric patterns on the gray walls with red, blue and green pencils. After the failed U.S. rescue mission in April, Metrinko was driven to the holy city of Qum and held for a week with two other hostages in a filthy, rat-infested prison cell whose windows were covered with blankets. He often heard the crack of a whip followed by screams; once, when a blanket fell, he caught a glimpse of some Iranians being flogged.

Metrinko passed the next two months in more pleasant quarters: a room in a onetime art gallery. He never seriously considered trying to escape, since even when he was allowed to stroll in the courtyard he was surrounded by 20 or more armed guards. Says Metrinko ruefully: "It was like a grade-B movie, but I'm not James Cagney." The Ayatullah Khomeini's son Seyyed Ahmed talked to the hostages for half an hour one day. Metrinko complained to him that the food consisted of "rice and grease" and that he was not allowed to exercise. Seyyed Ahmed ordered the guards to let the hostages go outside for regular exercise. Says Metrinko: "They didn't obey. In the next month and a half, we were only allowed outside three times."

GIVING THANKS: Metrinko attends a service at his hometown church after his release

After he was moved to a prison in Tehran in late June, Metrinko cursed his guards in Farsi as "thieves" and "liars" for taking away his watch and glasses, and denounced Khomeini as a "killer." The militants blindfolded Metrinko, punched and slapped him, and put him in an isolation cell. For two weeks he slept on its bare floor with no heat or light, except for what little came over the transom of the steel door.

Even at the last moment, Metrinko was defiant. When he was boarding the bus to go to the Algerian plane that was to fly the hostages to freedom, a guard called him an "American bastard." Replied Metrinko: "Shut up, you son of a prostitute." Guards dragged Metrinko off the bus; as it left for the airport, they punched him a few times. But he was finally taken to the airport in a car. Says Metrinko: "I was awfully close to missing the whole show."

When Metrinko got home last week, he went immediately to Sts. Cyril and Methodius Church, where he had been baptized as a child into the Ukrainian Catholic faith. He blew out the votive flame that had been lit on the 100th day of his captivity, and wept when the priest read the Sermon on the Mount. Metrinko now plans to retreat to a cabin deep in the woods for a few weeks. The hideaway has no phone or TV, but, he says, "there's a wonderful fireplace, and I'm going to spend my time chopping a lot of wood to keep the fire going." ■

HALLOWED GROUND:
A fire fighter digs through
the rubble of the Twin
Towers on Sept. 11. The
final body count: 2,823.

In Harm's Way

Thousands of innocent civilians are killed in a suicide assault as Islamist terrorists hijack U.S. jetliners and attack the symbols of America's might

Just as commuters began arriving at work on the morning of Sept. 11, 2001, New York City and Washington were hit by the most deadly strikes ever launched against America's homeland. Nineteen men, directed by Islamist militant Osama bin Laden and his international terror group, al-Qaeda, hijacked four U.S. airliners and crashed two of them into the Twin Towers of New York City's World Trade Center. A third was smashed into the Pentagon near Washington. A fourth, now thought to be intended to target the White House, was downed by passengers in Pennsylvania. For the first time since the attack on Pearl Harbor in 1941, U.S. soil became a war zone and medics, police, fire fighters and everyday citizens served as a new kind of American soldier.

September 14, 2001

Day of Infamy

On a normal day, we value heroism because it is uncommon. On Sept. 11, 2001, we valued heroism because it was everywhere. The fire fighters kept climbing the stairs of the tallest buildings in town, even as the steel moaned and the cracks spread in zippers through the walls, to get to the people trapped in the sky.

This was the bloodiest day on American soil since our Civil War, a modern Antietam played out in real time, not with soldiers but with secretaries, security guards, lawyers, bankers, janitors. It was strange that a day of war was a day we stood still. We couldn't move—that must have been the whole

idea—so we had no choice but to watch. Every city cataloged its targets; residents looked at their skylines, wondering if they would be different in the morning. It was as though someone had taken a huge brush and painted a bull's-eye around every place Americans gather, every icon we revere, every service we depend on, and vowed to take them out or shut them down, or force us to do it ourselves.

It was, of course, a perfect day: 70° and flawless skies, perfect for a nervous pilot who has stolen a huge jet and intends to turn it into a missile. It was a Boeing 767 from Boston, American Airlines Flight 11 bound for Los Angeles with 81 passengers, that first got the attention of air-traffic controllers. The plane took off at 7:59 a.m. and headed west, over the Adirondacks, before tak-

JAMES NACHTWEY—VII

ing a sudden turn south and diving down toward the heart of New York City. Meanwhile American Flight 757 had left Dulles, bound for Los Angeles; United Flight 175 left Boston for Los Angeles at 7:58, and United Flight 93 left Newark three minutes later, bound for San Francisco. All climbed into beautiful clear skies, all four planes on transcontinental flights, plump with fuel, ripe to explode. "They couldn't carry anything—other than an atom bomb—that could be as bad as what they were flying," observed a veteran investigator.

The first plane hit the World Trade Center's north tower at 8:46, ripping through the building's skin and setting its upper floors ablaze. People thought it was a sonic boom, or a construction accident, or freak lightning on a lovely fall day; at worst, a horrible airline accident, a plane losing altitude, out of control, a pilot trying to ditch in the river and missing. But as the gruesome rains came—bits of plane, a tire, office furniture, glass, a hand, a leg, whole bodies, began falling all around—people in the streets all stopped and looked,

and fell silent. As the smoke rose, the ash rained gently down, along with a whole lost flock of paper shuffling down from the sky to the street below, edges charred, plane tickets and account statements and bills and reports floating down to earth.

Almost instantly, a distant wail of sirens came from all directions, even as people poured from the building, even as a second plane bore down on lower Manhattan. Consultant Andy Perry grabbed his pal Nathan Shields from his office and they began to run down 46 flights. With each passing floor more and more people joined the flow down the steps. The lights stayed on, but the lower stairs were filled with water from burst pipes and sprinklers. The smell of jet fuel suffused the building. Hallways collapsed, flames shot out of a men's room. Perry and Shields raced into the street in time to see the second plane bearing down.

On the ground, workers tore off their shirts to make bandages and tourniquets for the wounded; others used bits of clothing as masks to help them breathe. Whole stretches of street were

slick with blood, and up and down the avenues you could hear the screams of people plunging from the burning tower. People watched in horror as a man tried to shimmy down the outside of the tower. He made it about three floors before flipping backward to the ground.

When United Flight 175, heading for California, passed the Massachusetts-Connecticut border, it made a 30-degree turn, and then an even sharper turn and swooped down on Manhattan, between the buildings, to impale the south tower at 9:02. This plane seemed to hit lower and harder; maybe that's because by now every camera in the city was trained on the towers, and the crowds in the street, refugees from the first explosion, were there to see it. Desks and chairs and people were sucked out the windows and rained down on the streets below. Men and women, cops and fire fighters watched and wept. As fire and debris fell, cars blew up; the air smelled of smoke and concrete, that smell that spits out of jackhammers chewing up pavement. You could taste the air, survivors said, more easily than you could breathe it.

ACT II: At 9:02 a.m., with the north tower of the World Trade Center already in flames, United Airlines Flight 175 slams into the south tower

IT'S FALLING! Though hit second, the south tower collapsed first, at 10:00 a.m., sending New Yorkers racing north to safety

ROBERT STOLARIK—GAMMA

The first crash had changed everything; the second changed it again. Anyone who thought the first was an accident now knew better. This was not some awful, isolated episode, not Oklahoma City, not even the first World Trade Center bombing in 1993. Now this felt like a war, and the system responded accordingly; the emergency plans came out of the drawers and clicked one by one into place. The city buckled up, the traffic stopped, the bridges and tunnels were shut down at 9:35 as warnings tumbled one after another; the Empire State Building was evacuated, then the United Nations. First the New York City airports were closed, then Washington's, and then the whole country was grounded for the first time in history.

At the moment the second plane was slamming into the south tower, President Bush was being introduced to the second-graders of Emma E. Booker Elementary in Sarasota, Fla. As he was getting ready to pose for pictures with the teachers and kids, chief of staff Andy Card entered the room, walked over to the President and whispered in his right ear. The President's face became visibly tense and serious. He nodded. Card left, and for several minutes the President seemed distracted and somber, but then he resumed his interaction with the class.

When the President emerged from the classroom, he spoke to waiting reporters. "This is a difficult time for America," he began. He ordered a mas-

sive investigation to "hunt down the folks who committed this act." Meanwhile the bomb dogs took a few extra passes through Air Force One, and an extra fighter escort was added. But the President too was going to have trouble getting home.

Even as the President spoke, the second front opened. Having hit the country's financial and cultural heart, the killers went for its political and military muscles. David Marra, 23, an information-technology specialist, had turned his BMW off an I-395 exit when he saw an American Airlines jet swooping in, its wings wobbly, looking as if it were going to slam right into the Pentagon: "It was 50 ft. off the deck when he came in. It sounded like the pilot had the throttle completely floored. The plane rolled left and then rolled right. Then he caught an edge of his wing on the ground." There is a helicopter pad right in front of the side of the Pentagon. The wing touched there, then the plane cartwheeled into the building.

But that was not all; there was a third front as well. At 9:58 the Westmoreland County emergency-operations center, 35 miles southeast of Pittsburgh, received a frantic cell-phone call from a man who said he was locked in the rest room aboard United Flight 93. Glenn Cramer, the dispatch supervisor, said the man was distraught and kept repeating: "We are being hijacked! We are being hijacked!" He also said this was not a hoax, and that the plane "was going down." Said Cramer: "He heard some sort of explosion and saw white smoke coming from the plane. Then we lost contact with him."

The plane had taken off at 8:01 from Newark, N.J., bound for San Francisco. But as it passed south of Cleveland, Ohio, it took a sudden, violent left turn and headed inexplicably back into Pennsylvania. As the 757 and its 38 passengers and seven crew members blew past Pittsburgh, air-traffic controllers tried frantically to raise the crew via radio. There was no response.

The rogue plane soared over woodland, cattle pastures and cornfields until it passed over Kelly Leverknight's home. She too was watching the news when she heard the plane rush by. "It was headed toward the school," she said, the school where her three children were.

Had Flight 93 stayed aloft a few seconds longer it would have plowed into Shanksville-Stonycreek School and its 501 students. Instead, at 10:06 a.m., the plane smashed into a reclaimed section of an old coal strip mine. [Later discoveries would confirm initial theories that the passengers aboard the flight had learned of the other attacks via telephone and had revolted against the hijackers to bring down the plane. *See* the Profiles in this section—ED.]

Back in New York City, the chaos was only beginning. Convoys of police vehicles raced downtown toward the cloud of smoke at the end of the avenues. The streets and parks filled with people, heads turned like sunflowers, all gazing south, at the clouds that were on the ground instead of in the sky, at the fighter jets streaking down the

Hudson River. The aircraft carriers U.S.S. *John F. Kennedy* and U.S.S. *George Washington* took up positions off the nation's East Coast.

Then the south tower of the World Trade Center turned into powder. The tower's structural strength had come largely from the 244 steel girders that formed the perimeter of each floor and bore most of the weight of all the floors above. Steel starts to bend at 1,000°. The floors above where the plane hit—each floor weighing millions of pounds—were resting on steel that was softening from the heat of the burning jet fuel, softening until the girders could no longer bear the load above. "All that steel turns into spaghetti," explained retired ATF investigator Ronald Baughn. "And then all of sudden that structure is untenable, and the weight starts bearing down on floors that were not designed to hold that weight, and you start having collapse." Each floor drops onto the one below, the weight becoming greater and greater, and eventually it all comes down. "It didn't topple. It came straight down. All the floors are pancaking down, and there are people on those floors."

The south tower collapsed at 10, fulfilling the prophecy of 1993, when terrorists first tried to bring it down. The north tower came down 29 minutes

CAPITAL STRIKE: With the spire of the Washington Monument looming in the background, fire fighters battle the blaze at the Pentagon, where 189 died

GREG WHITESELL—GETTY IMAGES

IN MEMORIAM: New Yorkers created impromptu shrines all around the city after the deadly attack

later, crushing itself like a piston. All that was left of the New York skyline was a chalk cloud. The towers themselves were reduced to jagged stumps; the atrium lobby arches looked like a bombed-out cathedral.

The streets filled with masked men and women, cloth and clothing torn to tie across their noses and mouths against the dense debris rain. The streets were eerily quiet. All trading had stopped on Wall Street, so those canyons were empty, the ash several inches thick. Fire fighters pushed people further back, back up north. Mayor Rudolph Giuliani took to the streets, walking through the raining dust and ordering people to evacuate the entire lower end of the island. Medical teams performed triage on the street corners of Tribeca, doling out medical supplies and tending the walking wounded. Doctors, nurses, EMTs, even lifeguards, were recruited to help.

The refugee march began at the base of the island and wound up the highways as far you could see, tens of thousands of people with clothes dusted, faces grimy, marching northward, away from the battlefield. There was not a single smile on a single face. But there was remarkably little panic as well—more steel and ingenuity. There were no strangers in town anymore, only sudden friends, sharing names, news and phones. At Bellevue Hospital, the city's largest trauma center, an extra burn unit was set up in the emergency room. The night shift was called in early. By 5:40, only 149 patients had

been admitted—which suggested not how few had been injured, but how few could be saved.

After Air Force One took off from Florida, the mood aboard could not have been more tense. Vice President Dick Cheney told the President that the White House and Air Force One were both targets. Bush, the Vice President insisted, should head to a safe military base as soon as possible. White House staff members, Air Force flight attendants and Secret Service agents all were subdued and shaken. One agent sadly reported that the Secret Service field office in New York City, with its 200 agents, was located in the World Trade Center. The plane's TV monitors were tuned in to local news programs. Bush was watching as the second tower collapsed. About 45 minutes after takeoff, a decision was made to fly to Offutt Air Force Base in Ne-

UNITED WE STAND: The President salutes a hero on his visit to ground zero three days after the attack

braska, site of the nation's nuclear command and one of the most secure military installations in the country. But Bush and his aides didn't want to wait that long before he could make a public statement. The plane touched down at Barksdale Air Force Base, outside of Shreveport, La., where, at 12:36, the President spoke from a windowless conference room, in front of two American flags dragged together by Air Force privates. "Freedom itself was attacked this morning by a faceless coward," he began, then spoke for two minutes before leaving the room. In the evening he returned to Washington, strode across the South Lawn of the White House and delivered a national address from the Oval Office. Earlier, Congressmen and Senators, Republicans hugging Democrats, had convened on the Capitol steps to sing *God Bless America*.

Even before the smoke had cleared, it was obvious that the culprits knew their way around a Boeing cockpit— and all the security weaknesses in the U.S. civil aviation system. The enemy had chosen the quietest day of the week for the operation, when there would be fewer passengers to subdue; they had boarded westbound transcontinental flights, planes fully loaded with fuel. They were armed with knives and box cutters, had gained access to the cockpits and herded everyone to the back of the plane. Once at the controls, they had turned off at least one of the aircraft's self-identifying beacons, known as transponders, a move that renders the planes somewhat less visible to air-traffic controllers. And each aircraft had gone through dramatic but carefully executed course corrections.

No group other than veteran Saudi terrorist Osama bin Laden's looseknit network of operatives in dozens of countries worldwide has ever shown the will, wallet or gall to attack the U.S. before. By nightfall, less than 12 hours after the attacks, U.S. officials told TIME that their sense that bin Laden was involved had got closer to what one senior official said was 90%.

One world ended at 8:46 on Tuesday morning and another was born, one we always trust in but never see, in which normal people become fierce heroes and everyone takes a test for which they haven't studied. ∎

December 31, 2001

Rudolph Giuliani

When the Twin Towers fell, New York City's gutsy mayor stood tall

SEPT. 12, 2001, 2:30 A.M. SIXTEEN HOURS AFTER THE Twin Towers of the World Trade Center collapsed, the exhausted Mayor of New York City, Rudolph Giuliani, finally arrived at the apartment of an old friend to shower and sleep. But he couldn't sleep, he later told TIME, so he reached for a new biography of TIME's Man of the Year 1940—Winston Churchill. In the words of Britain's proud, defiant wartime Prime Minister, Giuliani found inspiration. "I started thinking about Churchill," he said, "started thinking that we're going to have to rebuild the spirit of the city, and what better example than Churchill and the people of London during the Blitz in 1940, who had to keep up their spirit during this sustained bombing? It was a comforting thought."

The mayor arrived at the World Trade Center just after the second tower was struck; he watched human beings drop from the sky. Unable to use the city's emergency command center located within the complex, Giuliani and his aides were in the lobby of a nearby building when the first tower fell. The mayor took charge, leading city officials, reporters and civilians north through the blizzard of ash and smoke. A detective jimmied open the door to a firehouse so Giuliani could set up a command post. He then took to the airwaves to calm and reassure his people, made a few hundred rapid-fire decisions about the security and rescue operations, toured hospitals to comfort the families of the missing and made four more visits to the gruesome attack scene.

In the hours after the attacks, with the nation groping for meaning and reassurance, Giuliani became the voice of America. "We're going to rebuild, and we're going to be stronger than we were before," he said, his suit still coated with ashes from the collapse of the buildings. "I want the people of New York to be an example to the rest of the country, and the rest of the world, that terrorism can't stop us."

Sept. 11 was the day that Giuliani was supposed to begin his inevitable slide toward irrelevancy. It was primary-election day in the city, when people would go to the polls to begin choosing his successor. After two terms, his place in history seemed secure: great mayor, not-so-great guy. The first Republican to run the town in a generation, he had restored New York's spirit, cutting crime by two-thirds, moving 691,000 people off the welfare rolls, boosting property values and incomes in neighborhoods rich and poor, redeveloping great swaths of the city. But great swaths of the city were sick of him. People were tired of his Vesuvian temper and constant battles— against his political enemies, against some of his own appointees, against city-funded museums, against black leaders and street vendors and jaywalkers and finally even against his own wife. His marriage to television personality Donna Hanover had become a war: ugly headlines, dueling press conferences. Giuliani's girlfriend, a pharmaceutical-sales manager named Judith Nathan, had helped him get through a battle against prostate cancer, and his struggle touched off a wave of concern and appreciation for him. But most New Yorkers seemed ready for Rudy and Judi to leave the stage and melt into the crowd.

YA GOTTA HAVE HEART: Giuliani revealed his softer side after 9/11

Fate had another idea. When the day of infamy came, Giuliani seized it as if he had been waiting for it all his life, taking on half a dozen critical roles and performing each masterfully. Improvising on the fly, he became America's homeland-security boss, giving calm, informative briefings about the attacks and the extraordinary response to them. He was the gutsy decision maker, balancing security against symbolism, overruling those who wanted to keep the city buttoned up tight, pushing key institutions— from the New York Stock Exchange to Major League Baseball—to restart and prove that New Yorkers were getting on with life. He was the crisis manager, bringing together major players from city, state and federal governments for marathon daily meetings that got everyone working together. And he was the consoler in chief, strong enough to let his voice brim with pain, compassion and love. When he said, "The number of casualties will be more than any of us can bear," he showed a side of himself most people had never seen.

Giuliani's eloquence under fire made him a global symbol of healing and defiance. As Roy Jenkins, author of the biography that inspired Giuliani after Sept. 11, told TIME, "What Giuliani succeeded in doing is what Churchill succeeded in doing in the dreadful summer of 1940: he managed to create an illusion that we were bound to win." ∎

Mike Kehoe

A grieving fire fighter is called a hero—but he doesn't feel like one

O N THE MORNING OF SEPT. 11, 2001, NEW YORK CITY fire fighter Mike Kehoe and his wife E.J. drove into Manhattan together from their Staten Island home. Shortly after 7 a.m., he dropped her off at the downtown Manhattan radiologist whom she assists. At 8:46 a hijacked jetliner hit the north tower of the World Trade Center. The first and second alarms sounded in unison at 8:47 at firehouses across lower Manhattan. The third was transmitted at 8:48 as a 10-60, code for a major emergency. No fourth alarm was necessary; at 8:56 the blaze was upgraded to a five-alarm fire.

The noise of the first crash traveled two miles north to the Alphabet City firehouse that is shared by Mike's company, Engine 28, and Ladder 11. Mike remembers what followed only in spurts. The engine, which typically barrels straight to the scene, was doing a strange, slow zigzag as it approached the Twin Towers. When he climbed out Mike saw why: the street was already littered with bodies that had fallen from the sky. The fire fighters entered the lobby of 1 World Trade through blown-out windows and waited for orders at a desk that served as a makeshift command center.

While other squads extract people from burning buildings, the sole job of an engine company like Mike's is to lay the hose to douse the flames. As his team climbed upstairs to do that, a kind of eerie order presided in the stairwell. People were perspiring from the heat, but they were filing down calmly. Some, as if they were on the sidelines at a road race, even stopped to hand the fire fighters bottled water. "I have no idea how much time had passed," Mike says, "but we were up around floor 28 when it seemed like someone had grabbed hold of the towers, like King Kong was shaking the two towers." The south tower had collapsed. Within seconds, the call to evacuate came over the bullhorn. The members of Engine 28 turned and charged down the stairs. They lingered, breathless, in the lobby for an instant as some companies, ignoring the order, continued to run into the building. Roy Chelsen, a fireman with Engine 28, yelled, "We have to get out. Run!" Then King Kong returned. Mike dived under a battalion chief's cherry-red Suburban.

"The only way to describe it was like a blizzard, like a quiet blizzard where everything was black," he says. He tried to hold his breath until the dark storm passed. When he finally stood up, he saw an abandoned Poland Spring truck and helped himself to a bottle of water to wash the ash and grime from his throat.

For the first couple of days, Mike did not return home. He worked 24-hour shifts, much of it on the pile, the putrid 16-acre wasteland where the laws of time and space did not abide. "We'd be working in one place for a bit, and they'd blow the horn and tell us to run because another building might collapse on us, and then they'd bring us back to the same place two hours later," he recalls. The grim labor consisted of scooping handfuls of debris into 5-gal. white buckets. Mike picked through body parts and shoes and paperwork. He and his Engine 28 colleagues were on a special mission: to find their six missing housemates from Ladder 11. Rescuers eventually turned up the remains of Ladder 11, crushed like a Coke can, and later the bodies of three of its men.

SPOTLIGHT: This picture, widely circulated, made Mike Kehoe a hero—but he insists the day's real heroes are dead

JOHN LABRIOLA—AP/WIDE WORLD

In the meantime, Mike discovered he had become a hero. A Port Authority contractor had grabbed his digital camera on his rush down from the 71st floor and released the shutter on the 20th floor just as Mike was climbing to the scene of the blaze. On the Friday after that Tuesday, the photo hit the *Daily News*. Mike's picture was the one frozen frame to give the horrors inside the towers a face and a name. Suddenly everyone wanted a piece of him. There were 40 messages a day from reporters; well-wishers sent checks, whiskey, prayers.

The photograph fast became part of the redemptive fairy tale spun by Americans to make some rough sense of Sept. 11. The good guys like Mike saved the day, the evil ones were blotted out, and we all bought F.D.N.Y. caps to celebrate the victory. But to those who lived that story and now rub up against its shards every day, resolution is nothing more than a mass-marketed myth. The guys at work grumbled that all the attention was going to Mike instead of the six men lost in the calamity. Everyone wanted to know how many people the superhero pulled from the towers. Mike's answer: "I saved one person that day, and that was me, and it was by running for my life."

When Mike visited an elementary school in Pennsylvania, a teacher told him. "Before Sept. 11, a hero to these children was Superman on TV. After everything awful that happened, they need some good to come out of it, and you've been that for them. They need a hero they can see and touch." And they can't touch the six men of Ladder 11. ∎

September 24, 2001 • December 31, 2001

Heroes of Flight 93

"Let's roll!" one cried—and four men gave up their lives to save thousands

ON SEPT. 11, 2001, TOM BURNETT CALLED HIS WIFE DEENA with grim tidings. "I know we're all going to die. There's three of us who are going to do something about it." Burnett was one of the 38 passengers and seven crew members aboard hijacked United Airlines Flight 93, and he was not the only person to relay information to a loved one. In first-class seat 4D, public relations executive Mark Bingham used an airplane phone to call his mother. "Mom, this is Mark Bingham," he said, so rattled that he included his last name. "Three guys have taken over the plane, and they say they have a bomb." Back in coach, Jeremy Glick phoned his wife Lyzbeth to say, "Three Arab-looking men with red headbands" had taken over the cockpit of the plane.

Flight 93 was the last of the hijacked planes to meet its fate. The passengers knew about the attacks on the World Trade Center. Though we may never finally establish what took place in the last moments of the flight, it appears that four strangers—Burnett, Bingham, Glick and Todd Beamer, an executive with Oracle Computer—banded together to fight their captors and ditch the Boeing 757 before it could reach Washington and harm untold thousands. Did more assist? We may never know.

Other relatives of people on Flight 93 have spoken up too and assigned their loved ones a heroic narrative. Those of the captain, Jason Dahl, say he would never have allowed hijackers to take control of his plane without a fight. But there is something about the similarity of Burnett, Bingham, Glick and Beamer that makes the portrait of them as confederates perfectly imaginable. All four were large, athletic, decisive types. Bingham, 6 ft. 4 in., played rugby when at the University of California, Berkeley, and still played for the San Francisco Fog, a gay amateur team. Glick, 6 ft. 4 in., was a national collegiate judo champion, according to the website of the software firm for which he was a sales manager. Burnett, 6 ft. 1 in., was a former high school football player and an executive of a medical-devices firm. Beamer, 6 ft., 200 lbs., played baseball, basketball and soccer in high school, and at one time considered pursuing a career in professional baseball.

All four men were nimble, successful, charismatic, self-

elected leaders—the kind that have a knack for finding one another. Glick's last words to his wife Lyzbeth, like Burnett's vow of action to his wife, make us want to believe they prevailed. "We're going to rush the hijackers," said Glick. Then he put down the phone.

Todd Beamer's final message—overheard by a telephone company operator—was even more memorable. Unable to reach his family on the phone, he ended up talking with a GTE operator, who later recalled Beamer's fear—"Were going down!" he yelled at one point—and his prayers—"Jesus, help me," he cried. After Beamer put the phone down, the operator heard him say, "Are you guys ready? O.K. Let's roll."

No one is certain what happened next, but we do know two things: Todd Beamer "really didn't do much without a plan," as his wife says, and his plane crashed into rural Pennsylvania, not Pennsylvania Avenue. "Todd didn't take no for an answer in any area of life, whether it was on the athletic field or in some other situation," Lisa Beamer says. "He would say, 'I know we're in a bad situation, but let's do what we can.'"

Many diverse Americans latched onto Beamer's phrase to

BEAMER: He loved baseball—and the Cubs

BINGHAM: Gay, proud and still playing rugby

BURNETT: Like the others, a former athlete

symbolize that sort of strength of character. President George W. Bush used it to end a speech; rocker Neil Young released a song with that title; in the months after the attacks, there were "Let's roll" mouse pads, fireworks and backpacks. Many of the businesses producing the memorabilia donated their proceeds to charity. A lawyer for the newly formed Todd M. Beamer Foundation had to fire off occasional letters asking others not to market "Let's roll." "Unfortunately," said the lawyer, Paul Kennedy of Philadelphia, "the phrase has become instantly famous in light of a national tragedy."

A man of deeds and not words, Beamer would probably find the "Let's roll" sensation a little strange. His widow hopes the tchotchkes don't cheapen the message behind the two words: "It's about standing up for what you believe in and taking action without thought to the personal consequences." Or, as Lisa Beamer says on the Beamer Foundation website: "Todd and the other freedom fighters of Flight 93 brought the first victory in our nation's war against terrorism." ∎

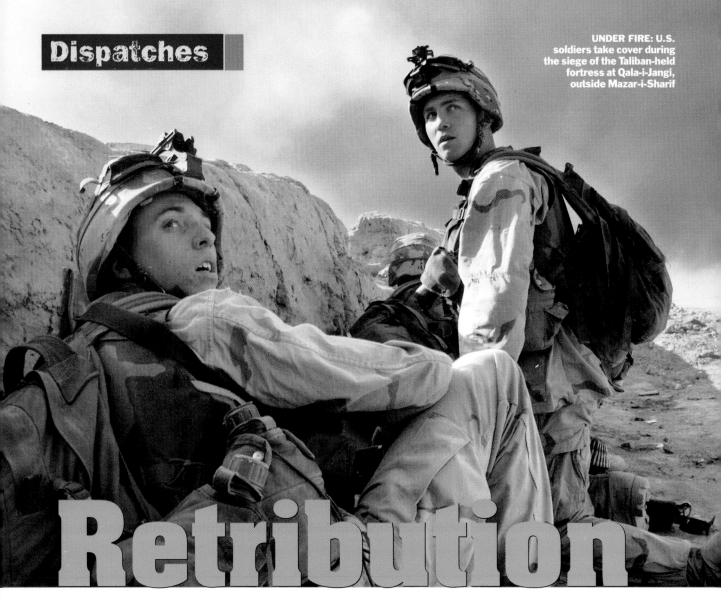

Retribution

Retaliating against the regime that harbored terrorist chief Osama bin Laden, the U.S. joins with local rebels to topple Afghanistan's Taliban

Determined to bring justice to the Muslim terrorists behind the attack on America in September 2001, U.S. President George W. Bush—emulating his father's strategy in the Gulf War—forged a worldwide coalition against terror. The first target: Afghanistan, whose fundamentalist Taliban regime sheltered Saudi-born terrorist Osama bin Laden, leader of the international terror network al-Qaeda, the group behind the 9/11 attacks. As in the Vietnam era, the U.S. fought in tandem with a proxy army of local troops, the Northern Alliance, a loose coalition of anti-Taliban warlords. Within months, U.S. air power and Alliance ground forces shattered the Taliban, but bin Laden wasn't nabbed.

October 1, 2001

"The Hour Is Coming"

For a new kind of war, it had an old sort of start. In the places where soldiers and sailors live—in Norfolk, Va.; Fort Bragg, N.C.; in a hundred other towns of the Republic and far beyond its shores—the rhetoric of impending battle was rendered into the humdrum details of military life. Bills were paid; kit bags packed; wives, husbands and children hugged. Patriotism hung in the air, as palpable as the first chills of fall; flags sprouted on a million lapels and fluttered from a thousand taxicabs in a wounded but defiant New York City. On television,

the reports came from Islamabad, not as they had a decade ago from Riyadh or Baghdad or Amman. And as predecessors in his high office—including his father—had done before, George W. Bush drove from the White House to the Capitol and in an address to Congress and a worldwide audience discharged the weightiest responsibility that any President can ever be asked to shoulder. "I've called the armed services to alert," Bush said, "and there is a reason. The hour is coming when America will act, and you will make us proud."

In his speech, Bush spoke directly to the Taliban, the radical Islamic regime that rules Afghanistan and harbors Osama bin Laden, leader of the al-Qaeda network, the prime suspect in the Sept. 11 atrocities. Bush demanded that the Taliban hand over all terrorist leaders to U.S. authorities. The Taliban has not done so, demanding, in turn, proof that bin Laden is guilty. If the Taliban does not shift from that position, a shooting war seems inevitable. ∎

October 22, 2001

Down and Dirty

It was the colors that Hamad Alokzai noticed. The gaunt Afghan, with a beard like matted wool and gaudy silver rings on his fingers, had returned to Afghanistan from exile in Quetta, Pakistan, to check on his former comrades. On Thursday night he sat with his old Taliban commander under blankets in a pickup truck, safely tucked away in the hills outside Kandahar. "The bombs make a sound, then you see green lights falling through the sky," the commander told Alokzai. "The missiles have flashing yellow lights." That night, Alokzai counted 30 missiles striking targets around the city. "It was like Kandahar was covered in a floating green dust," he told TIME.

Most of the Taliban fighters—including their supreme leader, Mullah Mohammed Omar—had already left town. On Wednesday night a single missile was fired on the village of Sangesar, destroying the mosque where Omar

started his movement in 1995. Even the war-hardened locals were impressed by that level of accuracy.

Though Kandahar's hospitals were filled with casualties, the only troops killed, Alokzai said, were boys "left behind at the airport as night watchmen." Where once 10,000 Taliban supporters had gathered to pray, now fewer than a hundred did. On just one day, more than 45 Taliban trucks left Kandahar for redoubts in the high mountains. They were filled with guns and ammunition.

This is the real thing. Last week the noisy war, the one marked by percussive blasts that shake mountains, by the rattle of small-arms fire and the air-sucking whump of a fuel-air explosive, finally started. Like all battles, it had an otherworldly quality. The cruise missiles and precision-guided bombs that thudded into Afghanistan, the B-2 Stealth bombers, half-circling the globe from Whiteman Air Force Base in Missouri to Central Asia, all seem more at home in a science-fiction novel than on the evening news.

Last week's bombing and missile attacks hit more than 60 targets, such as air-defense systems, weapons dumps and training camps run by both the Taliban and al-Qaeda. Pilots had it as easy as anyone flying a mobile-weapons platform ever will.

After six days, the bombing slowed, in part for observance of Friday prayers

KINGPIN: Osama bin Laden in a video taped after the attacks

at mosques. When it was resumed early Saturday, the conventional wisdom grew that Afghanistan is not, as they say in the Pentagon, a "target-rich environment." Secretary of Defense Donald Rumsfeld made the point in his inimitable style: "We're not running out of targets," he said. "Afghanistan is."

That was not entirely true. Politics intruded on the air war and prevented some targets from being attacked. To the north of Kabul, troops of the Northern Alliance are hungry and spoiling for a fight. Their commanders hoped the U.S. bombers would target the Taliban forces massed against them.

In the first week, that didn't happen. What had once been the expected strategy for combat—U.S. forces assisting the Northern Alliance in a proxy war against the Taliban—seems to have been put on hold as potential leaders squabble over the shape of a postwar government. ∎

AIRBORNE: A jet takes off from the U.S.S. *Enterprise* in the Persian Gulf as the bombing campaign against Afghanistan begins on Oct. 7, 2001

November 12, 2001

Bombs Away

On the front lines of the war, you learn about America's strategy by staring at the smoke. Above the peaks and ridges of northern Afghanistan last week, the plumes billowed thick and black in long, ragged lines—calling cards of the B-52 bombers that each dropped 25,000 lbs. of ordnance on Taliban positions. For Northern Alliance fighters scanning the sky, those clouds of smoke, dust and debris could mean only one thing: the long-awaited American order to take the fight to the Taliban had at last arrived.

"Forward air controllers" among the 100 U.S. commandos now on Afghan soil called in B-52 strikes to pound Taliban positions. Until now the Taliban's front lines have been spared, but last week the U.S. unleashed 80% of its firepower on Taliban soldiers in Mazar-i-Sharif and Kabul. ∎

MOB: Once begun, the Taliban collapse came quickly. Here, prisoners are crowded into a city square.

November 19, 2001

The Horse Soldiers

In the dead of night, horses poured from the hills. They came charging down from the craggy ridges in groups of 10, their riders dressed in flowing *shalwar kameez* and armed with AK-47s and grenade launchers. In the Kishindi Valley below, 35 miles south of the prized northern city of Mazar-i-Sharif, the few Taliban tanks in the area not destroyed by American bombs took aim at the Northern Alliance cavalry galloping toward them. But the 600 horsemen had been ordered to charge directly into the line of fire. The rebels were told to leap on top of the tanks, pull the Taliban gunners out through the open hatches and kill them.

The first land battle in the century's first war began with a showdown from a distant age: fearless men on horseback against modern artillery. America's money was on the ponies.

They won. According to accounts given to TIME by Alliance officials, 3,500 rebels serving under Uzbek warlord

Rashid Dostum, 47, pushed the Taliban out of Kishindi with a 16-hour assault that left 200 Taliban and an unknown number of Alliance troops dead. To the west, forces loyal to Alliance commander Ustad Atta Mohammed seized the outlying village of Aq Kuprik. From there the Alliance's long-promised and much delayed march on Mazar-i-Sharif gathered an irresistible momentum. One Taliban commander on the front lines secretly arranged to defect with a few hundred of his men and agreed to let the Alliance through his line. The advancing rebels found another Taliban commander, Mullah Qahir, trying to avoid capture by snipping off his beard with nail scissors. "From what I hear," said an Alliance officer, "it's a good time to be a razor salesman in Mazar."

Heavy rains slowed the rebel advance. Just west of the city, Taliban forces in the old citadel Qala-i-Jangi uncorked a final fusillade from cannons, multibarrel rocket launchers, mortars and fixed machine guns. Alliance troops found hundreds of Taliban fighters—most of them Arab and Pakistani volunteers—holed up in a girls' high school. They were zealots, primed for death: after the Alliance commanders failed to coax them into surrender, a two-hour fire fight broke out, and all the Taliban troops were killed or captured. It was their last stand; by nightfall Friday the Alliance stormed the city. ■

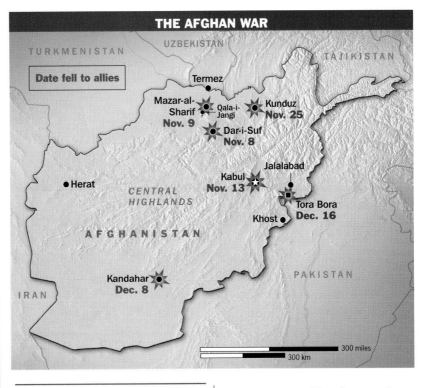

THE AFGHAN WAR

Date fell to allies

November 26, 2001

Witness to a Sudden And Bloody Liberation

Slowly, hesitantly, the four tanks and two armored fighting vehicles of the Northern Alliance's Guards Brigade rolled forward from their advance position 28 miles north of Kabul. It was last Monday afternoon, [Nov. 12] before the capital fell, and the crews were tensed for a barrage of enemy fire. But none came, so they pushed on faster, rumbling down narrow lanes in thick clouds of dust before turning onto the Old Road and heading south toward Kabul. This was once agricultural land, but now the landscape was lunar and blitzed: the remaining trees were shredded and the fields were pocked with the 10-ft.-deep footprints of 1,000-lb. American bombs.

The convoy passed abandoned bunkers, some manned by the corpses of Taliban troops. A few hundred yards ahead, Alliance infantrymen exchanged small-arms fire with Taliban stragglers. But the afternoon's fiercest fighting, a remarkably brief exchange of recoilless rifle and mortar, had tapered off shortly before, and by 4:30 the brigade rolled over what for two years had been the immovable front line in this war. By dusk all resistance had disappeared.

The battle for Kabul lasted less than three hours. Just three days before, an optimistic Alliance commander had been predicting it would last two weeks. The battle took place 28 miles to the city's north, but Taliban commanders mounted no counterattack.

Even before the sun rose Tuesday morning, the Alliance had resumed its advance, a triumphal convoy of jeeps, truck and tanks rumbling toward Kabul. Several Western reporters, includ-

FORWARD! Northern Alliance troops attack the fortress of Qala-i-Jangi, scene of some of the war's toughest fighting

ERIK DE CASTRO—REUTERS—TIMEPIX

FREE! Jubilant Afghans hail the Northern Alliance's entry into liberated Kabul, which fell after the Taliban mounted only token resistance

ing TIME's, made their way into town before the Alliance and encountered scenes of both celebration and violence. Jubilant crowds, giddy with relief that the fighting had passed them by, cheered foreigners, flew once banned kites and joyrode in their cars. From the back of one, a pretty teenage girl, her burka thrown off, laughed and waved.

Elsewhere there was gunplay and brutal mob justice. A pair of Arab jihadists barricaded themselves in a tiny kitchen of a house near the airport and fought off armed locals for an hour before crying out the *Shahadah* ("There is no god but God, and Muhammad is his Prophet") and killing themselves with their own grenades. Soldiers pulled

TIME's correspondent forward to watch as a civilian, his face contorted with hatred, fired short bursts from a Kalashnikov rifle into the still heaving chests of the wounded. Another man used his knife to gouge out the eyes of a third, mortally wounded foreign fighter.

As the sun set on a Taliban-free Kabul for the first time in five years, a pickup truck, blaring long-banned Afghan music, slowly circled a square. Men crowded onto its bed, clapping and dancing into the night. ∎

December 17, 2001

Into the Caves

HUNTERS: Still tracking down al-Qaeda members in April 2002, U.S. soldiers inspect a cave in eastern Afghanistan during Operation Mountain Lion

ADAM BUTLER—APWIDE WORLD

The White Mountains of Afghanistan are beautiful this time of year. Snow blankets the peaks from Kabul to the Khyber Pass, smothering the ancient smugglers' footpaths that lead out of the country and into Pakistan. Human traffic in the mountains comes to a halt and the terrain is enveloped in an otherworldly calm.

Last week the hush was shattered by the blasts of hundreds of American bombs, the rattle of Kalashnikovs and the roar of tanks and pickup trucks carrying about 1,000 anti-Taliban soldiers into the Tora Bora cave complex to deliver a final reckoning to Osama bin Laden. The Afghans crept through he valleys and into the caves in the wake of U.S. air strikes, hoping to nab enemy militants as they tried to scramble too higher ground.

But things did not proceed quite as planned. On Thursday, 60 Alliance fighters ventured past a front line near the village of Melawa and took up positions on a hill that offered a clear line of fire. Moments later al-Qaeda snipers protecting bin Laden began firing from a crest above. Six men were gravely wounded. The hunters then beat a retreat, done for the day. "We were thinking we'd be bold and courageous," said one. "They were waiting for us."

For the Taliban, for Osama bin Laden and his dwindling legion of lieutenants, Tora Bora is the last sanctuary. The Taliban's barbaric and medieval rule unraveled for good last week as the regime's soldiers fled from Kandahar, their last stronghold. Some skulked back to their home villages. Others, like Mullah Mohammed Omar, the Taliban's supreme leader, went missing.

There are bound to be more surprises lurking in the snow. In a war of bribes and secret deals, targets have a way of becoming more elusive the closer you get to them, and victory doesn't always bring the promised spoils. The conflict in Afghanistan has confounded expectations. Who anticipated that the Taliban's rule would disintegrate wholesale two months into the U.S. bombing campaign? Or that the regime's soldiers would abandon Kandahar as meekly and abruptly as they did, quitting the city in the dead of night? The next morning, amid much confusion, there was jubilation in the streets of Kandahar. Residents tore down the white Taliban flag; rebel Pashtun forces fired AK-47 rounds into the air.

But there was no champagne in the allies' high command: the U.S. and its allies were still embroiled in a two-front manhunt for the Taliban chief and his even more high-profile Saudi "guest," bin Laden. ∎

The Deadly Hunt

After weeks of fast triumphs, the war has drifted into a frustrating endgame, a double manhunt for Mullah Mohammed Omar and Osama bin Laden. Every day seems to bring a new theory about bin Laden's whereabouts. Is he dead in a Tora Bora cave? Hiding out along one side or the other of the Afghan border with Pakistan? The Pentagon has tabled plans to send additional U.S. troops to hunt in the mountains of Tora Bora. And there was never a chance that Pakistan would want the U.S. to deploy the troops necessary to seal off its 1,510-mile border with Afghanistan.

For many Afghans allied with the U.S., it seems that the fighting should be over. With the Taliban routed, their war aims have been accomplished. But the U.S. has a major goal still unsatisfied—to get both Taliban leader Mullah Omar and al-Qaeda chief bin Laden. ∎

MOPPING UP: U.S. troops scramble out of a Chinook MH-47 helicopter on March 5, 2002. Seven U.S. soldiers died in a fire fight the day before, but the operation destroyed an al-Qaeda buildup south of Kabul.

December 10, 2001

Johnny Spann, John W. Lindh

Two radically different American lives converge in an Afghan fortress

THE STRANGEST CULTURE CLASH OF THE WAR IN AFGHAN-istan took place on a bright Sunday morning in late November. In the Qala-i-Jangi prison fortress, a few miles west of Mazar-i-Sharif, CIA agent Johnny ("Mike") Spann was sorting through 300 surrendered Taliban soldiers in an attempt to determine which of them were al-Qaeda members. Dressed in blue jeans, with an AK-47 strapped across the back of his black sweater, Spann passed through several rows of Taliban before crouching in front of a prisoner who had been separated from the rest, a mass of tangled hair and tattered clothes once named John Walker. "What's your name?" Spann asked. No response. "Hey," he said, snapping his fingers twice in front of Walker's dirt-caked face. "Who brought you here? Wake up! How did you get here?"

Walker didn't answer. A few hours later, Spann became the first American casualty in Afghanistan, when dozens of surrendered Taliban soldiers overwhelmed their guards. During the uprising, John Walker hid, delaying the world's discovery of an American Taliban. After a week spent starving in a basement deep below the prison, Walker and 85 comrades were flushed out when their dungeon was flooded with ice-cold water. Spann was gone, but his questions for John Walker remained: "Who brought you here? How did you get here?

John Walker Lindh was a middle child who spent his first 10 years in Silver Spring, Md., in the happy, unremarkable manner that most parents wish for their children. John's father, attorney Frank Lindh, took the bus to his job at the Department of Justice. Marilyn Walker was a stay-at-home mom who kept her maiden name. They played with their three kids and went to Mass at St. Bernadette's Catholic Church. In 1991 the family moved to San Anselmo, Calif., in opulent, socially liberal Marin County. John was gentle and shy. After a semester at a local high school, he transferred to Tamiscal High, an alterna-tive school with 100 students and a self-directed, individual-ized course of study. Marilyn Walker had left Catholicism and become a Buddhist; John was intrigued by religion too.

Apparently it was *The Autobiography of Malcolm X* that in-spired Walker to convert to Islam. On Friday nights he would change out of his Western clothes and attend services at the Is-lamic Center of Mill Valley. In 1998 Walker passed a profi-ciency exam and graduated early from Tamiscal High. Soon he told Abdullah Nana, a new Islamic friend, that he had found an Arabic-language school in San'a, Yemen, on the Internet. In December 1998 he left for the Middle East.

From the ages of 16 to 18, John Walker had transformed himself from a quiet, smooth-cheeked American teenager to a devout, bearded Muslim studying in Yemen. Were his parents really onboard with all this? Frank Lindh says yes. "He was al-ways intellectually coherent, and he had a wonderful sense of humor," Lindh told reporters. When Walker returned to Cali-fornia around Christmas 1999, he found his parents had sep-arated. According to Nana, Yemen hadn't matched his ex-pectations: "They weren't as orthodox as [John] thought."

When the U.S.S. *Cole* was bombed in October 2000, Walker was back in Yemen. A month after the bombing, he left Yemen for Bannu, a vil-lage in Pakistan's northwest to attend an Islamic school, or *madrasah;* these are reputed to provide thousands of Tal-iban soldiers. John Walker's last contact with his family was in May 2001. He told his mother he was "moving some-where cooler for the summer." Sept. 11 came and went, and still John's parents heard nothing. Finally, on Dec. 1, Marilyn Walk-er and Frank Lindh saw their son, a captive, on television. As the footage played, Marilyn Walker burst into tears.

Tears were also shed in Winfield, Ala., where folks remem-ber hometown boy Johnny Micheal Spann as a polite kid who studied hard, played football for the Winfield High Pirates and didn't draw attention to himself. But there was one secret he would share with anyone who would listen: "I want to be in-volved in the FBI or CIA," he would say. "That's my goal."

Mike Spann realized his dream. After a stint as a Marine Corps artillery officer, he joined the CIA in 1999. In October 2001, the rookie covert officer packed off to Afghanistan, where he roamed the country in Afghan garb. His father recalls that his son once said, "Someone's got to do the things that no one else wants to do." And sometimes, those who make that choice will pay the ultimate price for it. ∎

LINDH: He will be tried as a traitor

SPANN: He fulfilled his dream in joining the CIA

NEWS INTERNATIONAL

CIA—AP/WIDE WORLD

Heroes

As of June 1, 2002, the most decorated soldier of the war in Afghanistan was Daniel A. Romero, 30. Sergeant First Class Romero, a member of the 19th Special Forces Group, was trying to disarm an unexploded rocket in Kandahar on April 15, 2002, when it detonated, killing him instantly. Romero was posthumously awarded nine medals, including the Bronze Star, the Legion of Merit and the Purple Heart.

Forty-four Americans had been killed in and around Afghanistan while taking part in Operation Enduring Freedom as of May 31, 2002.

After the Fall

The recovery of victims and removal of debris at the 16-acre site of the World Trade Center in lower Manhattan began on Sept. 11, 2001, and concluded on May 30, 2002. The clean-up excavated 1,642,698 tons of material, which was carted off in 108,444 truckloads. The work continued 24 hours a day, seven days a week, for 262 days and required 3.1 million man-hours of labor. Even so, the massive job was originally estimated to take three more months and cost $6 billion more than it did. The final price tag for the effort was approximately $750 million—almost 90% less than initial estimates of $7 billion. The end of the vast project was marked by a solemn memorial service.

> "We have never been braver. We have never been stronger."
> —New York City Mayor Rudolph Giuliani, 9/11/01

Hardware

DEPARTMENT OF DEFENSE

No Pilot, No Problem

The Predator (technically known as the RQ-1A Unmanned Aerial Vehicle) has been stalking the skies for the U.S. military since 1995, when it was deployed in Bosnia. Powered by a four-cylinder, 101-horsepower engine that drives a single rear-mounted propeller, the drone can fly for 40 hours without landing. Normal speed: 84 m.p.h. Predators usually operate in groups of four, requiring 55 people on the ground (working in three shifts from a windowless trailer) to pilot the planes, operate the sensors and interpret the data sent back.

Predators can carry several kinds of gear: a high-resolution video camera, a synthetic-aperture radar (which can see through clouds), a forward-looking infrared radar (which can map terrain and detect movement, day or night), a missile targeting system (to guide smart bombs launched from ships, tanks or other aircraft) and live missiles. When all of this equipment is deployed simultaneously, on several Predators, it gives battlefield commanders a multi-spectrum, real-time picture of the situation on the ground.

Casualties

The final death toll from the terrorist attacks of September 2001 stands at 3,056, including the 19 hijackers. This includes 2,823 people who died at the World Trade Center and aboard the planes that slammed into it, 189 at the Pentagon and aboard American Flight 77, and 44 passengers and crew on United Flight 93, which crashed in Pennsylvania. The remains of 1,722 of those who died at the Trade Center had not been recovered by May 31, 2002.

Price Tags

Three Black Hawk helicopters went down during the 1993 incident in Somalia that left 15 Americans dead—two crashed and burned, while a third, though badly damaged, limped home.

The price of one Sikorsky UH-60 chopper in 1993 dollars: $6.7 million, without such extras as side-mounted artillery and cargo hoists. When Hollywood re-created the incident for the 2001 film *Black Hawk Down*, the movie's budget was $90 million.

Index